465 —

100 —

{ who — what
when
where
why + how

{ remille
remillon
pr. remillez

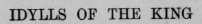

IDYLLS OF THE KING

Macmillan's Pocket American and English Classics

A Series of English Texts, edited for use in Elementary and Secondary Schools, with Critical Introductions, Notes, etc.

16mo   Cloth   28 cents each

Addison's Sir Roger de Coverley.
American Democracy from Washington to Wilson. •
American Patriotism in Prose and Verse.
Andersen's Fairy Tales.
Arabian Nights' Entertainments.
Arnold's Sohrab and Rustum.
Austen's Pride and Prejudice.
Austen's Sense and Sensibility.
Bacon's Essays.
Baker's Out of the Northland.
Bible (Memorable Passages).
Blackmore's Lorna Doone.
Boswell's Life of Johnson. Abridged.
Browning's Shorter Poems.
Mrs. Browning's Poems (Selected).
Bryant's Thanatopsis, etc.
Bryce on American Democracy.
Bulwer-Lytton's Last Days of Pompeii.
Bunyan's The Pilgrim's Progress.
Burke's Speech on Conciliation.
Burns' Poems (Selections).
Byron's Childe Harold's Pilgrimage.
Byron's Shorter Poems.
Carlyle's Essay on Burns.
Carlyle's Heroes and Hero Worship.
Carroll's Alice's Adventures in Wonderland.
Chaucer's Prologue and Knight's Tale.
Church's The Story of the Iliad.
Church's The Story of the Odyssey.
Coleridge's The Ancient Mariner.
Cooper's The Deerslayer.
Cooper's The Last of the Mohicans.
Cooper's The Spy.
Dana's Two Years Before the Mast.
Defoe's Robinson Crusoe. Part I.
Defoe's Robinson Crusoe. Abridged.
De Quincey's Confessions of an English Opium-Eater.
De Quincey's Joan of Arc, and The English Mail-Coach.
Dickens' A Christmas Carol, and The Cricket on the Hearth.
Dickens' A Tale of Two Cities.
Dickens' David Copperfield. (Two vols.)
Dickens' Oliver Twist.
Dryden's Palamon and Arcite.
Early American Orations, 1760-1824.

Edwards' Sermons.
Eliot's Mill on the Floss.
Eliot's Silas Marner.
Emerson's Essays.
Emerson's Early Poems.
Emerson's Representative Men.
English Essays.
English Narrative Poems.
Epoch-making Papers in U. S. History.
Franklin's Autobiography.
Mrs. Gaskell's Cranford.
Goldsmith's The Deserted Village, and Other Poems.
Goldsmith's The Vicar of Wakefield.
Gray's Elegy, etc., and Cowper's John Gilpin, etc.
Grimm's Fairy Tales.
Hale's The Man Without a Country.
Hawthorne's Grandfather's Chair.
Hawthorne's Mosses from an Old Manse.
Hawthorne's Tanglewood Tales.
Hawthorne's The House of the Seven Gables.
Hawthorne's Twice-told Tales (Selections).
Hawthorne's Wonder-Book.
Holmes' Poems.
Holmes' Autocrat of the Breakfast Table.
Homer's Iliad (Translated).
Homer's Odyssey (Translated).
Hughes' Tom Brown's School Days.
Hugo's Les Miserables. Abridged.
Huxley's Selected Essays and Addresses
Irving's Life of Goldsmith.
Irving's Knickerbocker's History.
Irving's Sketch Book.
Irving's The Alhambra.
Irving's Tales of a Traveller.
Keary's Heroes of Asgard.
à Kempis : The Imitation of Christ.
Kingsley's The Heroes.
Kingsley's Westward Ho!
Lamb's The Essays of Elia.
Lamb's Tales from Shakespeare.
Letters from Many Pens.
Lincoln's Addresses, Inaugurals, and Letters.
Lockhart's Life of Scott. Abridged.
London's Call of the Wild.

Macmillan's Pocket American and English Classics

A SERIES OF ENGLISH TEXTS, EDITED FOR USE IN ELEMENTARY AND SECONDARY SCHOOLS, WITH CRITICAL INTRODUCTIONS, NOTES, ETC.

16mo   Cloth   28 cents each

Longfellow's Evangeline.
Longfellow's Hiawatha.
Longfellow's Miles Standish.
Longfellow's Miles Standish and Minor Poems.
Longfellow's Tales of a Wayside Inn.
Lowell's The Vision of Sir Launfal.
Lowell's Earlier Essays.
Macaulay's Essay on Addison.
Macaulay's Essay on Hastings.
Macaulay's Essay on Lord Clive.
Macaulay's Essay on Milton.
Macaulay's Lays of Ancient Rome.
Macaulay's Life of Samuel Johnson.
Malory's Le Morte d'Arthur.
Milton's Minor Poems.
Milton's Paradise Lost, Books I and II.
Old English Ballads.
Old Testament Selections.
Palgrave's Golden Treasury.
Parkman's Oregon Trail.
Plutarch's Lives of Cæsar, Brutus, and Mark Antony.
Poe's Poems.
Poe's Prose Tales (Selections).
Poems, Narrative and Lyrical.
Pope's Homer's Iliad.
Pope's Homer's Odyssey.
Pope's The Rape of the Lock.
Representative Short Stories.
Rossetti's (Christina) Selected Poems.
Ruskin's Sesame and Lilies.
Ruskin's The Crown of Wild Olive and Queen of the Air.
Scott's Ivanhoe.
Scott's Kenilworth.
Scott's Lady of the Lake.
Scott's Lay of the Last Minstrel.
Scott's Marmion.
Scott's Quentin Durward.
Scott's The Talisman.
Select Orations.
Selected Poems, for Required Reading in Secondary Schools.
Selections from American Poetry.
Selections for Oral Reading.

Shakespeare's As You Like It.
Shakespeare's Hamlet.
Shakespeare's Henry V.
Shakespeare's Julius Cæsar.
Shakespeare's King Lear.
Shakespeare's Macbeth.
Shakespeare's Merchant of Venice.
Shakespeare's Midsummer Night's Dream.
Shakespeare's Richard II.
Shakespeare's Richard III.
Shakespeare's Romeo and Juliet.
Shakespeare's The Tempest.
Shakespeare's Twelfth Night.
Shelley and Keats: Poems.
Sheridan's The Rivals and The School for Scandal.
Short Stories.
Short Stories and Selections.
Southern Orators: Selections.
Southern Poets: Selections.
Southey's Life of Nelson.
Spenser's Faerie Queene, Book I.
Stevenson's Kidnapped.
Stevenson's The Master of Ballantrae.
Stevenson's Travels with a Donkey, and An Inland Voyage.
Stevenson's Treasure Island.
Swift's Gulliver's Travels.
Tennyson's Idylls of the King.
Tennyson's In Memoriam.
Tennyson's The Princess.
Tennyson's Shorter Poems.
Thackeray's English Humorists.
Thackeray's Henry Esmond.
Thoreau's Walden.
Trevelyan's Life of Macaulay. Abridged.
Virgil's Æneid.
Washington's Farewell Address, and Webster's First Bunker Hill Oration.
Whittier's Snow-Bound and Other Early Poems.
Wister's The Virginian.
Woolman's Journal.
Wordsworth's Shorter Poems.

THE MACMILLAN COMPANY
NEW YORK · BOSTON · CHICAGO
SAN FRANCISCO

MACMILLAN & CO., Limited
LONDON · BOMBAY · CALCUTTA
MELBOURNE

THE MACMILLAN CO. OF CANADA, Ltd.
TORONTO

ALFRED LORD TENNYSON.

TENNYSON'S

IDYLLS OF THE KING

EDITED

WITH INTRODUCTION AND NOTES

BY

CHARLES W. FRENCH, A.M.

New York

THE MACMILLAN COMPANY

1919

Norwood Press
J. S. Cushing Co. — Berwick & Smith Co.
Norwood, Mass., U.S.A.

CONTENTS

INTRODUCTION:

PAGE

    Alfred, Lord Tennyson ix
    Idylls of the King xv

IDYLLS OF THE KING:

    The Coming of Arthur 1
    Gareth and Lynette 22
    The Marriage of Geraint 81
    Geraint and Enid 115
    Lancelot and Elaine 154
    The Holy Grail 210
    The Last Tournament 247
    Guinevere 278
    The Passing of Arthur 306

NOTES 325

INDEX TO NOTES 425

INTRODUCTION

ALFRED, LORD TENNYSON

It is often the case that the life of a poet is best read in his works; for a true poet is not often a man of action, or one who throws himself, to any large extent, into the great movements of the day; consequently the facts of importance in his biography may be told in few words. The Tennyson whom the world knows and loves to-day is not the man who lived in Somersby or Farringford, but the pure sweet spirit who comes to us in the mystic beauty of *The Lady of Shalott* and *Sir Galahad*, the calm faith and high philosophy of *In Memoriam*, the musical harmony of many a perfect lyric, the romantic tales of the *Idylls*, or the tranquil trust of the *Crossing the Bar*. His life had little of incident, yet in his great utterances he lived more truly and exerted more potent and lasting influences than many a hero whose life has filled chapters of the world's history.

Alfred Tennyson was born in 1809 in Somersby, in Lincolnshire, where his father was rector. In the healthful life of this beautiful country district he

passed his boyhood days. He attended for four years
the grammar school at Louth and went to Trinity College, Cambridge, in 1828, where he stayed three years.
After this he lived at various places, supporting himself on his own small income, until 1845, when he was
given a state pension. In 1850 he married Miss Emily
Sellwood, to whom he had been engaged for many
years, and was appointed poet laureate of England to
succeed Wordsworth, who had recently died. Three
years later he bought a house at Farringford, in the
Isle of Wight, where he lived the most of the time
until 1869, when he occupied another house at Aldworth, near Haslemere, in order to be more remote
from the great crowds of visitors whom his increasing
popularity attracted in large numbers to Farringford.
In 1884 he was raised to the peerage under the title of
Baron Tennyson of Aldworth and Farringford. He
died in October, 1892, and was buried in Westminster
Abbey, with great ceremonial.

In personal appearance Tennyson was a man of
unusual dignity and distinction. Jowett said of him,
after his death, that he was a magnificent man, who
stood before you in all his native refinement and
strength. He was naturally of a shrinking disposition, in spite of his splendid physique, and could seldom be persuaded to go anywhere where he would be
brought into contact with crowds of people. Like

Wordsworth, he was a devout worshipper of nature and of nature's God. He delighted in long walks in solitary places and was a close and discriminating student of plants and birds, as well as of the various phenomena of nature. More than any other poet of recent years he went to nature for his subjects, his illustrations, and his inspiration. His works are very numerous. For fifty years his pen never wearied, and no poet has ever been accorded a more genuine and widespread appreciation. Among the great galaxy of English poets of the past two centuries, including such names as Scott, Wordsworth, Keats, Shelley, Coleridge, Byron, and Browning, he ranks easily first in the breadth and quality of his work, and there are those who think that in coming years he will be known as one of the five or six greatest poets of the world.

A complete account of the works of Tennyson, with the circumstances attendant upon their production and publication, would be too long for this sketch. Only the more important will be named.

While in Trinity College he won the Chancellor's medal by a poem on *Timbuctoo*, which was published in 1829. Previously, in 1827, a book entitled *Poems by Two Brothers* had appeared, written by his brother Charles and himself. The poems in this book were without special merit, and gave little promise of the future greatness which was to be his.

In 1830 appeared his second book of *Poems, chiefly Lyrical*, and in 1832 a third, containing *The Lady of Shalott* and other poems now famous. After this he remained silent for ten years. During this time, however, he was hard at work perfecting his art by unwearying study. Everything he wrote was re-written, revised, mercilessly criticised, and corrected, until he had acquired a perfection and finish of technique which no poet of any age has ever ex-celled and few have equalled. It was not until he felt himself sure of the high excellence of his work that he ventured to publish another book. Conse-quently his next book, published in 1842, was a masterpiece and at once leaped into an enduring popularity. It contained many poems which are now classed among his best, and from this time on he was firmly fixed in public favor. In 1847 he published *The Princess*, which contains some of the most beau-tiful and perfect lyrics in the English language. In 1855 *Maud* appeared, and in 1859 the first instalment of the *Idylls*. In 1864 came *Enoch Arden*, of which seventeen thousand copies were sold on the day of publication. From that time on appeared in rapid succession volume after volume, containing much that the world loves to-day and will continue to love as long as literature lasts. Beginning in 1875, he pub-lished a series of dramas, among which were *Queen*

Mary, Harold, and the *Foresters.* While they contain much brilliant work, they are among the least popular of his works. The *Idylls* were published from time to time until the last, *Balin and Balan,* appeared in 1885. His later work was marked by the production of the superb lyric, *Crossing the Bar,* a short time before his death.

In his early days Tennyson formed an intimate friendship with Arthur Henry Hallam, whose death in 1833 affected him profoundly and lastingly. He began at once to write a monumental elegy, which should not only express fittingly his unspeakable grief, but should also embody his philosophy of the great problems of life and death. In 1850 *In Memoriam* was published, and at once became the most widely read and most profoundly admired poem of its time in the English language, a distinction which perhaps it retains to the present day.

Tennyson paid great attention to the technique of his poetry, and composed with the most painstaking care. He rewrote his poems many times, changing words and reconstructing lines, until he reached perfection of form and rhythm. He was especially careful in his choice of words, and employed many rhetorical devices to add to the beauty and effectiveness of his work. He employed all kinds of meter known to rhetoric, and originated many besides. Very many of his lyric poems may be set to music without change, for, as some one has said, "they sing themselves." While he lived aloof from the world, he kept in touch with the thought of the day, and was intensely interested in the great progressive movements which took place in the social and economic life of the time, and much of the newer thought reflected itself in his poetry. Yet his genius was distinctively mystic and romantic, and the emotional element was never lacking, even in the most didactic and philosophical of his poetry. In all his work, whatever the subject, there is a peculiar charm which attracts many who are not otherwise lovers of poetry, and which once experienced can never be thrown off.

Tennyson early became interested in the Arthurian legends, and spent much time in reading the various versions to be found in the works of the great mediæval romancers. In 1832 he published the first of his Arthurian poems, *The Lady of Shalott*, which was followed in 1842 by the other lyrics, *Sir Lancelot and Queen Guinevere*, and *Sir Galahad*. In the same volume appeared the *Morte d'Arthur*, which now forms a part of the *Passing of Arthur*. In 1859 he published *Enid*, *Vivien*, *Elaine*, and *Guinevere*. In 1869 appeared the *Coming of Arthur*, *The Holy Grail*, *Pelleas and Ettarre*, and the *Passing of Arthur*. In 1871 the *Last Tournament* was published, and

the next year *Gareth and Lynette*. In 1885 the
"twelve books" were completed by the publication
of *Balin and Balan*. He felt that the theme of
the *Idylls* was "the greatest of all poetical subjects,"
and no one can read them carefully without seeing
that in his treatment of them he has risen to the high
level of his subject.

Many lives of the poet have been written, but by
far the best, and the one which, naturally, gives the
most intimate and sympathetic view of his life and
personality is the *Memoir of Tennyson* by his
son, Hallam, Lord Tennyson, who has also edited
and published his works in six volumes, which
contain many interesting annotations and expla-
nations from the hand of the poet himself, and
never before published. These books are published
by The Macmillan Company, and have been referred to by the editor with permission of the
publishers.

THE IDYLLS OF THE KING

The *Idylls* are a group of romantic poems in blank
verse, written at various times, and with several different minor heroes; but all inspired by and celebrat-
ing the personality and achievement of the mythic
King Arthur. They are based on a cycle of great

mediæval romances, but are written with the evident
intention of inculcating great moral and social truths,
of which, in the belief of the poet, the age needs to be
strongly reminded. The poet himself said of them:
"The whole is the dream of man coming into practical
life and ruined by one sin. Birth is a mystery and
death is a mystery, and in the midst lies the tableland
of life and its struggles and performances. It is not
the history of one man or of one generation, but of a
whole cycle of generations."

Through all the *Idylls* may be traced one constantly
developing theme, the ruin of a great and noble ideal
by the broadening and deepening influence of a single
sin, and that one of which the hero is himself guiltless. Through all the episodes the gathering power
of evil and its blighting influence upon the whole
community is clearly brought out, and the final overthrow of Arthur's great constructive scheme and of
his high ideals appears as the direct result of the sin
of her who should have been his most powerful helper.
The *Idylls* contain many of the elements of a great
epic poem, but are lacking in that essential unity
which, with the final triumph of the hero and the
principles for which he contends, are the necessary
elements of all great epic poems. Yet a careful study
will undoubtedly show that all the apparently discon-
nected episodes are contributory, directly or indirectly,

to the development of the great central theme. The action is epic, in that it exemplifies the great and heroic struggle of the soul, with high purposes and ideals, against the aggressive evil of the world; and while this struggle seems to end in defeat, a final vision comes of a better world, where its defeat shall be turned into a glorious triumph, and the dying king hailed as a world-victor. The materials of which the *Idylls* were constructed were taken mainly from old romances; but the poet has brought them together with a perfect art, has colored them with the brilliant hues of his high artistic sense, and has so wrought them into new patterns and exalted themes that the resulting poem is a new creation, wholly the poet's own, and not the mere recrudescence of oft-repeated legends of the past.

During the earlier Middle Ages, when the pursuit of literature was confined to the bards and minstrels, who wandered through the length and breadth of the land, entertaining people by the recital of heroic deeds, many of which they had learned from their predecessors and some of which they composed themselves, there was a tendency to group scattered romances and tales around the names of certain well-known heroes, until there were built up a number of great romantic and heroic cycles, named from the heroes whose deeds they celebrated. Thus came into existence the Gawain

romances, and those which centred around Merlin,
Tristram, Lancelot, and Arthur. In some cases there
resulted an interchange of tales, until many belonging
strictly to one cycle are found connected with another.
Thus the Arthurian cycle has drawn largely from those
of Gawain and Lancelot, and especially from the Grail
legends.

The Arthurian cycle is probably the most comprehensive, varied, and widely disseminated of them all.
These romances have entered into nearly all literatures
of Europe, being found in French, German, Spanish,
and Italian, as well as in the English and Welsh.
With them, in addition to many others, have been
combined the Grail legends; and the various romances
which formed the groundwork of Wagner's great music
dramas are merely variations of the romances of the
Arthurian cycle.

The historic material upon which these legends are
based is very slight, if indeed there is any at all.
During the latter part of the fifth century the Britons
for a time made a successful stand against the Saxon
invaders, who had overrun the land, and under the
leadership of a captain, named Arthur, they had
nearly broken their power, in twelve great battles, and
gained a glorious victory, not far from the year 500,
on Mount Badon. But the tide was only checked, and
the Saxons soon regained their power and swept the

discomfited Britons back into the remoter regions of Wales and Scotland.

Arthur is mentioned by early chroniclers, such as Nennius and Gildas, but the first extended tale of his achievements was written by Geoffrey of Monmouth, in his *Historia*, about 1140, who undoubtedly invented a considerable part of his history. Some years later Wace wrote on the same subject, adding much imaginative material to that of Geoffrey; and later, by some fifty years, Layamon rewrote the romance and added many incidents which were original with himself. Then followed lays, metrical romances, and prose romances, which crystallized the many floating tales and gave them greater dignity and currency. One of the most gifted and famous of the Arthurian romancers was Chrétien de Troyes, a Frenchman, who wrote six great Arthurian poems, among which was *Erec and Enid*, which was indirectly the source of Tennyson's *Geraint Idylls*. Another was the story of *Tristram*, which was the source of much material found in later writers.

The greatest single writer of Arthurian romances was Sir Thomas Malory, who wrote the *Morte Darthur*. Little is known about the man except that he was born about 1400, and that his great work was not published until some years after his death. It is an interesting fact that the book was published by Caxton on the first press ever set up in England, and was one of the first books to be so published.

Although the *Idylls* were not written consecutively, and though more than forty years elapsed between the publication of the first and the last, yet in a remarkable way they show the development of a single theme. And although they introduce many episodes and many heroes not connected with Arthur, except remotely, yet his great personality pervades the whole work and looms high above the greatest of the circle of knights who formed his Round Table. For instance, in *Gareth and Lynette* Gareth is easily the central figure of the idyll, and comparatively little is seen of Arthur, yet his personality pervades the whole poem, inspires Gareth to do his noblest deeds, and terrifies wrongdoers by the mere thought of his unswerving justice. So in *Geraint and Enid* the cruel and causeless jealousy of Geraint stands out in black relief against the sweetness and high nobility of the king, which is thus strongly glorified. A careful analysis of all the *Idylls* would show that the dominating character in each is Arthur. The consummate power of the poet is shown clearly in his ability to keep the chief character constantly before the eye even when he does not appear in the lines.

It has been observed that the action of the poem seems to follow closely the seasons of the year, though really it covers a number of years. In the *Coming of Arthur* we have the early springtime. The winter has passed away in the passing of the fierce wars against the pagans, and the clearing up of the waste lands for occupation. It is the joyous Maytime when Arthur sends for his beautiful bride, and the altar before which their vows are taken is bright and fragrant with the May-blooms. In *Gareth and Lynette* we find the warmer suns of June, with the strong constructive energies of the early summer in full activity, in the state as well as in nature. The king is busy establishing order and law, and in laying the deep and strong foundations of his kingdom. The trees are in full leaf, the birds fill the air with their music, and the whole atmosphere of the idyll is full of activity and sweetness and the pure joy of living. In the *Geraint Idylls* the season has advanced. The hay and the grain in the fields are ready for the harvester. The sun shines with its full power, and the weary laborer takes his siesta at noon in the grateful shade. The sky at times is overcast, and the sultry air, with its threatening storms, weakens the energies and at times gives birth to fearful forebodings.

In *Merlin and Vivien* and *Balin and Balan* comes the full summer-time with its overpowering heats, its unrestrained passions, and the unchaining of the fearful forces of the tempest, which bring ruin and the crushing of hope. In *Lancelot and Elaine* the season is passing into the late summer and already are coming the dark forebodings of winter, wherein the energies of earth and sky are chilled into the sleep of death. The shadows have begun to lengthen and the death of all things is at hand.

In the *Holy Grail* we reach the early fall, not in its beauty of autumnal colorings, but in the bleakness and loneliness of that season when the harvests have failed and the early blight of a fruitless year overshadows every soul with the certainty of failure. In *Pelleas and Etarre* the shadows are still deepening and the impending doom is seen and felt in every heart. The *Last Tournament* speaks the last word of bitter condemnation. The skies are thick and murky, the leaves have fallen, all hopes have fled. Evil abides in every life, and doom is pronounced.

Guinevere ushers in the winter-tide of failure, disappointment, and death. Heavy mists fill the air and remorse gnaws the heart. The time for repentance is past, and there remains only the fearful looking for the appointed end of all things. One ray of light, only, penetrates the gloom, and that comes with the blameless king, who brings with him, in the darkness of the night, — the death of the year, — the promise of a brighter dawning, — a cheerier springtide, — in some distant, better land. In the *Passing of Arthur* the doom has fallen, and the icy hand of winter, the cheerless season of death, has fallen upon the land and upon every life. Passion has spent its force, the warmth of the sun has withdrawn itself, and there remains silence, desolation, death.

Thus the story of human life is told from the springtime of youth to the snows of age. The higher motives which should control all life are exemplified in the character of the blameless king, and the destructive influences of sin are shown with all the power of poetic genius and the fascination of romantic tales coupled with that profound philosophy of high living which, after all, is one of the great features of the genius of Tennyson.

Whether the *Idylls* are read as simple tales of mediæval life, or as allegories, which figure the virtues and vices of life in the seductive garb of Chivalry, or as a presentation of a noble philosophy of life, with all the vividness and coloring with which art can clothe it, the *Idylls* must always remain among the most fascinating and suggestive of modern poems and as a supreme illustration of the high perfection of poetic art.

The student will find the following books especially helpful in the study of the *Idylls: Essays on Tennyson's Idylls of the King*, Littledale, The Macmillan Co., from which frequent quotations have been made by the editor, with the permission of the publishers; *The Arthur of the English Poets*, Howard Maynadier, Houghton and Mifflin; and *Tennyson, His Art and Relation to Modern Life*, Stopford Brooke, Putnam. An excellent account of the literature can be found in Schofield's *English Literature from the Norman Conquest to Chaucer*, The Macmillan Co.

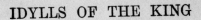

IDYLLS OF THE KING

IDYLLS OF THE KING

IDYLLS OF THE KING

THE COMING OF ARTHUR

LEODOGRAN,° the King of °Cameliard,
Had one fair daughter, and none other child;
And she was fairest of all flesh on earth,
Guinevere, and in her his one delight.

  For many a petty king ere Arthur came   **5**
Ruled in this isle and, ever waging war
Each upon other, wasted all the land;
And still from time to time the °heathen host
Swarm'd over-seas, and harried what was left.
And so there grew great tracts of wilderness,   **10**
Wherein the beast was ever more and more,
But man was less and less, till Arthur came.
For first °Aurelius lived and fought and died,
And after him King Uther fought and died,
But either fail'd to make the kingdom one.   **15**
And after these King Arthur for a space,
And thro' the °puissance of his °Table Round,
Drew all their petty princedoms under him,
Their king and head, and made a realm, and reign'd.

And thus the land of Cameliard was waste,   20
Thick with wet woods, and many a beast therein,
And none or few to scare or chase the beast;
So that wild dog and wolf and boar and bear
Came night and day, and rooted in the fields,
And wallow'd in the gardens of the King.   25
And ever and anon the °wolf would steal
The children and devour, but now and then,
Her own brood lost or dead, lent her fierce teat
To human sucklings; and the children, housed
In her foul den, there at their meat would growl,   30
And mock their foster-mother on four feet,
Till, straighten'd, they grew up to wolf-like men
Worse than the wolves.   And King Leodogran
°Groan'd for the Roman legions here again
And Cæsar's eagle: then his brother king,   35
°Urien, assail'd him : last a heathen horde,
Reddening the sun with smoke and earth with blood,
And on the spike that split the mother's heart
Spitting the child, brake on him, till, °amazed,
He knew not whither he should turn for aid.   40

But — for he heard of Arthur newly crown'd,
Tho' not without an uproar made by those
Who cried, 'He is not Uther's son' — the King
Sent to him, saying, 'Arise, and help us thou !
For here between the man and beast we die.'   45

And Arthur yet had done no deed of arms,
But heard the call and came: and °Guinevere
Stood by the castle walls to watch him pass;
But since he neither wore on helm or shield
The °golden symbol of his kinglihood,   50
But rode a simple knight among his knights,
And many of these in richer arms than he,
She saw him not, or mark'd not, if she saw,
One among many, tho' his face was bare.
But Arthur, looking downward as he past,   55
Felt the light of her eyes into his life
Smite on the sudden, yet rode on, and pitch'd
His tents beside the forest. Then he °drave
The heathen; after, slew the beast, and fell'd
The forest, letting in the sun, and made   60
Broad pathways for the hunter and the knight,
And so return'd.

        For while he linger'd there,
A doubt that ever smoulder'd in the hearts
Of those great lords and barons of his realm
Flash'd forth and into war; for most of these,   65
Colleaguing with a score of petty kings,
Made head against him, crying: 'Who is he
That he should rule us? who hath proven him
King Uther's son? for lo! we look at him,
And find nor face nor bearing, limbs nor voice,   70

Are like to those of Uther whom we knew.
This is the son of °Gorloïs, not the king;
This is the son of °Anton, not the King."

And Arthur, passing thence to battle, felt
°Travail, and throes and agonies of the life,   75
Desiring to be °join'd with Guinevere,
And thinking as he rode: ' Her father said
That there between the man and beast they die.
Shall I not lift her from this land of beasts
Up to my throne and side by side with me?   80
What happiness to reign a lonely king,
Vext — O ye stars that shudder over me,
O earth that soundest hollow under me,
Vext with waste dreams? for saving I be join'd
To her that is the fairest under heaven,   85
I seem as nothing in the mighty world,
And cannot will my will nor work my work
Wholly, nor make myself in mine own realm
Victor and lord.   But were I join'd with her,
Then might we live together as one life,   90
And reigning with one will in everything
Have power on this °dark land to lighten it,
And power on this °dead world to make it live.'

Thereafter — as °he speaks who tells the tale —
When Arthur reach'd a field of battle bright   95

With pitch'd pavilions of his foe, the world
Was all so clear about him that he saw
The smallest rock far on the faintest hill,
And even in high day the °morning star.
So when the King had set his banner broad,   100
At once from either side, with trumpet-blast,
And shouts, and clarions shrilling unto blood,
The °long-lanced battle let their horses run.
And now the barons and the kings prevail'd,
And now the King, as here and there that war   105
Went swaying; but the Powers who walk the world
Made lightnings and great thunders over him,
And dazed all eyes, till Arthur by main might,
And mightier of his hands with every blow,
And leading all his knighthood, threw the °kings   110
Carádos, Urien, Cradlemont of Wales,
Claudius, and Clariance of Northumberland,
The King Brandagoras of Latangor,
With Anguisant of Erin, Morganore,
And Lot of Orkney.   Then, before a voice   115
As °dreadful as the shout of one who sees
To one who sins, and deems himself alone
And all the world asleep, they swerved and brake
Flying, and Arthur call'd to stay the brands
That hack'd among the flyers, °'Ho! they yield!'   120
So like a °painted battle the war stood
Silenced, the living quiet as the dead,

And in the heart of Arthur joy was lord.
He laugh'd upon his °warrior whom he loved
And honor'd most. 'Thou dost not doubt me King, 125
So well thine arm hath wrought for me to-day.'
'Sir and my °liege,' he cried, 'the fire of God
Descends upon thee in the battle-field :
°I know thee for my King!' Whereat the two,
For each had warded either in the fight, 130
Sware on the field of death a deathless love.
And Arthur said, °'Man's word is God in man:
Let chance what will, °I trust thee to the death.'

Then quickly from the °foughten field he sent
Ulfius, and Brastias, and Bedivere, 135
His new-made knights, °to King Leodogran,
Saying, 'If I in aught have served thee well,
Give me thy daughter Guinevere to wife.'

Whom when he heard, Leodogran in heart
Debating—'How should I that am a king, 140
However much he holp me at my need,
Give my one daughter saving to a king,
And a king's son?'—lifted his voice, and call'd
A hoary man, his chamberlain, to whom
He trusted all things, and of him required 145
His counsel: 'Knowest thou aught of Arthur's
   birth?'

Then spake the hoary chamberlain and said:
Sir King, there be but two old men that know;
And each is twice as old as I: and one
Is °Merlin, the wise man that ever served   150
King Uther thro' his magic art; and one
Is Merlin's master — so they call him — Bleys,
Who taught him magic; but the scholar ran
Before the master, and so far that Bleys
Laid magic by, and sat him down, and °wrote   155
All things and whatsoever Merlin did
In one great annal-book, where after-years
Will learn the secret of our Arthur's birth.'

To whom the King Leodogran replied:
'O °friend, had I been holpen half as well   160
By this King Arthur as by thee to-day,
Then beast and man had had their share of me;
But summon here before us yet once more
Ulfius, and Brastias, and Bedivere.'

Then, when they came before him, the King said: 165
'I have seen the °cuckoo chased by lesser fowl,
And reason in the chase; but wherefore now
Do these your lords stir up the heat of war,
Some calling Arthur born of Gorloïs,
Others of Anton?   Tell me, ye yourselves,   170
Hold ye this Arthur for King Uther's son?'

And Ulfius and Brastias answer'd, 'Ay.'
Then Bedivere, the first of all his knights
Knighted by Arthur at his crowning, spake —
For bold in heart and act and word was he,   175
Whenever slander breathed against the King —

'Sir, there be many rumors on this head:
For there be those who hate him in their hearts,
Call him baseborn, and since his ways are sweet,
And theirs are bestial, hold him less than man;   180
And there be those who deem him more than man,
And dream he dropt from heaven: but my belief
In all this matter — so ye care to learn —
Sir, for ye know that in King Uther's time
The prince and warrior Gorloïs, he that held   185
°Tintagil castle by the Cornish sea,
Was wedded with a winsome wife, °Ygerne;
And daughters had she borne him, — one whereof,
Lot's wife, the Queen of Orkney, °Bellicent,
Hath ever like a loyal sister cleaved   190
To Arthur, — but a son she had not borne.
And Uther cast upon her eyes of love;
But she, a stainless wife to Gorloïs,
So loathed the °bright dishonor of his love
That Gorloïs and King Uther went to war,   195
And overthrown was Gorloïs and slain.
°Then Uther in his wrath and heat besieged

Ygerne within Tintagil, where her men,
Seeing the mighty swarm about their walls,
Left her and fled, and Uther enter'd in,   200
And there was none to call to but himself.
So, compass'd by the power of the King,
Enforced she was to wed him in her tears,
And with a shameful swiftness; afterward,
Not many moons, King Uther died himself,   205
Moaning and wailing for an heir to rule
After him, lest the realm should go to °wrack.
And that same night, the night of the new year,
By reason of the bitterness and grief
That vext his mother, all before his time   210
Was Arthur born, and all as soon as born
Deliver'd at a secret postern-gate
To Merlin, to be holden far apart
Until his hour should come; because the lords
Of that fierce day were as the lords of this,   215
Wild beasts, and surely would have torn the child
Piecemeal among them, had they known; for each
But sought to rule for his own self and hand,
And many hated Uther for the sake
Of Gorloïs.   Wherefore Merlin took the child,   220
And gave him to Sir Anton, an old knight
And ancient friend of Uther; and his wife
Nursed the young prince, and rear'd him with her
    own;

And no man knew. And ever since the lords
Have foughten like wild beasts among themselves, 225
So that the realm has gone to wrack ; but now,
This year, when Merlin — for his hour had come —
°Brought Arthur forth, and set him in the hall,
Proclaiming, "Here is Uther's heir, your king,"
A hundred voices cried : "Away with him !   230
No king of ours ! a son of Gorloïs he ;
Or else the child of Anton, and no king,
Or else baseborn." Yet Merlin thro' his craft,
And while the people clamor'd for a king,
Had Arthur crown'd ; but after, the great lords   235
Banded, and so brake out in open war.'

Then while the King debated with himself
If Arthur were the child of shamefulness,
Or born the son of Gorloïs after death,
Or Uther's son and born before his time,   240
Or whether there were truth in anything
Said by these three, there came to Cameliard,
With Gawain and young Modred, her two sons,
Lot's wife, the Queen of °Orkney, Bellicent ;
Whom as he could, not as he would, the King   245
Made feast for, saying, as they sat at meat :
°'A doubtful throne is ice on summer seas.
Ye come from Arthur's court. Victor his men
Report him ! Yea, but ye — think ye this king —

So many those that hate him, and so strong,   25e
So few his knights, however brave they be —
Hath body enow to hold his foemen down?'

'O King,' she cried, 'and I will tell thee: few,
Few, but all brave, all of one mind with him;
For I was near him when the savage yells   255
Of Uther's peerage died, and Arthur sat
Crowned on the daïs, and his warriors cried,
"Be thou the king, and we will work thy will
Who love thee."   Then the King in low deep tones,
And simple words of great authority,   260
Bound them by so strait vows to his own self
That when they rose, knighted from kneeling, some
Were pale as at the passing of a ghost,
Some flush'd, and others dazed, as one who wakes
Half-blinded at the coming of a light.   265

'But when he spake, °and cheer'd his Table Round
With large, divine, and comfortable words,
Beyond my tongue to tell thee — I beheld
From eye to eye thro' all their Order flash
A momentary likeness of the King;   270
And ere it left their faces, thro' the cross
And those around it and the Crucified,
Down from the casement over Arthur, smote
Flame-color, vert, and azure, in three rays,

Faith, hope, & charity

One falling upon each of three fair queens   275
Who stood in silence near his throne, the friends
Of Arthur, gazing on him, tall, with bright
Sweet faces, who will help him at his need.

'And there I saw °mage Merlin, whose vast wit
And hundred winters are but as the hands   280
Of loyal vassals toiling for their liege.

'And near him stood the °Lady of the Lake,
Who knows a subtler magic than his own —
Clothed in white °samite, mystic, wonderful.
She gave the King his °huge cross-hilted sword,   285
Whereby to drive the heathen out: a mist
Of incense curl'd about her, and her face
Wellnigh was hidden in the minster gloom;
But there was heard among the holy hymns
A °voice as of the waters, for she dwells   290
Down in a deep — calm, whatsoever storms
May shake the world — and when the surface rolls,
Hath power to walk the waters like our Lord.

'There likewise I beheld °Excalibur
Before him at his crowning borne, the sword   295
That rose from out the bosom of the lake,
And Arthur row'd across and took it — rich
With jewels, °elfin Urim, on the hilt,

Bewildering heart and eye — the °blade so bright
That men are blinded by it — on one side,   300
Graven in the oldest tongue of all this world,
" Take me," but turn the blade and ye shall see,
And written in the speech ye speak yourself,
" Cast me away!"   And sad was Arthur's face
Taking it, but old Merlin counsell'd him,   305
" Take thou and strike! the time to cast away
Is yet far-off."   So this great brand the King
Took, and by this will beat his foemen down.'

Thereat Leodogran rejoiced, but thought
To sift his doubtings to the last, and ask'd,   310
Fixing full eyes of question on her face,
' The °swallow and the swift are near akin,
But thou art closer to this noble prince,
Being his own dear sister;' and she said,
' Daughter of Gorloïs and Ygerne am I;'   315
' And therefore Arthur's sister?' ask'd the King.
She answer'd, ' These be secret things,' and sign'd
To those two sons to pass, and let them be.
And Gawain went, and breaking into song
Sprang out, and follow'd by his flying hair   320
Ran like a colt, and leapt at all he saw;
But Modred laid his ear beside the doors,
And there half-heard — the same that afterward
Struck for the throne, and striking found his doom.

And then the Queen made answer: 'What know I ?
For dark my mother was in eyes and hair,   326
And dark in hair and eyes am I ; and dark
Was Gorloïs ; yea, and dark was Uther too,
Wellnigh to blackness ; but this °king is fair
Beyond the race of Britons and of men.   330
Moreover, always in my mind I hear
A cry from out the dawning of my life,
A mother weeping, and I hear her say,
"O that ye had some brother, pretty one,
To guard thee on the rough ways of the world." '   335

'Ay,' said the King, 'and hear ye such a cry ?
But when did Arthur chance upon thee first ? '

'O King!' she cried, 'and I will tell thee true :
He found me first when yet a little maid :
Beaten I had been for a little fault   340
Whereof I was not guilty ; and out I ran
And flung myself down on a bank of heath,
And hated this fair world and all therein,
And wept, and wish'd that I were dead ; and he —
I know not whether of himself he came,   345
Or brought by Merlin, who, they say, can walk
Unseen at pleasure — he was at my side,
And spake sweet words, and comforted my heart,
And dried my tears, being a child with me.

And many a time he came, and evermore   350
As I grew greater grew with me; and sad
At times he seem'd, and sad with him was I,
Stern too at times, and then I loved him not,
But sweet again, and then I loved him well.
And now of late I see him less and less,   355
But those first days had golden hours for me,
For then I surely thought he would be king.

    'But let me tell thee now another tale:
For Bleys, our Merlin's master, as they say,
Died but of late, and sent his cry to me,   360
To hear him speak before he left his life.
Shrunk like a °fairy changeling lay the mage;
And when I enter'd told me that himself
And Merlin ever served about the King,
Uther, before he died; and on the night   365
When Uther in Tintagil past away
Moaning and wailing for an heir, the two
Left the still King, and passing forth to breathe,
Then from the castle gateway by the chasm
Descending thro' the dismal night — a night   370
In which the bounds of heaven and earth were lost —
Beheld, so high upon the dreary deeps
It seem'd in heaven, a ship, the shape thereof
A dragon wing'd, and all from stem to stern
Bright with a shining people on the decks,   375

And gone as soon as seen.   And then the two
Dropt to the cove, and watch'd the great sea fall,
Wave after wave, each mightier than the last,
Till last, a °ninth one, gathering half the deep
And full of voices, slowly rose and plunged   380
Roaring, and all the wave was in a flame:
And down the wave and in the flame was borne
A naked babe, and rode to Merlin's feet,
Who stoopt and caught the babe, and cried, "The
      King!
Here is an heir for Uther!"   And the fringe   385
Of that great breaker, sweeping up the strand,
Lash'd at the wizard as he spake the word,
And all at once all round him rose in fire,
So that the child and he were clothed in fire.
And presently thereafter follow'd calm,   390
Free sky and stars: "And this same child," he said,
"Is he who reigns; nor could I part in peace
Till this were told."   And saying this the seer
Went thro' the strait and dreadful pass of death,
Not ever to be question'd any more   395
Save on the further side; but when I met
Merlin, and ask'd him if these things were truth —
The shining dragon and the naked child
Descending in the glory of the seas —
He laugh'd as is his wont, and answer'd me   400
In °riddling triplets of old time, and said: —

'"Rain, rain, and sun! a rainbow in the sky!
A young man will be wiser by and by;
An old man's wit may wander ere he die.

Rain, rain, and sun! a rainbow on the lea!　405
And truth is this to me, and that to thee;
And truth or clothed or naked let it be.

Rain, sun, and rain! and the free blossom blows:
Sun, rain, and sun! and where is he who knows?
From the °great deep to the great deep he goes."　410

'So Merlin riddling anger'd me; but thou
Fear not to give this King thine only child,
Guinevere: so great bards of him will sing
Hereafter; and dark sayings from of old
Ranging and ringing thro' the minds of men,　415
And echo'd by old folk beside their fires
For comfort after their wage-work is done,
Speak of the King; and Merlin in our time
Hath spoken also, not in jest, and sworn
Tho' men may wound him that he will not die,　420
But pass, again to come, and then or now
Utterly smite the heathen underfoot,
Till these and all men hail him for their king.'

She spake and King Leodogran rejoiced,
But musing 'Shall I answer yea or nay?'　425

c

Doubted, and drowsed, nodded and slept, and saw,
Dreaming, a slope of land that ever grew,
Field after field, up to a height, the peak
Haze-hidden, and thereon a phantom king,
Now looming, and now lost; and on the slope   430
The sword rose, the hind fell, the herd was driven,
Fire glimpsed; and all the land from roof and rick,
In drifts of smoke before a rolling wind,
Stream'd to the peak, and mingled with the haze
And made it thicker; while the phantom king   435
Sent out at times a voice; and here or there
Stood one who pointed toward the voice, the rest
Slew on and burnt, crying, 'No king of ours,
No son of Uther, and no king of ours;'
Till with a wink his dream was changed, the haze   440
Descended, and the solid earth became
As nothing, but the King stood out in heaven,
Crown'd.   And Leodogran awoke, °and sent
Ulfius, and Brastias, and Bedivere,
Back to the court of Arthur answering yea.   445

   Then Arthur charged his warrior whom he loved
And honor'd most, °Sir Lancelot, to ride forth
And bring the Queen, and watch'd him from the gates;
And Lancelot past away among the flowers —
For then was latter April — and return'd   450
Among the flowers, in May, with Guinevere.

To whom arrived, by °Dubric the high saint,
Chief of the church in Britain, and before
The stateliest of her °altar-shrines, the King
That morn was married, while in stainless white,   455
°The fair beginners of a nobler time,
And glorying in their vows and him, his knights
Stood round him, and rejoicing in his joy.
Far shone the fields of May thro' open door,
The sacred altar blossom'd white with May,   460
The Sun of May descended on their King,
They gazed on all earth's beauty in their Queen,
Roll'd incense, and there passed along the hymns
A voice as of the waters, while the two
Sware at the shrine of Christ a deathless love :   465
And Arthur said, 'Behold, thy doom is mine.
Let chance what will, I love thee to the death!'
To whom the Queen replied with drooping eyes,
'King and my lord, I love thee to the death!'
And holy Dubric spread his hands and spake :   470
'Reign ye, and live and love, and make the world
Other, and may thy Queen be one with thee,
And all this Order of thy Table Round
Fulfil the boundless purpose of their King!'

So Dubric said; but when they left the shrine   475
Great lords °from Rome before the portal stood,
In scornful stillness gazing as they past ;

Then while they paced a city all on fire
With sun and cloth of gold, the trumpets blew,
And Arthur's knighthood sang before the King : — 480

'Blow trumpet, °for the world is white with May !
Blow trumpet, the long night hath roll'd away !
Blow thro' the living world — "Let the King reign !"

'Shall Rome or Heathen rule in Arthur's realm ?
Flash brand and lance, fall battle-axe on helm,   485
Fall battle-axe, and flash brand ! Let the King
    reign !

'Strike for the King and live ! his knights have
    heard
That God hath told the King a secret word.
Fall battle-axe, and flash brand ! Let the King
    reign !

'Blow trumpet ! he will lift us from the dust.   490
Blow trumpet ! live the strength and die the lust !
Clang battle-axe, and clash brand ! Let the King
    reign !

'Strike for the King and die ! and if thou diest,
The King is king, and ever wills the highest.
Clang battle-axe, and clash brand ! Let the King
    reign !
                                            495

· Blow, for our Sun is mighty in his May!
Blow, for our Sun is mightier day by day!
Clang battle-axe, and clash brand! Let the King
  reign!

'The King will follow Christ, and we the King,
In whom high God hath breathed a secret thing. 500
Fall battle-axe, and clash brand! Let the King
  reign!

So sang the knighthood, moving to their hall.
There at the banquet those great lords from Rome,
The slowly-fading mistress of the world, *personifacates*
Strode in and claim'd their tribute as of yore. 505
But Arthur spake: 'Behold, for these have sworn
To wage my wars, and worship me their King;
The old order changeth, yielding place to new;
And we that fight for our fair father Christ,
Seeing that ye be grown too weak and old 510
To drive the heathen from your °Roman wall,
No tribute will we pay.' So those great lords
Drew back in wrath, and Arthur strove with Rome.

And Arthur and his knighthood for a space
Were all one will, and thro' that strength the King 515
Drew in the petty princedoms under him,
Fought, and in °twelve great battles overcame
The heathen hordes, and made a realm and reign'd.

GARETH AND LYNETTE

THE last tall son of Lot and Bellicent,
And tallest, °Gareth, in a °showerful spring
Stared at the °spate.   A slender-shafted pine
°Lost footing, fell, and so was whirl'd away.
'How he went down,' said Gareth, 'as a false knight 5
Or evil king before my lance, if lance
Were mine to use — O senseless cataract,
Bearing all down in thy precipitancy —
And yet thou art but swollen with cold snows
And mine is living blood: thou dost His will, 10
The Maker's, and not knowest, and I that know,
Have strength and wit, in my good mother's hall
Linger with vacillating obedience,
Prison'd, and kept and coax'd and whistled to —
Since the good mother holds me still a child! 15
Good mother is bad mother unto me!
A worse were better; yet no worse would I.
Heaven °yield her for it, but in me put force
To weary her ears with one continuous prayer,
Until she let me fly °discaged to sweep 20
In °ever-highering eagle-circles up
To the great Sun of Glory, and thence swoop

Down upon all things base, and dash them dead,
A knight of Arthur, working out his will,
To cleanse the world. Why, Gawain, when he came 25
With Modred hither in the summer-time,
Ask'd me to tilt with him, the proven knight.
Modred for want of worthier was the judge.
Then I so shook him in the saddle, he said,
"Thou hast half prevail'd against me," said so—
    he— 30
Tho' Modred biting his thin lips was mute,
For he is always sullen: what care I?'

And Gareth went, and hovering round her chair
Ask'd, 'Mother, tho' ye count me still the child,
Sweet mother, do ye love the child?' She laughed, 35
'Thou art but a wild-goose to question it.'
'Then, mother, an ye love the child,' he said,
'Being a goose and rather tame than wild,
Hear the child's story.' 'Yea, my well-beloved,
An 'twere but of the °goose and golden eggs.' 40

And Gareth answer'd her with kindling eyes:
'Nay, nay, good mother, but this egg of mine
Was finer gold than any goose can lay;
For this an eagle, a royal eagle, laid
Almost beyond eye-reach, on such a palm 45
As glitters gilded in thy °Book of Hours.

And there was ever °haunting round the palm
A lusty youth, but poor, who often saw
The splendor sparkling from aloft, and thought,
" An I could climb and lay my hand upon it,   5c
Then were I wealthier than a °leash of kings."
But ever when he reach'd a hand to climb,
One that had loved him from his childhood caught
And stay'd him, " Climb not lest thou break thy neck,
I charge thee by my love," and so the boy,   55
Sweet mother, neither °clomb nor brake his neck,
But brake his very heart in pining for it,
And past away.'

              To whom the mother said,
' True love, sweet son, had risk'd himself and climb'd,
And handed down the golden treasure to him.'   60

    And Gareth answer'd her with kindling eyes:
' Gold ? said I gold ? — ay then, why he, or she,
Or whosoe'er it was, or half the world
Had ventured — *had* the thing I spake of been
Mere gold — but this was all of that true steel   65
Whereof they forged the brand Excalibur,
And lightnings play'd about it in the storm,
And all the little fowl were flurried at it,
And there were cries and clashings in the nest,
That sent him from his senses : let me go.'   70

Then Bellicent bemoan'd herself and said:
' Hast thou no pity upon my loneliness?
Lo, where thy father °Lot beside the hearth
Lies like a log, and all but smoulder'd out!
For ever since when traitor to the King   75
He fought against him in the barons' war,
And Arthur gave him back his territory,
His age hath slowly droopt, and now lies there
A yet-warm corpse, and yet unburiable,
No more; nor sees, nor hears, nor speaks, nor knows. 80
And both, thy brethren are in Arthur's hall,
Albeit neither loved with that full love
I feel for thee, nor worthy such a love.
Stay therefore thou; °red berries charm the bird,
And thee, mine innocent, the °jousts, the wars,   85
Who never knewest finger-ache, nor pang
Of wrench'd or broken limb — an °often chance
In those brain-stunning shocks, and tourney-falls,
Frights to my heart; but stay: follow the deer
By these tall firs and our fast-falling °burns;   90
So make thy manhood mightier day by day;
Sweet is the chase: and I will seek thee out
Some °comfortable bride and fair, to grace
Thy climbing life, and cherish my prone year,
Till falling into Lot's forgetfulness   95
I know not thee, myself, nor anything.
Stay, my best son! ye are yet more boy than man.'

Then Gareth: 'An ye hold me yet for child,
Hear yet once more the story of the child.
°For, mother, there was once a king, like ours.   100
The prince his heir, when tall and marriageable,
Ask'd for a bride; and thereupon the king
Set two before him. One was fair, strong, arm'd —
°But to be won by force — and many men
Desired her; one, °good lack, no man desired.   105
And these were the conditions of the king:
That save he won the first by force, he needs
Must wed that other, whom no man desired,
A red-faced bride who knew herself so vile
That evermore she long'd to hide herself,   110
Nor fronted man or woman, eye to eye —
Yea — some she cleaved to, but they died of her.
And one — they call'd her Fame; and one — O
    mother,
How can ye keep me tether'd to you? — °Shame.
Man am I grown, a man's work must I do.   115
Follow the deer? follow the Christ, the King,
Live pure, speak true, right wrong, follow the
    King —
Else, wherefore born?'

              To whom the mother said:
'Sweet son, for there be many who deem him not,
Or will not deem him, wholly proven King —   120

Albeit in mine own heart I knew him King
When I was °frequent with him in my youth,
And heard him kingly speak, and doubted him
No more than he, himself; but felt him mine,
Of closest kin to me: yet — wilt thou leave   125
Thine easeful biding here, and risk thine all,
Life, limbs, for one that is not proven King?
Stay, till the cloud that settles round his birth
Hath lifted but a little.   Stay, sweet son.'

    And Gareth answer'd quickly: ° ' Not an hour,   130
So that ye yield me — I will walk thro' fire,
Mother, to gain it — your full leave to go.
°Not proven, who swept the dust of ruin'd Rome
From off the threshold of the realm, and crush'd
The idolaters, and made the people free?   135
Who should be king save him who makes us free?'

    So when the Queen, who long had sought in vain
To break him from the intent to which he grew,
Found her son's will unwaveringly °one,
She answer'd craftily: °' Will ye walk thro' fire?   140
Who walks thro' fire will hardly heed the smoke.
Ay, go then, an ye must: only one proof,
Before thou ask the King to make thee knight,
Of thine obedience and thy love to me,
Thy mother. — I demand.'   145

                              And Gareth cried:
'A hard one, or a hundred, so I go.
Nay — °quick! the proof to prove me to the quick!'

    But slowly spake the mother looking at him:
'Prince, thou shalt go disguised to Arthur's hall,
And hire thyself to °serve for meats and drinks   150
Among the scullions and the °kitchen-knaves,
And those that hand the dish across the °bar.
Nor shalt thou tell thy name to any one.
And thou shalt serve a twelvemonth and a day.'

    For so the Queen believed that when her son   155
Beheld his only way to glory lead
Low down thro' °villain kitchen-vassalage,
Her own true Gareth was too princely-proud
To pass thereby; so should he rest with her,
Closed in her castle from the sound of arms.   160

    Silent awhile was Gareth, then replied:
'The thrall in person may be free in soul,
And I shall see the jousts.   Thy son am I,
And, since thou art my mother, must obey.
I therefore yield me freely to thy will;   165
For hence will I, disguised, and hire myself
To serve with scullions and with kitchen-knaves;
Nor tell my name to any — no, not the King.'

Gareth awhile linger'd. The mother's eye
Full of the wistful fear that he would go,   170
And turning toward him wheresoe'er he turn'd,
Perplext his outward purpose, till an hour
When, waken'd by the wind which with full voice
Swept bellowing thro' the darkness on to dawn,
He rose, and out of slumber calling two   175
That still had tended on him from his birth,
Before the wakeful mother heard him, went.

The three were clad like tillers of the soil.
Southward they set their faces. The birds made
Melody on branch and melody in mid air.   180
The damp hill-slopes were quicken'd into green,
And the live green had kindled into flowers,
For it was past the time of Easter-day.

So, when their feet were planted on the plain
That broaden'd toward the base of °Camelot,   185
Far off °they saw the silver-misty morn
Rolling her smoke about the royal mount,
That rose between the forest and the field.
At times the summit of the high city flash'd;
At times the spires and turrets half-way down   190
Prick'd thro' the mist; at times the great gate shone
Only, that open'd on the field below:
Anon, the whole fair city had disappear'd.

Then those who went with Gareth were amazed,
One crying, 'Let us go no further, lord: 195
Here is a city of enchanters, built
By fairy kings.'   The second echo'd him,
'Lord, we have heard from our wise man at home
To northward, that this king is not the King,
But only changeling out of Fairyland,   200
Who drave the heathen hence by sorcery
And Merlin's glamour.'   Then the first again,
'Lord, there is no such city anywhere,
But all a vision.'

                  Gareth answer'd them
With laughter, swearing he had glamour enow   205
In his own blood, his princedom, youth, and hopes,
°To plunge old Merlin in the Arabian sea;
So push'd them all unwilling toward the gate.
And there was no gate like it under heaven.
For barefoot on the keystone, which was lined   210
And rippled like an ever-fleeting wave,
°The Lady of the Lake stood: all her dress
Wept from her sides as water flowing away;
But like the cross her great and goodly arms
Stretch'd under all the cornice and upheld: 215
And drops of water fell from either hand;
And down from one a sword was hung, from one
A censer, either worn with wind and storm;

And o'er her breast floated the sacred fish;
And in the space to left of her, and right,   220
Were Arthur's wars in weird devices done,
New things and old co-twisted, as if Time
Were nothing, so °inveterately that men
Were giddy gazing there; and over all
High on the top were those three queens, the
     friends   225
Of Arthur, who should help him at his need.

   Then those with Gareth for so long a space
Stared at the figures that at last it seem'd
The °dragon-boughts and elvish emblemings
Began to move, seethe, twine, and curl: they call'd 230
To Gareth, 'Lord, the gateway is alive.'

   And Gareth likewise on them fixt his eyes
So long that even to him they seem'd to move.
Out of the city a blast of music peal'd.
Back from the gate started the three, to whom   235
From out thereunder came an °ancient man,
Long-bearded, saying, 'Who be ye, my sons?'

   Then Gareth: 'We be tillers of the soil,
Who leaving share in furrow came to see
The glories of our King: but these, my men, —   240
Your city moved so weirdly in the mist, —

Doubt if the King be king at all, or come
From Fairyland; and whether this be built
By magic, and by fairy kings and queens;
Or whether there be any city at all,   245
Or all a vision: and this music now
Hath scared them both, but tell thou these the truth.'

  Then that old °Seer made answer, °playing on him
And saying: 'Son, I have °seen the good ship sail
Keel upward and mast downward, in the heavens,   250
And solid turrets topsy-turvy in air:
°And here is truth; but an it please thee not,
Take thou the truth as thou hast told it me.
For truly, as thou sayest, a fairy king
And fairy queens have built the city, son;   255
They came from out a °sacred mountain-cleft
Toward the sunrise, each with harp in hand,
And built it to the music of their harps.
And, as thou sayest, it is enchanted, son,
For there is nothing in it as it seems   260
Saving the °King; tho' some there be that hold
The King a shadow, and the city real:
Yet take thou heed of him, for, so thou pass
Beneath this archway, then wilt thou become
A thrall to his enchantments, for the King   265
Will bind thee by such vows as is a shame
A man should not be bound by, yet the which

No man can keep; but, so thou dread to swear,
Pass not beneath this gateway, but abide
Without, among the cattle of the field.   270
For an ye heard a music, like anow
They are building still, seeing the city is built
To music, therefore °never built at all,
And therefore built for ever.'

                    Gareth spake
Anger'd: 'Old master, °reverence thine own beard 275
That looks as white as utter truth, and seems
Wellnigh as long as thou art statured tall!
Why mockest thou the stranger that hath been
To thee fair-spoken?'

                    But the Seer replied:
'Know ye not then the Riddling of the Bards: 280
"Confusion, and illusion, and relation,
Elusion, and occasion, and evasion"?
I mock thee not but as thou mockest me;
And all that see thee, for thou art not who
Thou seemest, but I know thee who thou art.   285
And now thou goest up to mock the King,
Who cannot brook the shadow of any lie.'

   Unmockingly the mocker ending here,
Turn'd to the right, and past along the plain;

   D

Whom Gareth looking after said: ' My men,   290
Our one white lie sits like a little ghost
Here on the threshold of our enterprise.
°Let love be blamed for it, not she, nor I:
Well, we will make amends.'

                With all good cheer
He spake and laugh'd, then enter'd with his twain 295
Camelot, a city of shadowy palaces
And stately, rich in emblem and the work
Of ancient kings who °did their days in stone;
Which Merlin's hand, °the Mage at Arthur's court,
Knowing all arts, had touch'd, and everywhere,   300
At Arthur's ordinance, tipt with lessening peak
And pinnacle, and had made it °spire to heaven.
And ever and anon a knight would pass
Outward, or inward to the hall: his arms
Clash'd; and the sound was good to Gareth's ear. 305
°And out of bower and casement shyly glanced
Eyes of pure women, wholesome stars of love;
And all about a healthful people stept
As in the presence of a gracious king.

Then into hall Gareth ascending heard   310
A voice, the voice of Arthur, and beheld
Far over heads in that long-vaulted hall
The splendor of the presence of the King

Throned, and delivering °doom — and look'd no more —
But felt his young heart hammering in his ears,   315
And thought, 'For this half-shadow of a lie
The truthful King will doom me when I speak.'
Yet pressing on, tho' all in fear to find
°Sir Gawain or Sir Modred, saw nor one
Nor other, but in all the listening eyes   320
Of those tall knights that ranged about the throne
Clear honor shining like the dewy star
Of dawn, and faith in their great King, with pure
Affection, and the light of victory,
And glory gain'd, and evermore to gain.   325

Then came a widow crying to the King:
'A boon, Sir King! Thy father, Uther, reft
From my dead lord a field with violence;
For howsoe'er at first he proffer'd gold,
Yet, for the field was pleasant in our eyes,   330
We yielded not; and then he reft us of it
Perforce and left us neither gold nor field.'

Said Arthur, °'Whether would ye? gold or field?'
To whom the woman weeping, 'Nay, my lord,
The field was pleasant in my husband's eye.'   335

And Arthur: 'Have thy pleasant field again,'
And thrice the gold for Uther's use thereof,

According to the years.   No boon is here,
But justice, so thy say be proven true.
Accursed, who from the wrongs his father did   340
Would shape himself a right!'

                And while she past,
Came yet another widow crying to him:
'A boon, Sir King!   °Thine enemy, King, am I.
With thine own hand thou slewest my dear lord,
A knight of Uther in the barons' war,   345
When Lot and many another rose and fought
Against thee, saying thou wert basely born.
I held with these, and loathe to ask thee aught.
Yet lo! my husband's brother had my son
Thrall'd in his castle, and hath starved him dead,   350
And °standeth seized of that inheritance
Which thou that slewest the sire hast left the son,
So, tho' I scarce can ask it thee for hate,
Grant me some knight to do the battle for me,
Kill the foul thief, and wreak me for my son.'   35r

  Then strode a good knight forward, crying to him,
'A boon, Sir King!   I am her kinsman, I.
Give me to right her wrong, and slay the man.'

  Then came °Sir Kay, the seneschal, and cried,
'A boon, Sir King! even that thou grant her none,   360

This railer, that hath mock'd thee in full hall —
None; or the wholesome boon of °gyve and gag.'

But Arthur: ' We sit King, to help the wrong'd
Thro' all our realm.   The woman loves her lord.
Peace to thee, woman, with thy loves and hates!   365
The kings of old had doom'd thee to the flames;
°Aurelius Emrys would have scourged thee dead,
And Uther slit thy tongue: but get thee hence —
Lest that rough °humor of the kings of old
Return upon me!   Thou that art her kin,   370
Go likewise; lay him low and slay him not,
But bring him here, that I may judge the right,
According to the justice of the King:
Then, be he guilty, by that deathless King
Who lived and died for men, the man shall die.'   375

Then came in hall the messenger of °Mark,
A name of evil savor in the land,
The Cornish king.   In either hand he bore
What dazzled all, and shone far-off as shines
A field of °charlock in the sudden sun   380
Between two showers, a cloth of palest gold,
Which down he laid before the throne, and knelt,
°Delivering that his lord, the vassal king,
Was even upon his way to Camelot;
For having heard that Arthur of his grace   385

Had made his goodly °cousin Tristram knight,
And, for himself was of the greater state,
Being a king, he trusted his liege-lord
Would yield him this large honor all the more;
So pray'd him well to accept this cloth of gold,   390
In token of true heart and fealty.

   Then Arthur cried to rend the cloth, to rend
In pieces, and so cast it on the hearth.
An oak-tree smoulder'd there. 'The goodly knight!
What! shall the shield of Mark stand among
   these?'
For, midway down the side of that long hall,   396
A stately pile, — whereof along the front,
Some blazon'd, some but carven, and some blank,
There ran a treble range of stony shields, —
Rose, and high-arching over-brow'd the hearth.   400
And under every shield a knight was named.
For this was Arthur's custom in his hall.
When some good knight had done one noble deed,
His arms were carven only; but if twain,
His arms were blazon'd also; but if none,   405
The shield was blank and bare, without a sign
Saving the name beneath: and Gareth saw
The shield of Gawain blazon'd rich and bright,
And Modred's blank as death; and Arthur cried
To rend the cloth and cast it on the hearth.   410

' More like are we to °reave him of his crown
Than make him knight because men call him king.
The kings we found, ye know we stay'd their hands
From war among themselves, but left them kings;
Of whom were any bounteous, merciful, 415
Truth-speaking, brave, good livers, them we enroll'd
Among us, and they sit within our hall.
But Mark hath tarnish'd the great name of king,
As Mark would sully the low state of churl;
And, seeing he hath sent us cloth of gold, 420
Return, and meet, and hold him from our eyes,
Lest we should °lap him up in cloth of lead,
Silenced for ever — °craven — a man of plots,
Craft, poisonous counsels, wayside ambushings —
No fault of thine: let Kay the seneschal 425
Look to thy wants, and send thee satisfied —
Accursed, who strikes nor lets the hand be seen!'

And many another suppliant crying came
With noise of ravage wrought by beast and man,
And °evermore a knight would ride away. 430

Last,° Gareth leaning both hands heavily
Down on the shoulders of the twain, his men,
Approach'd between them toward the King, and ask'd,
'A boon, Sir King,' — his voice was all ashamed, —

'For see ye not how weak and hunger-worn   435
I seem — leaning on these? grant me to serve
For meat and drink among thy kitchen-knaves
A twelvemonth and a day, nor seek my name.
Hereafter I will fight.'

          To him the King:
'A goodly youth and worth a goodlier boon!   440
But so thou wilt no goodlier, then must Kay,
The master of the meats and drinks, be thine.'

   He rose and past; then Kay, a man of mien
°Wan-sallow as the plant that feels itself
Root-bitten by white lichen:

          °'Lo ye now!   445
This fellow hath broken from some abbey, where,
God °wot, he had not beef and °brewis enow,
However that might chance! but °an he work,
Like any pigeon will I cram his crop,
And sleeker shall he shine than any hog.'   450

   Then °Lancelot standing near: 'Sir Seneschal,
'Sleuth-hound thou knowest, and grey, and all the
      hounds;
A horse thou knowest, a man thou dost not know:
Broad brows and fair, a °fluent hair and fine,

High nose, a nostril large and fine, and hands   455
Large, fair, and fine! — Some young lad's mystery —
But, or from sheepcot or king's hall, the boy
Is noble-natured. Treat him with all grace,
Lest he should come to shame thy judging of him.'

Then Kay: 'What murmurest thou of mystery?   46
Think ye this fellow °will poison the King's dish?
Nay, for he spake too fool-like: mystery!
Tut, an the lad were noble, he had ask'd
For horse and armor: fair and fine, forsooth!
Sir Fine-face, °Sir Fair-hands? but see thou to it   465
That thine own fineness, Lancelot, some fine day
Undo thee not — and leave my man to me.'

So Gareth all for glory underwent
The sooty yoke of kitchen-vassalage,
Ate with young lads his portion by the door,   470
And couch'd at night with grimy kitchen-knaves.
And Lancelot ever spake him pleasantly,
But Kay the seneschal, who loved him not,
Would hustle and harry him, and labor him
Beyond his comrade of the hearth, and set   475
To turn the °broach, draw water, or hew wood.
Or grosser tasks; and Gareth bow'd himself
With all obedience to the King, and wrought
All kind of service with a noble ease

That graced the lowliest act in doing it.   480
And when the thralls had talk among themselves,
And one would praise the love that linkt the King
And Lancelot — how the King had saved his life
In battle twice, and Lancelot once the King's —
For Lancelot was the first in tournament,   485
But Arthur mightiest on the battle-field —
Gareth was glad.   Or if some other told
How once the wandering forester at dawn,
Far over the blue °tarns and hazy seas,
On °Caer-Eryri's highest found the King,   490
A °naked babe, of whom the Prophet spake,
' He passes to the °Isle Avilion,
He passes and is heal'd and cannot die ' —
Gareth was glad.   But if their talk were foul,
Then would he whistle rapid as any lark,   495
Or carol some old °roundelay, and so loud
That first they mock'd, but, after, reverenced him.
Or Gareth, telling some °prodigious tale
Of Knights who sliced a red life-bubbling way
Thro' twenty folds of twisted dragon, held   500
All in a °gap-mouth'd circle his good mates
Lying or sitting round him, idle hands,
Charm'd; till Sir Kay, the seneschal, would come
Blustering upon them, °like a sudden wind
Among dead leaves, and drive them all apart.   505
Or when the thralls had sport among themselves,

So there were any trial of mastery,
He, °by two yards in casting bar or stone,
Was counted best; and if there chanced a joust,
So that Sir Kay nodded him leave to go,   510
Would hurry thither, and when he saw the knights
Clash like the coming and retiring wave,
And the spear spring, and good horse reel, the boy
Was half beyond himself for ecstasy.

So for a month he wrought among the thralls;   515
But in the weeks that follow'd, the good Queen,
Repentant of the word she made him swear,
And saddening in her childless castle, sent,
Between the °in-crescent and de-crescent moon,
Arms for her son, and loosed him from his vow.   520

This, Gareth hearing from a squire of Lot
With whom he used to play at tourney once,
When both were children, and in lonely haunts
Would scratch a °ragged oval on the sand,
And each at either dash from either end —   525
Shame never made girl redder than Gareth joy.
He laugh'd; he sprang.   'Out of the smoke, at once
I leap from Satan's foot to Peter's knee —
These °news be mine, none other's — nay, the King's —
Descend into the city:' whereon he sought   530
The King alone, and found, and told him all.

'I have °stagger'd thy strong Gawain in a tilt
For pastime; yea, he said it: joust can I.
Make me thy knight — in secret! let my name
Be hidden, and give me the first quest, I spring   535
Like flame from ashes.'

                    Here the °King's calm eye
Fell on, and check'd, and made him flush, and bow
Lowly, to kiss his hand, who answer'd him:
'Son, the good mother let me know thee here,
And sent her wish that I would yield thee thine.   540
Make thee my knight? my knights are sworn to vows
Of utter hardihood, utter gentleness,
And, loving, utter faithfulness in love,
And uttermost obedience to the King.'

Then Gareth, lightly springing from his knees: 545
'My King, for hardihood I can promise thee.
For uttermost obedience make demand
Of whom ye gave me to, the Seneschal,
No mellow master of the meats and drinks!
And as for love, God wot, I love not yet,   550
But love I shall, God willing.'

                    And the King:
'Make thee my knight in secret? yea, but he,
Our noblest brother, and our truest man,
And one with me in all, he needs must know.'   554

'Let Lancelot know, my King, let Lancelot know,
Thy noblest and thy truest!'

                    And the King:
'But wherefore would ye men should wonder at you?
Nay, rather for the sake of me, their King,
And the deed's sake my knighthood do the deed,
Than to be noised of.'

                    Merrily Gareth ask'd: 560
°'Have I not earn'd my cake in baking of it?
Let be my name until I make my name!
My deeds will speak: it is but for a day.'
So with a kindly hand on Gareth's arm
Smiled the great King, and half-unwillingly   565
Loving his °lusty youthhood yielded to him.
Then, after summoning Lancelot privily:
'I have given him the first °quest: he is not proven.
Look therefore, when he calls for this in hall,
Thou get to horse and follow him far away.   570
Cover the °lions on thy shield, and see,
Far as thou mayest, he be nor ta'en nor slain.'

Then that same day there past into the hall
A damsel of high lineage, and a brow
°May-blossom, and a cheek of apple-blossom,   575
Hawk-eyes; and lightly was her slender nose

°Tip-tilted like the petal of a flower:
She into hall past with her page and cried:

'O King, °for thou hast driven the foe without,
See to the foe within! bridge, ford, beset   580
By bandits, every one that owns a tower
°The lord of half a league. Why sit ye there?
Rest would I not, Sir King, an I were king,
Till even the °lonest hold were all as free
From cursed bloodshed as thine altar-cloth   585
From that °best blood it is a sin to spill.'

'Comfort thyself,' said Arthur, 'I nor mine
Rest: so my knighthood keep the vows they swore,
The wastest moorland of our realm shall be
Safe, damsel, as the centre of this hall.   590
What is thy name? thy need?'

                        'My name?' she said —
°Lynette, my name; °noble; my need, a knight
To combat for my sister, °Lyonors,
A lady of high lineage, of great lands,
And comely, yea, and comelier than myself.   595
She lives in °Castle Perilous: a river
Runs in three loops about her living-place;
And o'er it are three passings, and three knights
Defend the passings, brethren, and a fourth,

And of that four the mightiest, holds her stay'd   600
In her own castle, and so besieges her
To break her will, and make her wed with him ·
And but delays his °purport till thou send
To do the battle with him thy chief man
Sir Lancelot, whom he trusts to overthrow;   505
Then wed, with glory: but she will not wed
Save whom she loveth, or a °holy life.
Now therefore have I come for Lancelot.'

Then Arthur mindful of Sir Gareth ask'd:
'Damsel, ye know this °Order lives to crush   610
All wrongers of the realm.   But say, these four,
Who be they ?   What the fashion of the men?'

'They be of foolish fashion, O Sir King,
The fashion of that °old knight-errantry
Who ride abroad, and do but what they will;   615
Courteous or bestial °from the moment, such
As have nor law nor king; and three of these
Proud in their °fantasy call themselves the Day,
°Morning-Star, and °Noon-Sun, and °Evening-Star,
Being strong fools; and never a whit more wise   620
The fourth, who alway rideth arm'd in black,
A huge man-beast of boundless savagery.
He names himself the Night and oftener Death,
And wears a helmet mounted with a skull,

And bears a skeleton figured on his arms,   625
To show that who may slay or °scape the three,
Slain by himself, shall enter endless night.
And all these four be fools, but mighty men,
And therefore am I come for Lancelot.'

   Hereat Sir Gareth call'd from where he rose,   630
A head with kindling eyes above the throng,
' A boon, Sir King — this quest!' then — for he mark'd
Kay near him groaning like a wounded bull —
' Yea, King, thou knowest thy kitchen-knave am I,
And mighty thro' thy meats and drinks am I,   635
And I can °topple over a hundred such.
Thy promise, King,' and Arthur glancing at him,
°Brought down a momentary brow. ' Rough, sudden,
And pardonable, °worthy to be knight —
Go therefore,' and all hearers were amazed.   640

   But on the damsel's forehead shame, pride, wrath
Slew the °may-white: she lifted either arm,
' Fie on thee, King! I ask'd for thy chief knight,
And thou hast given me but a kitchen-knave.'
Then ere a man in hall could stay her, turn'd,   645
Fled down the lane of access to the King,
Took horse, descended the slope street, and past
The weird white gate, and paused without, beside
The field of tourney, murmuring ' kitchen-knave!'

Now two great entries open'd from the hall,   650
At one end one that °gave upon a range
Of level pavement where the King would pace
At sunrise, gazing over plain and wood;
And down from this a lordly stairway sloped
Till lost in blowing trees and tops of towers;   655
And out by this main doorway past the King.
°But one was counter to the hearth, and rose
High that the highest-crested helm could ride
Therethro' nor graze; and by this entry fled
The damsel in her wrath, and on to this   660
Sir Gareth strode, and saw without the door
King Arthur's gift, the worth of half a town,
A war-horse of the best, and near it stood
The two that out of north had follow'd him.
This bare a maiden shield, a casque; that held   665
The horse, the spear; whereat Sir Gareth loosed
A cloak that dropt from collar-bone to heel,
A cloth of roughest web, and cast it down,
And from it, like a °fuel-smother'd fire
That lookt half-dead, brake bright, and flash'd as those
°Dull-coated things, that making slide apart   670
Their dusk wing-cases, all beneath there burns
A jewell'd harness, ere they pass and fly.
So Gareth ere he parted flash'd in arms.
Then as he donn'd the helm, and took the shield   675
And mounted horse and graspt a spear, of grain

E

°Storm-strengthen'd on a windy site, and tipt
With °trenchant steel, around him slowly prest
The people, while from out of kitchen came
The thralls in throng, and seeing who had work'd   680
Lustier than any, and whom they could but love,
Mounted in arms, threw up their caps and cried,
' God bless the King, and all his fellowship!'
And on thro' lanes of shouting Gareth rode
Down the slope street, and past without the gate   585

    So Gareth past with joy, °but as the cur
Pluckt from the cur he fights with, ere his cause
Be cool'd by fighting, follows, being named,
His owner, but remembers all, and growls
Remembering, so Sir Kay beside the door   690
Mutter'd in scorn of Gareth whom he used
To harry and hustle.

                    ' Bound upon a quest
With horse and arms — the King °hath past his
    time —
My scullion knave!   Thralls, to your work again,
°For an your fire be low ye kindle mine!   695
Will there be dawn in West and eve in East?
Begone! — my knave! — belike and like enow
Some old head-blow not heeded in his youth
So shook his wits they wander in his prime —

°Crazed! How the villain lifted up his voice,   700
Nor shamed to brawl himself a kitchen-knave!
Tut, he was tame and meek enow with me,
Till °peacock'd up with Lancelot's noticing.
Well — I will after my loud knave, and learn
Whether he know me for his master yet.   705
Out of the smoke he came, and °so my lance
Hold, by God's grace, he shall into the mire —
Thence, if the King awaken from his craze,
Into the smoke again.'

           But Lancelot said:
'Kay, wherefore wilt thou go against the King,   710
For that did never he whereon ye rail,
But ever meekly served the King in thee?
Abide: take counsel; for this lad is great
And lusty, and knowing both of lance and sword.'
'Tut, tell not me,' said Kay, ° 'ye are overfine   715
To mar stout knaves with foolish courtesies:'
Then mounted, on thro' silent faces rode
Down the slope city, and out beyond the gate.

    But by the field of tourney lingering yet
Mutter'd the damsel: 'Wherefore did the King   720
Scorn me? for, were Sir Lancelot lackt, at least
He might have yielded to me one of those
Who tilt for lady's love and glory here,

Rather than — O sweet heaven!   O fie upon him !—
His kitchen-knave.'

    To whom Sir Gareth drew — 725
And there were none but few goodlier than he —
Shining in arms, 'Damsel, the quest is mine.
Lead, and I follow.'   She thereat, as one
That smells a foul-flesh'd °agaric in the °holt,
And deems it °carrion of some woodland thing, 730
Or shrew, or weasel, nipt her slender nose
With petulant thumb and finger, °shrilling, ' Hence !
°Avoid, thou smellest all of kitchen-grease.
And look who comes behind ;' for there was Kay.
' Knowest thou not me ? thy master ?   I am Kay. 735
We lack thee by the hearth.'

    And Gareth to him,
' Master no more ! too well I know thee, ay —
The most °ungentle knight in Arthur's hall.'
' Have at thee then,' said Kay : they shock'd, and Kay
Fell shoulder-slipt, and Gareth cried again, 740
' Lead, and I follow,' and fast away she fled.

 But after °sod and shingle ceased to fly
Behind her, and the heart of her good horse
Was nigh to burst with violence of the beat,
Perforce she stay'd, and overtaken spoke: 745

'What doest thou, scullion, in my fellowship?
Deem'st thou that I accept thee aught the more
Or love thee better, that by some device
Full cowardly, or by mere unhappiness,
Thou hast overthrown and slain thy master — thou!
Dish-washer and broach-turner, °loon! — to me   751
Thou smellest all of kitchen as before.'

'Damsel,' Sir Gareth answer'd gently, 'say
Whate'er ye will, but whatsoe'er ye say,
I leave not till I finish this fair quest,
Or die therefor.'

                    'Ay, wilt thou finish it?
Sweet lord, how like a noble knight he talks!
The listening rogue hath caught the manner of it.
But, knave, anon thou shalt be met with, knave,
And then by such a one that thou for all   760
The kitchen brewis that was ever supt
Shalt not once dare to look him in the face.'

'I shall assay,' said Gareth with a smile
That madden'd her, and away she flash'd again
Down the long avenues of a boundless wood,   765
And Gareth following was again °beknaved:

'Sir Kitchen-knave, I have miss'd the only way
Where Arthur's men are set along the wood;

The wood is nigh as full of thieves as leaves :
If both be slain, I am rid of thee ; but yet,   770
Sir Scullion, canst thou use that °spit of thine ?
Fight, an thou canst : I have miss'd the only way.'

So till the dusk that follow'd evensong
Rode on the two, reviler and reviled ;
Then after one long slope was mounted, saw,   775
Bowl-shaped, thro' tops of many thousand pines
A gloomy-gladed hollow slowly sink
To westward — in the deeps whereof a mere,
Round as the red eye of an °eagle-owl,
Under the half-dead sunset glared ; and shouts   780
Ascended, and there brake a servingman°
Flying from out of the black wood, and crying,
' They have bound my lord to cast him in the mere.'
Then Gareth, ' Bound am I to right the wrong'd,
But straitlier bound am I to bide with thee.'   785
And when the damsel spake contemptuously,
' Lead, and I follow,' Gareth cried again,
' Follow, I lead !' so down among the pines
He plunged ; and there, black-shadow'd nigh the mere,
And mid-thigh-deep in bulrushes and reed,   790
Saw six tall men °haling a seventh along,
A stone about his neck to drown him in it.
Three with good blows he quieted, but three
Fled thro' the pines ; and Gareth loosed the stone

From off his neck, then in the mere beside   795
Tumbled it; °oilily bubbled up the mere.
Last, Gareth loosed his bonds and on free feet
Set him, a stalwart baron, Arthur's friend.

  ' Well that ye came, or else these °caitiff rogues
Had °wreak'd themselves on me; good cause is theirs
To hate me, for my wont hath ever been   801
To catch my thief, and then like vermin here
Drown him, and with a stone about his neck;
And under this °wan water many of them
Lie rotting, but at night let go the stone,   805
And rise, and flickering in a °grimly light
Dance on the mere.   °Good now, ye have saved a life
Worth somewhat as the cleanser of this wood.
And fain would I reward thee worshipfully.
What guerdon will ye ? '

                      Gareth sharply spake: 810
' None ! for the deed's sake have I done the deed,
In uttermost obedience to the King.
But wilt thou yield this damsel harborage ?

  Whereat the baron saying, ' I well believe
You be of Arthur's Table,' °a light laugh   815
Broke from Lynette : ' Ay, truly of a truth,
And in a sort, being Arthur's kitchen-knave ! —

But deem not I accept thee aught the more,
Scullion, for running sharply with thy spit
Down on a °rout of craven foresters.　　　　820
A thresher with his flail had scatter'd them.
Nay — for thou smellest of the kitchen still.
But an this lord will yield us harborage,
Well.'

　　　So she spake.　A league beyond the wood,
All in a full-fair manor and a rich,　　　　825
His towers, where that day a feast had been
Held in high hall, and many a viand left,
And many a costly °cate, received the three.
And there they placed a °peacock in his pride
Before the damsel, and the baron set　　　　830
Gareth beside her, but at once she rose.

　　°' Meseems, that here is much discourtesy,
Setting this knave, Lord Baron, at my side.
Hear me — this morn I stood in Arthur's hall,
And pray'd the King would grant me Lancelot　　　　835
To fight the brotherhood of Day and Night —
The last a monster unsubduable
Of any save of him for whom I call'd —
Suddenly bawls this °frontless kitchen-knave,
"The quest is mine; thy kitchen-knave am I,　　　　840
And mighty thro' thy meats and drinks am I."

Then Arthur all at once gone mad replies,
" Go therefore," and so gives the quest to him —
Him — here — a villain fitter to °stick swine
Than ride abroad redressing women's wrong,   845
Or sit beside a noble gentlewoman.'

Then half-ashamed and part-amazed, the lord
Now look'd at one and now at other, left
The damsel by the peacock in his pride,
And, seating Gareth at another board,   850
Sat down beside him, ate and then began :

' Friend, whether thou be kitchen-knave, or not,
Or whether it be the maiden's fantasy,
And whether she be mad, or else the King,
Or both or neither, or thyself be mad,   855
I ask not : but thou strikest a strong stroke,
For strong thou art and goodly therewithal
And saver of my life; and therefore now,
For here be mighty men to joust with, weigh
Whether thou wilt not with thy damsel back   860
To crave again Sir Lancelot of the King.
Thy pardon; I but speak for thine °avail,
The saver of my life.'

                    And Gareth said,
Full pardon, but I follow up the quest,
Despite of Day and Night and Death and Hell.'   865

So when, next morn, the lord whose life he saved
Had, some brief space, convey'd them on their way
And left them with God-speed, Sir Gareth spake,
'Lead, and I follow.'   Haughtily she replied :

'I fly no more : I allow thee for an hour.   870
°Lion and stoat have isled together, knave,
In time of flood.   Nay, furthermore, methinks
Some °ruth is mine for thee.   Back wilt thou, fool ?
For hard by here is one will overthrow
And slay thee; then will I to court again,   875
And shame the King for only yielding me
My champion from the ashes of his hearth.'

To whom Sir Gareth answer'd courteously :
'Say thou thy say, and I will do my deed.
Allow me for mine hour, and thou wilt find   880
My fortunes all as fair as hers who lay
°Among the ashes and wedded the King's son.'

Then to the shore of one of those long loops
Wherethro' the serpent river coil'd, they came.
Rough-thicketed   were   the   banks   and steep;   the
    stream
Full, narrow; this a bridge of single arc   886
°Took at a leap; and on the further side
Arose a silk pavilion, gay with gold

In streaks and rays, and all °Lent-lily in hue,
Save that the dome was purple, and above, 890
Crimson, a slender banneret fluttering.
And therebefore the lawless warrior paced
Unarm'd, and calling, 'Damsel, is this he,
The champion thou hast brought from Arthur's hall?
For whom we let thee pass.'   'Nay, nay,' she said, 895
'°Sir Morning-Star.   The King in utter scorn
Of thee and thy much folly hath sent thee nere
His kitchen-knave: and look thou to thyself:
See that he fall not on thee suddenly,
And slay thee unarm'd; he is not knight but knave.' 900

Then at his call, 'O daughters of the Dawn,
And servants of the Morning-Star, approach,
Arm me,' from out the silken curtain-folds
Bare-footed and bare-headed three fair girls
In gilt and rosy raiment came: their feet 905
In dewy grasses glisten'd; and the hair
All over glanced with dewdrop or with gem
Like sparkles in the stone °Avanturine.
These arm'd him in blue arms, and gave a shield
Blue also, and thereon the morning star. 910
And Gareth silent gazed upon the knight,
Who stood a moment, ere his horse was brought,
Glorying; and in the stream beneath him shone,
Immingled with Heaven's azure waveringly,

The gay pavilion and the naked feet,   915
His arms, the rosy raiment, and the star.

  Then she that watched him: 'Wherefore stare
      ye so?
Thou shakest in thy fear: there yet is time:
Flee down the valley before he get to horse.
Who will cry shame? Thou art not knight but knave.' 920

  Said Gareth: 'Damsel, whether knave or knight,
Far liefer had I fight a score of times
Than hear thee so missay me and revile.
Fair words were best for him who fights for thee;
But truly foul are better, for they send   925
That strength of anger thro' mine arms, I know
That I shall overthrow him.'

                            And he that bore
The star, when mounted, cried from o'er the bridge:
'A kitchen-knave, and sent in scorn of me!
Such fight not I, but answer scorn with scorn.   930
For this were shame to do him further wrong
Than set him on his feet, and take his horse
And arms, and so return him to the King.
Come, therefore, leave thy lady °lightly, knave.
Avoid: for it beseemeth not a knave   935
To ride with such a lady.'

                'Dog, thou liest!
I spring from loftier lineage than thine own.'
He spake; and all at fiery speed the two
Shock'd on the °central bridge, and either spear
Bent but not brake, and either knight at once,   940
Hurl'd as a stone from out of a catapult
Beyond the horse's crupper and the bridge,
Fell, as if dead; but quickly rose and drew,
And Gareth lash'd so fiercely with his brand
He drave his enemy backward down the bridge,   945
The damsel crying, 'Well-stricken, kitchen-knave!'
Till Gareth's shield was cloven; but one stroke
Laid him that clove it grovelling on the ground.

     Then cried the fallen, 'Take not my life: I yield.'
And Gareth, 'So this damsel ask it of me   950
Good — I accord it easily as a grace.'
She reddening, 'Insolent scullion! I of thee?
I bound to thee for any favor ask'd!'
'Then shall he die.' And Gareth there unlaced
His helmet as to slay him, but she shriek'd   955
'Be not so hardy, scullion, as to slay
One nobler than thyself.' 'Damsel, thy charge
Is an abounding pleasure to me. Knight,
Thy life is thine at her command. Arise
And quickly pass to Arthur's hall, and say   960
His kitchen-knave hath sent thee. See thou crave

His pardon for thy breaking of his laws.
Myself when I return will plead for thee.
Thy shield is mine — farewell; and, damsel, thou,
Lead, and I follow.'

               And fast away she fled;   965
Then when he came upon her, spake: ' Methought,
Knave, when I watch'd thee striking on the bridge,
The savor of thy kitchen came upon me
A little faintlier: but the wind hath changed;
I scent it twenty-fold.' And then she sang, °   970
' " O morning star " — not that tall felon there,
Whom thou, by sorcery or unhappiness
Or some device, hast foully overthrown, —
" O morning star that smilest in the blue,
O star, my morning dream hath proven true,   975
Smile sweetly, thou! my love hath smiled on me."

  ' But thou begone, take counsel, and away,
For hard by here is one that guards a ford —
The second brother in their fool's parable —
Will pay thee all thy wages, and to boot.   980
Care not for shame: thou art not knight but knave.'

  To whom Sir Gareth answer'd, laughingly:
' Parables? Hear a parable of the knave.
When I was kitchen-knave among the rest,

Fierce was the hearth, and one of my co-mates   985
Own'd a rough dog, to whom he cast his coat,
"Guard it," and there was none to meddle with it.
And such a coat art thou, and thee the King
Gave me to guard, and such a dog am I,
To worry, and not to flee; and — knight or knave —   990
The knave that doth thee service as full knight
Is all as good, meseems, as any knight
Toward thy sister's freeing.'

                     ' Ay, Sir Knave!
Ay, knave, because thou strikest as a knight,
Being but knave, I hate thee all the more.'   995

    ' Fair damsel, you should worship me the more,
That, being but knave, I throw thine enemies.'

    ' Ay, ay,' she said, ' but thou shalt meet thy
       match.'

    So when they touch'd the second river-loop,
Huge on a high red horse, and all in mail   1000
Burnish'd to blinding, shone the °Noonday Sun
Beyond a raging shallow. As if the °flower
That blows a globe of after arrowlets
Ten-thousand-fold had grown, flash'd the fierce
       shield,
All sun; and Gareth's eyes had flying blots   1005

Before them when he turn'd from watching him.
He from the roaring shallow roar'd,
'What doest thou, °brother, in my marches here?'
And she athwart the shallow shrill'd again,
'Here is a kitchen-knave from Arthur's hall   1010
Hath overthrown thy brother, and hath his arms.'
'Ugh!' cried the Sun, and, vizoring up a red
And cipher face of rounded foolishness,
Push'd horse across the foamings of the ford,
Whom Gareth met mid-stream; no room was there   1015
For lance or tourney-skill; four strokes they struck
With sword, and these were mighty; the new knight
Had fear he might be shamed; but as the Sun
Heaved up a ponderous arm to strike the fifth,
The hoof of his horse slipt in the stream, the stream   1020
Descended, and the Sun was wash'd away.

   Then Gareth laid his lance athwart the ford;
So drew him home; but he that fought no more,
As being all bone-batter'd on the rock,
Yielded; and Gareth sent him to the King.   1025
'Myself when I return will plead for thee.
'Lead, and I follow.'   Quietly she led.
'Hath not the good wind, damsel, changed again?'
'Nay, not a point; nor art thou victor here.
There lies a ridge of slate across the ford;   1030
His horse thereon stumbled — ay, for I saw it.

'"O sun"—not this strong fool whom thou, Sir Knave,
Hast overthrown thro' mere unhappiness —
"O sun, that wakenest all to bliss or pain,
O moon, that layest all to sleep again, 1035
Shine sweetly : twice my love hath smiled on me."

'What knowest thou of love-song or of love?
Nay, nay, God wot, so thou wert nobly born,
Thou hast a pleasant presence. Yea, perchance, —

'"O dewy flowers that open to the sun, 1040
O dewy flowers that close when day is done,
Blow sweetly : twice my love hath smiled on me."

'What knowest thou of flowers, except, belike,
To garnish meats with ? hath not our good King
Who lent me thee, the flower of kitchendom, 1045
A foolish love for flowers ? what stick ye round
The pasty ? wherewithal deck the boar's head ?
Flowers ? nay, the boar hath °rosemaries and bay.

'"O birds that warble to the morning sky,
O birds that warble as the day goes by, 1050
Sing sweetly : twice my love hath smiled on me."

'What knowest thou of birds, lark, °mavis, merle,
Linnet ? what dream ye when they utter forth

F

May-music growing with the growing light,
Their sweet sun-worship? these be for the snare —
So runs thy fancy — these be for the spit,   1056
Larding and basting.   See thou have not now
Larded thy last, except thou turn and fly.
There stands the third fool of their allegory.'

For there beyond a bridge of treble bow,   1060
All in a rose-red from the west, and all
Naked it seem'd, and glowing in the broad
°Deep-dimpled current underneath, the knight
That named himself the Star of Evening stood.

And Gareth, 'Wherefore waits the madman there
Naked in open dayshine?' 'Nay,' she cried,   1066
'Not naked, only wrapt in °harden'd skins
That fit him like his own; and so ye cleave
His armor off him, these will turn the blade.'

Then the third brother shouted o'er the bridge, 1070
'O brother-star, why shine ye here so low?
Thy ward is higher up: but have ye slain
The damsel's champion?' and the damsel cried:

'No star of thine, but shot from Arthur's heaven
With all disaster unto thine and thee!   1075
For both thy younger brethren have gone down

Before this youth ; and so wilt thou, Sir Star ;
Art thou not old ? '

(Gareth said) : ' Old, damsel, old and hard,
Old, with the might and breath of twenty boys.'
Said Gareth, ' Old, and over-bold in brag !   1080
But that same strength which threw the Morning Star
Can throw the Evening.'

                  Then that other blew
A hard and deadly note upon the horn.
' Approach and arm me ! '   With slow steps from out
An old storm-beaten, russet, many-stain'd   1085
Pavilion, forth a grizzled damsel came,
And arm'd him in old arms, and brought a helm
With but a drying evergreen for crest,
And gave a shield whereon the star of even
Half-tarnish'd and half-bright, his emblem, shone.   1090
But when it glitter'd o'er the saddle-bow,
They madly hurl'd together on the bridge ;
And Gareth overthrew him, lighted, drew,
There met him drawn, and overthrew him again,
But up like fire he started : and as oft   1095
As Gareth brought him grovelling on his knees,
So many a time he vaulted up again ;
Till Gareth panted hard, and his great heart,
Foredooming all his trouble was in vain,

Labor'd within him, for he seem'd as one   1100
That all in later, sadder age begins
To war against ill uses of a life,
But these from all his life arise, and cry,
'Thou hast made us lords, and canst not put us down!'
He half despairs; so Gareth seem'd to strike   1105
Vainly, the damsel clamoring all the while,
'Well done, °knave-knight, well stricken, O good knight-
       knave —
O knave, as noble as any of all the knights —
Shame me not, shame me not. I have prophesied —
Strike, thou art worthy of the Table Round —   1110
His arms are old, he trusts the harden'd skin —
Strike — strike — the wind will never change again.'
And Gareth hearing ever stronglier smote,
And hew'd great pieces of his armor off him,
But lash'd in vain against the harden'd skin,   1115
And could not wholly bring him under, more
Than loud °Southwesterns, rolling ridge on ridge,
The buoy that rides at sea, and dips and springs
For ever; till at length Sir Gareth's brand
Clash'd his, and brake it utterly to the hilt.   1120
'I have thee now;' but forth that other sprang,
And, all unknightlike, writhed his wiry arms
Around him, till he felt, despite his mail,
Strangled, but straining even his uttermost
Cast, and so hurl'd him headlong o'er the bridge 1125

Down to the river, sink or swim, and cried,
'Lead and I follow.'

          But the damsel said:
'I lead no longer; ride thou at my side;
Thou art the kingliest of all kitchen-knaves.

'"O trefoil, °sparkling on the rainy plain,   1130
O rainbow with three colors after rain,
Shine sweetly: thrice my love hath smiled on me."

'Sir,—and, good faith, I fain had added—Knight,
But that I heard thee call thyself a knave,—
Shamed am I that I so rebuked, reviled,   1135
Missaid thee; noble I am; and thought the King
Scorn'd me and mine; and now thy pardon, friend,
For thou hast ever answer'd courteously,
And wholly bold thou art, and meek withal
As any of Arthur's best, but, being knave,   1140
°Hast mazed my wit: I marvel what thou art.'

'Damsel,' he said, 'you be not all to blame,
Saving that you mistrusted our good King
Would handle scorn, or yield you, asking, one
Not fit to cope your quest. You said your say;   1145
Mine answer was my deed. Good sooth! I hold
He scarce is knight, yea but half-man, nor meet

To fight for gentle damsel, he, who lets
His heart be stirr'd with any foolish heat
At any gentle damsel's waywardness.   1150
Shamed? care not! thy foul sayings fought for me:
And seeing now thy words are fair, methinks
There rides no knight, not Lancelot, his great self,
Hath force to quell me.'

                   Nigh upon that hour
When the lone hern forgets his melancholy,   1155
°Lets down his other leg, and stretching dreams
Of goodly supper in the distant pool,
Then turn'd the noble damsel smiling at him,
And told him of a cavern hard at hand,
Where bread and baken meats and good red wine   1160
Of Southland, which the Lady Lyonors
Had sent her coming champion, waited him.

  Anon they past a narrow °comb wherein
Were slabs of rock with figures, knights on horse
Sculptured, and deckt in slowly-waning hues.   1165
' Sir Knave, my knight, a hermit once was here
Whose holy hand hath fashion'd on the rock
The war of Time against the soul of man,
And yon four fools have suck'd their allegory
From these damp walls, and taken but the form.   1170
Know ye not these?' and Gareth lookt and read—

In letters like to those the °vexillary
Hath left crag-carven o'er the streaming Gelt —
°'PHOSPHORUS,' then 'MERIDIES,' — 'HESPERUS' —
'NOX' — 'MORS,' beneath five figures, armed men, 1175
Slab after slab, their faces forward all,
And running down the Soul, a shape that fled
With broken wings, torn raiment, and loose hair,
For help and shelter to the hermit's °cave.
'Follow the faces, and we find it.   Look,   1180
Who comes behind ?'

　　　　　　　　　For one — delay'd at first
Thro' helping back the dislocated Kay
To Camelot, then by what thereafter chanced,
The damsel's headlong °error thro' the wood —
Sir Lancelot, having swum the river-loops —   1185
His blue shield-lions cover'd — softly drew
Behind the twain, and when he saw the star
Gleam, on Sir Gareth's turning to him, cried,
'Stay, felon knight, I avenge me for my friend.'
And Gareth crying prick'd against the cry ;   1190
But when they closed — in a moment — at one touch
Of that skill'd spear, the wonder of the world —
Went sliding down so easily, and fell,
That when he found the grass within his hands
He laugh'd ; the laughter jarr'd upon Lynette :   1195
Harshly she ask'd him, 'Shamed and overthrown,

And tumbled back into the kitchen-knave,
Why laugh ye?   that ye blew your boast in vain?'
'Nay, noble damsel, but that I, the son
Of old King Lot and good Queen Bellicent,   1200
And victor of the bridges and the ford,
And knight of Arthur, here lie thrown by whom
I know not, all thro' mere unhappiness —
Device and sorcery and unhappiness —
Out, sword; we are thrown!' And Lancelot answer'd: 1205
     'Prince,
O Gareth — thro' the mere unhappiness
Of one who came to help thee, not to harm,
Lancelot, and all as glad to find thee whole
As on the day when Arthur knighted him.'   1209

     Then Gareth: 'Thou — Lancelot! — thine the hand
That threw me?   An some chance to mar the boast
Thy brethren of thee make — which could not chance —
Had sent thee down before a lesser spear,
Shamed had I been, and sad — O Lancelot — thou!'

     Whereat the maiden, petulant: 'Lancelot,   1215
Why came ye not, when call'd? and wherefore now
Come ye, not call'd?   I gloried in my knave,
Who being still rebuked would answer still
Courteous as any knight — but now, if knight,
The marvel dies, and leaves me fool'd and trick'd,   1220

And only wondering wherefore played upon ;
And doubtful whether I and mine be scorn'd.
Where should be truth if not in Arthur's hall,
In Arthur's presence? Knight, knave, prince and
  fool,
I hate thee and forever.'

      And Lancelot said: 1225
' Blessed be thou, Sir Gareth ! knight art thou
To the King's best wish. O damsel, be you wise,
To call him shamed who is but overthrown ?
Thrown have I been, nor once, but many a time.
Victor from vanquish'd issues at the last, 1230
And overthrower from being overthrown.
With sword we have not striven ; and thy good horse
And thou are weary ; yet not less I felt
Thy manhood thro' that wearied lance of thine.
Well hast thou done ; for all the stream is freed, 1235
And thou hast wreak'd his justice on his foes,
And when reviled hast answer'd graciously,
And makest merry when overthrown. Prince, knight,
Hail, knight and prince, and of our Table Round !'

 And then when turning to Lynette he told 1240
The tale of Gareth, petulantly she said :
' Ay, well — ay, well — for worse than being fool'd
Of others, is to fool one's self. A cave,

Sir Lancelot, is hard by, with meats and drinks
And forage for the horse, and flint for fire.   1245
But all about it flies a honeysuckle.
Seek, till we find.'   And when they sought and found,
Sir Gareth drank and ate, and all his life
Past into sleep; on whom the maiden gazed:
'Sound sleep be thine! sound cause to sleep hast
      thou.
Wake lusty!   Seem I not as tender to him   1251
As any mother?   Ay, but such a one
As all day long hath rated at her child,
And vext his day, but blesses him asleep —
Good lord, how sweetly smells the honeysuckle   1255
In the hush'd night, as if the world were one
Of utter peace, and love, and gentleness!
O Lancelot, Lancelot,' — and she clapt her hands —
'Full merry am I to find my goodly knave
Is knight and noble.   See now, sworn have I,   1260
Else yon black felon had not let me pass,
To bring thee back to do the battle with him.
Thus an thou goest, he will fight thee first;
Who doubts thee victor? so will my knight-knave
Miss the full flower of this accomplishment.'   1265

      Said Lancelot: 'Peradventure he you name
May know my shield.   Let Gareth, an he will,
Change his for mine, and take my charger, fresh,

Not to be spurr'd, loving the battle as well
As he that rides him.' ' Lancelot-like,' she said,   1270
'Courteous in this, Lord Lancelot, as in all.'

And Gareth, wakening, fiercely clutch'd the shield:
'Ramp, ye lance-splintering lions, on whom all spears
Are rotten sticks! ye seem agape to roar!
Yea, ramp and roar at leaving of your lord! —   1275
Care not, good beasts, so well I care for you.
O noble Lancelot, °from my hold on these
Streams virtue — fire — thro' one that will not shame
Even the shadow of Lancelot under shield.
Hence: let us go.'

                Silent the silent field   1280
They traversed. °Arthur's Harp tho' summer-wan,
In counter motion to the clouds, allured
The glance of Gareth dreaming on his liege.
A star shot: ' Lo,' said Gareth, ' the foe falls!'
An owl whoopt: ' Hark the victor pealing there!' 1285
Suddenly she that rode upon his left
Clung to the shield that Lancelot lent him, crying:
' Yield, yield him this again; 'tis he must fight:
I curse the tongue that all thro' yesterday
Reviled thee, and hath wrought on Lancelot now   1290
To lend thee horse and shield: wonders ye have done;
Miracles ye cannot: here is glory enow

In having flung three: I see thee maim'd,
Mangled: I swear thou canst not fling the fourth.'

'And wherefore, damsel? tell me all ye know.   1295
You cannot scare me; nor rough face, or voice,
Brute bulk of limb, or boundless savagery
Appal me from the quest.'

        'Nay, prince,' she cried,
'God wot, I never look'd upon the face,
Seeing he never rides abroad by day;   1300
But watch'd him have I like a phantom pass
Chilling the night: nor have I heard the voice.
Always he made his mouthpiece of a page
Who came and went, and still reported him
As closing in himself the strength of ten,   1305
And when his anger tare him, massacring
Man, woman, lad, and girl — yea, the soft babe!
Some hold that he hath swallow'd infant flesh,
Monster!   O prince, I went for Lancelot first,
The quest is Lancelot's: give him back the shield.' 1310
  Said Gareth laughing, 'An he fight for this,
Belike he wins it as the better man:
°Thus — and not else!'

        But Lancelot on him urged
All the °devisings of their chivalry
When one might meet a mightier than himself;   1315

How best to manage horse, lance, sword, and shield,
And so fill up the gap where force might fail
With skill and °fineness.   Instant were his words.

Then Gareth : ' Here be rules.   I know but one —
To dash against mine enemy and to win.   1320
Yet have I watch'd thee victor in the joust,
And seen thy way.' ' Heaven help thee !' sigh'd Lynette.

Then for a space and under cloud that grew
To thunder-gloom palling all stars, they rode
In converse till she made her palfrey halt,   1325
Lifted an arm, and softly whisper'd, ' There.'
And all the three were silent seeing, pitch'd
Beside the Castle Perilous on the flat field,
A huge pavilion like a mountain peak
Sunder the glooming crimson on the marge,   1330
Black, with black banner, and a long black horn
Beside it hanging ; which Sir Gareth graspt,
And so, before the two could hinder him,
Sent all his heart and breath thro' all the horn.
Echo'd the walls, a light twinkled ; anon   1335
°Came lights and lights, and once again he blew ;
Whereon were hollow tramplings up and down
And muffled voices heard, and shadows past ;
Till high above him, circled with her maids,
The Lady Lyonors at a window stood,   1340

Beautiful among lights, and waving to him
White hands and courtesy; but when the prince
Three times had blown — after long hush — at
    last —
The huge pavilion slowly yielded up,
Thro' those black foldings, that which housed therein.
High on a night-black horse, in night-black arms,   1346
With °white breast-bone, and barren ribs of Death,
And °crown'd with fleshless laughter — some ten
    steps —
In the half-light — thro' the dim dawn — advanced
The monster, and then paused, and spake no word.   1350

But Gareth spake and all indignantly:
'Fool, for thou hast, men say, the strength of ten,
Canst thou not trust the limbs thy God hath given,
But must, to make the terror of thee more,
Trick thyself out in ghastly imageries   1355
Of that which Life had done with, and the clod,
Less dull than thou, will hide with mantling flowers
As if for pity?'   But he spake no word;
Which set the horror higher: a maiden swoon'd;
The Lady Lyonors wrung her hands and wept,   1360
As doom'd to be the bride of Night and Death;
Sir Gareth's head prickled beneath his helm;
And even Sir Lancelot thro' his warm blood felt
Ice strike, and all that mark'd him were aghast.

At once Sir Lancelot's charger fiercely neigh'd,   1365
And Death's dark war-horse bounded forward with
    him.
Then those that did not °blink the terror saw
That Death was cast to ground, and slowly rose.
But with one stroke Sir Gareth split the skull.
Half fell to right and half to left and lay.   1370
Then with a stronger buffet he clove the helm
As thoroughly as the skull; °and out from this
Issued the bright face of a blooming boy
Fresh as a flower new-born, and crying, 'Knight,
Slay me not: my three brethren bade me do it,   1375
To make a horror all about the house,
And °stay the world from Lady Lyonors;
They never dream'd the passes would be past.'
Answer'd Sir Gareth graciously to one
Not many a moon his younger, 'My fair child,   1380
What madness made thee challenge the chief knight
Of Arthur's hall?' 'Fair Sir, they bade me do it.
They hate the King and Lancelot, the King's friend;
They hoped to slay him somewhere on the stream,
They never dream'd the passes could be past.'   1385

Then sprang the happier day from underground;
And Lady Lyonors and her house, with dance
And revel, and song, made merry over Death,
As being after all their foolish fears

And horrors only proven a blooming boy.   1390
So large mirth lived, and Gareth won the quest.

    And °he that told the tale in older times
Says that Sir Gareth wedded Lyonors,
But °he that told it later says Lynette.

Gareth & Lynette
Intro
I. Gareth's resolve
II. Conversation with his mother
    A. Gareth's pleading. Consent
    B. the condition of his mother's
Body
I. Gareth's trip to Camelot.
II. Gareth's experiences as a kitchen-knav
III. Knighting of Gareth.
IV. Gareth's first quest.
    A. Lynette's quest.
    B. the combat with Sir Kay.
    C.   "   rescue of the baron.
    C.   "   overthrow of the 4 brothers
Conclusion
I. the merriment at the castle
    of Lady Lyonors.
II. Gareth's marriage.

THE MARRIAGE OF GERAINT

THE brave Geraint, a knight of Arthur's court,
A tributary prince of Devon, one
Of that great Order of the Table Round,
Had married Enid, Yniol's only child,
And loved her as he loved the light of heaven.   5
And as the light of heaven varies, now
At sunrise, now at sunset, now by night
With moon and trembling stars, so loved Geraint
To make her beauty vary day by day,
In crimsons and in purples and in gems.   10
And Enid, but to please her husband's eye,
Who first had found and loved her in a state
Of broken fortunes, daily fronted him
In some fresh splendor; and the Queen herself,
Grateful to Prince Geraint for service done,   15
Loved her, and often with her own white hands
Array'd and deck'd her, as the loveliest,
Next after her own self, in all the court.
And Enid loved the Queen, and with true heart
Adored her, as the stateliest and the best   20
And loveliest of all women upon earth.
And seeing them so tender and so close,

Long in their common love rejoiced Geraint.
But when a rumor rose about the Queen,
Touching her guilty love for Lancelot,   25
Tho' yet there lived no proof, nor yet was heard
The world's loud whisper breaking into storm,
Not less Geraint believed it, and there fell
A horror °on him lest his gentle wife,
Thro' that great tenderness for Guinevere,   30
Had suffer'd or should suffer any taint
In nature: wherefore, going to the King,
He made this pretext, that his princedom lay
Close on the borders of a territory
Wherein were bandit earls, and caitiff knights,   35
Assassins and all flyers from the hand
Of Justice, and whatever loathes a law;
And therefore, till the King himself should please
To cleanse this °common sewer of all his realm,
He craved a °fair permission to depart,   40
And there defend his marches: and the King
Mused for a little on his plea, but, last,
Allowing it, the prince and Enid rode,
And fifty knights rode with them, to the shores
Of Severn, and they past to their own land;   45
Where, thinking that, if ever yet was wife
True to her lord, mine shall be so to me,
He compass'd her with sweet observances
And °worship, never leaving her, and grew

°Forgetful of his promise to the King,⁣   50
Forgetful of the falcon and the hunt,
Forgetful of the tilt and tournament,
Forgetful of his glory and his name,
Forgetful of his princedom and its cares.
And this forgetfulness was hateful to her.   55
And by and by the people, when they met
In twos and threes, or fuller companies,
Began to scoff and jeer and babble of him
As of a prince whose manhood was all gone,
And °molten down in mere uxoriousness.   60
And this she gather'd from the people's eyes;
This too the women who attired her head,
To please her, dwelling on his boundless love,
Told Enid, and they sadden'd her the more:
And day by day she thought to tell Geraint,   65
But could not out of bashful delicacy;
While he, that watch'd her sadden, was the more
Suspicious that her nature had a °taint.

At last, it chanced that on a summer morn —
They sleeping °each by either — the new sun   70
Beat thro' the blindless casement of the room,
And heated the strong warrior in his dreams;
Who, moving, cast the coverlet aside,
And bared the knotted column of his throat,
The massive square of his heroic breast,   75

And arms on which the standing muscle sloped,
°As slopes a wild brook o'er a little stone,
Running too vehemently to break upon it.
And Enid woke and sat beside the couch,
Admiring him, and thought within herself,　　80
Was ever man so grandly made as he?
Then, like a shadow, past the people's talk
And accusation of uxoriousness
Across her mind. and, bowing over him,
Low to her own heart piteously she said:　　85

'O noble breast and all-puissant arms,
Am I the cause. I the poor cause that men
Reproach you, saying all your force is gone?
I am the cause, because I dare not speak
And tell him what I think and what they say.　　90
And yet I hate that he should linger here;
I cannot love my lord and not his name.
Far liefer had I gird his harness on him,
And ride with him to battle and stand by,
And watch his mightful hand striking great blows　　95
At caitiffs and at wrongers of the world.
Far better were I laid in the dark earth,
Not hearing any more his noble voice,
Not to be folded more in these dear arms,
And darken'd from the high light in his eyes,　　100
Than that my lord through me should suffer shame.

Am I so bold, and could I so stand by,
And see my dear lord wounded in the strife,
Or maybe pierced to death before mine eyes,
And yet not dare to tell him what I think,
And how men slur him, saying all his force
Is melted into mere effeminacy ?
O me, I fear that I am no true wife ! '

Half inwardly, half audibly she spoke,
And the strong passion in her made her weep   110
True tears upon his broad and naked breast,
And these awoke him, and by great mischance
He heard but fragments of her later words,
And that she fear'd she was not a true wife.
And then he thought, ' In spite of all my care,   115
°For all my pains, poor man, for all my pains,
She is not faithful to me, and I see her
Weeping for some gay knight in Arthur's hall.'
Then, tho' he loved and reverenced her too much
To dream she could be guilty of foul act,   120
Right thro' his manful breast darted the pang
That makes a man, in the sweet face of her
Whom he loves most, lonely and miserable.
At this he °hurl'd his huge limbs out of bed,
And shook his drowsy squire awake and cried   125
' My charger and her °palfrey ;' then to her,
' I will ride forth into the wilderness ;

For, tho' it seems my °spurs are yet to win,
I have not fallen so low as some would wish.
And thou, put on thy worst and meanest dress   130
And ride with me.'   And Enid ask'd, amazed,
'If Enid errs, let Enid learn her fault.'
But he, 'I charge thee, ask not, but obey.'
Then she bethought her of a faded silk,
A faded mantle and a faded veil,   135
And moving toward a °cedarn cabinet,
Wherein she kept them folded reverently
With °sprigs of summer laid between the folds,
She took them, and array'd herself therein,
Remembering when first he came on her   140
Drest in that dress, and how he loved her in it,
And all her foolish fears about the dress,
And all his journey to her, as himself
Had told her, and their coming to the court.

°For Arthur on the °Whitsuntide before   145
Held court at old °Caerleon upon Usk.
There cn a day, he sitting high in hall,
Before him came a °forester of Dean,
Wet from the woods, with notice of a hart
Taller than all his fellows, milky-white,   150
First seen that day: these things he told the King.
Then the good King gave order to let blow
His horns for hunting on the morrow morn,

And when the Queen petition'd for his leave
To see the hunt, allow'd it easily.   155
So with the morning all the court were gone.
But Guinevere lay late into the morn,
Lost in sweet dreams, and °dreaming of her love
For Lancelot, and forgetful of the hunt,
But rose at last, a single maiden with her,   160
Took horse, and forded Usk, and gain'd the wood;
There, on a little knoll beside it, stay'd
Waiting to hear the hounds, but heard instead
A sudden sound of hoofs, for Prince Geraint,
Late also, wearing neither hunting-dress   165
Nor weapon save a golden-hilted brand
Came quickly flashing thro' the shallow ford
Behind them, and so gallop'd up the knoll.
A purple scarf, at either end whereof
There swung an apple of the purest gold,   170
Sway'd round about him as he gallop'd up
To join them, glancing like a dragon-fly
In summer suit and silks of holiday.
Low bow'd the tributary prince, and she,
Sweetly and statelily, and with all grace   175
Of womanhood and queenhood, answer'd him:
' Late, late, Sir Prince,' she said, ' later than we!'
' Yea, noble Queen,' he answer'd, ' and so late
That I but come like you to see the hunt,
Not join it.' 'Therefore wait with me,' she said;   180

'For on this little knoll, if anywhere,
There is good chance that we shall hear the hounds:
Here often they break covert at our feet.'

And while they listen'd for the distant hunt,
And chiefly for the baying of °Cavall,   285
King Arthur's hound of deepest mouth, there rode
Full slowly by a knight, lady, and dwarf;
Whereof the dwarf lagg'd latest, and the knight
Had visor up, and show'd a youthful face,
Imperious, and of haughtiest lineaments.   190
And Guinevere, not mindful of his face
In the King's hall, desired his name, and sent
Her maiden to demand it of the dwarf;
Who being vicious, old, and irritable,
And doubling all his master's vice of pride,   195
Made answer sharply that she should not know.
'Then will I ask it of himself,' she said.
'Nay, by my faith, thou shalt not,' cried the dwarf;
'Thou art not worthy even to speak of him;'
And when she put her horse toward the knight,   200
Struck at her with his whip, and she return'd
Indignant to the Queen; whereat Geraint
Exclaiming, 'Surely I will learn the name,'
Made sharply to the dwarf, and ask'd it of him,
Who answer'd as before; and when the prince   205
Had put his horse in motion toward the knight,

Struck at him with his whip, and cut his cheek.
The prince's blood spirted upon the scarf,
Dyeing it; and his quick, °instinctive hand
Caught at the hilt, as to abolish him: 210
But he, from his exceeding manfulness
And pure nobility of temperament,
°Wroth to be wroth at such a worm, refrain'd
From even a word, and so returning said:

   ' I will avenge this insult, noble Queen,   215
Done in your maiden's person to yourself;
And I will track °this vermin to their earths:
For tho' I ride unarm'd, I do not doubt
To find, at some place I shall come at, arms
On loan, or else for °pledge; and, being found,   220
Then will I fight him, and will break his pride,
And on the third day will again be here,
So that I be not fallen in fight.   Farewell.'

   ' Farewell, fair prince,' answer'd the stately Queen.
' Be prosperous in this journey, as in all;   225
And may you light on all things that you love,
And live to wed with her whom first you love:
But ere you wed with any, bring your bride,
And I, were she the daughter of a king,
Yea, tho' she were a °beggar from the hedge,   230
Will clothe her for her °bridals like the sun.'

And Prince Geraint, now thinking that he heard
The noble hart at bay, now the far horn,
A little vext at losing of the hunt,
A little at the °vile occasion, rode,   235
By ups and downs, thro' many a grassy glade
And valley, with fixt eye following the three.
At last they issued from the world of wood,
And climb'd upon a fair and even ridge,
And show'd themselves against the sky, and sank.   240
And thither came Geraint, and underneath
Beheld the long street of a little town
In a long valley, on one side whereof,
White from the mason's hand, a fortress rose;
And on one side a castle in decay,   245
Beyond a bridge that spann'd a dry ravine:
And out of town and valley came a noise
As of a broad brook o'er a shingly bed
Brawling, or like a clamor of the rooks
At distance, ere they settle for the night.   250

And onward to the fortress rode the three
And enter'd, and were lost behind the walls.
'So,' thought Geraint, 'I have track'd him to nis
    earth.'
And down the long street riding wearily,
Found every °hostel full, and everywhere   255
Was hammer laid to hoof, and the hot hiss

And bustling whistle of the youth who scour'd
His master's armor; and of such a one
He ask'd, 'What means the tumult in the town?'
Who told him, scouring still, 'The °sparrow-hawk!' 260
Then riding close behind an ancient churl,
Who, smitten by the °dusty sloping beam,
Went sweating underneath a sack of corn,
Ask'd yet one more what meant the hubbub here?
Who answer'd gruffly, 'Ugh! the sparrow-hawk!' 265
Then riding further past an armorer's,
Who, with back turn'd, and bow'd above his work,
Sat riveting a helmet on his knee,
He put the selfsame query, but the man
Not turning round, nor looking at him said: 270
'Friend, he that labors for the sparrow-hawk
Has little time for idle questioners.'
Whereat Geraint flashed into sudden °spleen;
'A thousand °pips eat up your sparrow-hawk!
Tits, wrens, and all wing'd nothings peck him dead! 275
Ye think the °rustic cackle of your bourg
The murmur of the world! What is it to me?
O wretched set of sparrows, one and all,
Who pipe of nothing but of sparrow-hawks!
Speak, if ye be not like the rest, hawk-mad, 280
Where can I get me harborage for the night?
And °arms, arms, arms to fight my enemy? Speak!'
Whereat the armorer turning all amazed

And seeing one so gay in purple silks,
Came forward with the helmet yet in hand   285
And answer'd: 'Pardon me, O stranger knight;
We hold a tourney here to-morrow morn,
And there is scantly time for half the work.
Arms? truth! I know not: all are wanted here.
Harborage? truth, good truth, I know not, save,   290
It may be, at Earl Yniol's, o'er the bridge
Yonder.'   He spoke and fell to work again.

     Then rode Geraint, a little spleenful yet,
Across the bridge that spann'd the dry ravine.
There musing sat the hoary-headed earl —   295
His dress a suit of fray'd magnificence,
Once fit for feasts of ceremony — and said
'Whither, fair son?' to whom Geraint replied,
'O friend, I seek a harborage for the night.'
Then Yniol, 'Enter therefore and partake   300
The slender entertainment of a house
Once rich, now poor, but ever open-door'd.'
'Thanks, venerable friend,' replied Geraint;
'So that ye do not serve me sparrow-hawks
For supper, I will enter, I will eat   305
With all the °passion of a twelve hours' fast.'
Then sigh'd and smiled the hoary-headed earl,
And answer'd, 'Graver cause than yours is mine
To curse this hedgerow thief, the sparrow-hawk:

But in, go in; for save yourself desire it,   310
We will not touch upon him even in jest.'

Then rode Geraint into the castle court,
His charger trampling many a prickly star
Of sprouted thistle on the broken stones.
He look'd and saw that all was ruinous.   315
Here stood a shatter'd archway plumed with fern:
And here had fallen a great part of a tower,
Whole, like a crag that tumbles from the cliff,
And like a crag was gay with °wilding flowers:
And high above a piece of turret stair,   320
Worn by the feet that now were silent, wound
Bare to the sun, and °monstrous ivy-stems
Claspt the gray walls with hairy-fibred arms,
And suck'd the joining of the stones, and look'd
A knot, beneath, of snakes, aloft, a grove.   325

And while he waited in the castle court,
The voice of Enid, Yniol's daughter, rang
Clear thro' the open casement of the hall,
Singing; and as the sweet voice of a bird,
Heard by the °lander in a lonely isle,   330
Moves him to think what kind of bird it is
That sings so delicately clear, and make
Conjecture of the plumage and the form,
So the sweet voice of Enid moved Geraint;

And made him like a man abroad at morn   335
When first the °liquid note beloved of men
Comes flying over many a windy wave
To Britain, and in April suddenly
Breaks from a °coppice gemm'd with green and red,
And he suspends his converse with a friend,   340
Or it may be the labor of his hands,
To think or say, 'There is the nightingale:'
So fared it with Geraint, who thought and said,
° 'Here, by God's grace, is the one voice for me.'

It chanced the °song that Enid sang was one   345
Of Fortune and her wheel, and Enid sang:

'Turn, Fortune, turn thy wheel and lower the
    proud;
Turn thy wild wheel thro' sunshine, storm, and
    cloud;
Thy wheel and thee we neither love nor hate.

'Turn, Fortune, turn thy wheel with smile or frown;
With that wild wheel we go not up or down;   350
Our hoard is little, but our hearts are great.

'Smile and we smile, the lords of many lands;
Frown and we smile, the lords of our own hands;
For man is man and master of his fate.   355

Turn, turn thy wheel above the staring crowd;
Thy wheel and thou are shadows in the cloud;
Thy wheel and thee we neither love nor hate.'

'Hark, by the bird's song ye may learn the nest,'
Said Yniol; 'enter quickly.' Entering then,   360
Right o'er a mount of newly-fallen stones,
The dusky-rafter'd many cobweb'd hall,
He found an ancient dame in °dim brocade;
And near her, like a blossom °vermeil-white
That lightly breaks a faded flower-sheath,   365
Moved the fair Enid, all in faded silk,
Her daughter. In a moment thought Geraint,
'Here, by °God's rood, is the one maid for me.'
But none spake word except the hoary earl:

'Enid, the good knight's horse stands in the court;
Take him to the stall, and give him corn, and then, 371
Go to the town and buy us flesh and wine;
And we will make us merry as we may.
Our hoard is little, but our hearts are great.'

He spake: the prince, as Enid past him, fain   375
To follow, strode a stride, but Yniol caught
His purple scarf, and held, and said, 'Forbear!
Rest! the good house, tho' ruin'd, O my son,
Endures not that her guest should serve himself.'

And, reverencing the custom of the house,   380
Geraint, from utter courtesy, forebore.

    So Enid took his charger to the stall,
And after went her way across the bridge,
And reach'd the town, and while the prince and earl
Yet spoke together, came again with one,   385
A youth that, following with a °costrel, bore
The means of goodly welcome, flesh and wine.
And Enid brought sweet cakes to make them cheer,
And, in her veil enfolded, °manchet bread.
And then, because their hall must also serve   390
For kitchen, boil'd the flesh, and spread the board,
And stood behind, and waited on the three.
And, seeing her so sweet and serviceable,
Geraint had longing in him evermore
To stoop and kiss the tender little thumb   395
That crossed the trencher as she laid it down :
But after all had eaten, then Geraint,
For now the wine made summer in his veins,
Let his eye rove in following, or rest
On Enid at her lowly handmaid-work,   400
Now here, now there, about the dusky hall ;
Then suddenly addrest the hoary earl :

    ' Fair host and earl, I pray your courtesy ;
This sparrow-hawk, what is he ? tell me of him.

His name? but no, good faith, I will not have it: 405
For if he be the knight whom late I saw
Ride into that new fortress by your town,
White from the mason's hand, then have I sworn
From his own lips to have it — I am Geraint
Of Devon — for this morning, when the Queen 410
Sent her own maiden to demand the name,
His dwarf, a vicious °under-shapen thing,
Struck at her with his whip, and she return'd
Indignant to the Queen; and then I swore
That I would track this caitiff to his hold, 415
And fight and break his pride, and have it of him.
And all unarm'd I rode, and thought to find
Arms in your town, where all the men are mad
°They take the rustic murmur of their bourg
For the great wave that echoes round the world: 420
They would not hear me speak: but if ye know
Where I can fight on arms, or if yourself
Should have them, tell me, seeing I have sworn
That I will break his pride and learn his name,
Avenging this great insult done the Queen.' 425

Then cried Earl Yniol: 'Art thou he indeed,
Geraint, a name far-sounded among men
For noble deeds? and truly I, when first
I saw you moving by me on the bridge,
Felt ye were somewhat, yea, and by your state 430

H

And presence might have guess'd you one of those
That eat in Arthur's hall at Camelot.
Nor speak I now from foolish flattery ;
For this dear child hath often heard me praise
Your feats of arms, and often when I paused   435
Hath ask'd again, and ever loved to hear ;
So grateful is the noise of noble deeds
To noble hearts who see but acts of wrong.
O never yet had woman such a pair
Of suitors as this maiden : first °Limours,   440
A creature wholly given to brawls and wine,
Drunk even when he woo'd ; and be he dead
I know not, but he past to the °wild land.
The second was your foe, the sparrow-hawk,
My curse, my nephew — I will not let his name   445
Slip from my lips if I can help it — he,
When I that knew him fierce and turbulent
Refused her to him, then his pride awoke ;
And since the proud man often is the mean,
He sow'd a slander in the common ear,   450
°Affirming that his father left him gold,
And in my charge, which was not render'd to him ;
Bribed with large promises the men who served
About my person, the more easily
Because my means were somewhat broken into   455
Thro' open doors and hospitality ;
Rais'd my own town against me in the night

Before my Enid's birthday, sack'd my house;
From mine own earldom foully ousted me;
Built that new fort to overawe my friends,   460
For truly there are those who love me yet;
And keeps me in this ruinous castle here,
Where doubtless he would put me soon to death
But that his pride too much despises me:
And I myself sometimes despise myself;   465
For I have let men be and have their way,
Am much too gentle, have not used my power;
Nor know I whether I be very base
Or very manful, whether very wise
Or very foolish: only this I know,   470
That whatsoever evil happen to me,
I seem to suffer nothing heart or limb,
But can endure it all most patiently.'

'Well said, true heart,' replied Geraint, 'but arms,
That if the sparrow-hawk, this nephew, fight   475
In next days' tourney I may break his pride.'

And Yniol answered: 'Arms, indeed, but old
And rusty, old and rusty, Prince Geraint,
Are mine, and therefore, at thine asking, thine.
But in this tournament can no man tilt,   480
°Except the lady he loves best be there.
Two forks are fixt into the meadow ground,

And over these is placed a silver wand,
And over that a golden sparrow-hawk,
The prize of beauty for the fairest there.   485
And this, what knight soever be in field
Lays claim to for the lady at his side,
And tilts with my good nephew thereupon,
Who being apt at arms and big of bone
Has ever won it for the lady with him,   490
And toppling over all antagonism
Has earn'd himself the name of sparrow-hawk.
But thou, that hast no lady, canst not fight.'

To whom Geraint with eyes all bright replied,
Leaning a little toward him: 'Thy leave!   495
Let me lay lance in rest, O noble host,
For this dear child, because I never saw,
Tho' having seen all beauties of our time,
Nor can see elsewhere, anything so fair.
And if I fall her name will yet remain   500
Untarnish'd as before; but if I live,
So aid me Heaven when at mine uttermost
As I will make her truly my true wife!'

Then, howsoever patient, Yniol's heart
Danced in his bosom, seeing better days.   505
And looking round he saw not Enid there —
Who hearing her own name had stolen away —

But that old dame, to whom full tenderly
And fondling all her hand in his he said:
'Mother, a maiden is a tender thing,   510
And best by her that bore her understood.
Go thou to rest, but ere thou go to rest
Tell her, and °prove her heart toward the prince.'

So spake the kindly-hearted earl, and she
With frequent smile and nod departing found,   515
Half disarray'd as to her rest, the girl;
Whom first she kiss'd on either cheek, and then
On either shining shoulder laid a hand,
And kept her off and gazed upon her face,
And told her all their converse in the hall,   520
Proving her heart: but never light and shade
Coursed one another more on open ground
Beneath a troubled heaven, than red and pale
Across the face of Enid hearing her;
While slowly falling as a scale that falls,   525
When weight is added only grain by grain,
Sank her sweet head upon her gentle breast;
Nor did she lift an eye nor speak a word,
Rapt in the fear and in the wonder of it:
So moving without answer to her rest   530
She found no rest, and ever fail'd to draw
The quiet night into her blood, but lay
Contemplating her own unworthiness;

And when the pale and bloodless east began
To °quicken to the sun, arose, and raised   535
Her mother too, and hand in hand they moved
Down to the meadow where the °jousts were held,
And waited there for Yniol and Geraint.

And thither came the °twain, and when Geraint
Beheld her first in field, awaiting him,   540
He felt, were she the prize of bodily force,
Himself beyond the rest pushing could move
The °Chair of Idris.   Yniol's rusted arms
Were on his princely person, but thro' these
Prince-like his bearing shone ; and °errant knights   545
And ladies came, and by and by the town
°Flow'd in and settling circled all the lists.
And there they fixt the forks into the ground,
And over these they placed the silver wand,
And over that the golden sparrow-hawk.   550
Then Yniol's nephew, after trumpet blow,
Spake to the lady with him and proclaim'd,
' Advance and take, the fairest of the fair,
What I these two years past have won for thee,
The prize of beauty.'   Loudly spake the prince,   555
' Forbear : there is a worthier,' and the knight
With some surprise and thrice as much disdain
Turn'd, and beheld the four, and all his face
Glow'd like the heart of a great fire at Yule,

So burnt he was with passion, crying out,   560
'Do battle for it then,' no more; and thrice
They clash'd together, and thrice they brake their
      spears.
Then each, dishorsed and drawing, lash'd at each
So often and with such blows that all the crowd
Wonder'd, and now and then from °distant walls   565
There came a clapping as of phantom hands.
So twice they fought, and twice they breathed, and still
The dew of their great labor and the blood
Of their strong bodies, flowing, drain'd their force.
But either's force was match'd till Yniol's cry,   570
'Remember that great insult done the Queen,'
Increased Geraint's, who heaved his blade aloft,
And crack'd the helmet thro', and bit the bone,
And fell'd him, and set foot upon his breast,
And said, 'Thy name?'   To whom the fallen man   575
Made answer, groaning: 'Edyrn, son of Nudd!
Ashamed am I that I should tell it thee.
My pride is broken: men have seen my fall.'
'Then, °Edyrn, son of Nudd,' replied Geraint,
'These two things shalt thou do, or else thou diest.   580
First, thou thyself, with damsel and with dwarf,
Shalt ride to Arthur's court and, coming there,
Crave pardon for that insult done the Queen,
And shalt abide her judgment on it; next,
Thou shalt give back their earldom to thy kin.   585

These two things shalt thou do, or thou shalt die.'
And Edyrn answer'd, 'These things will I do,
For I have never yet been overthrown,
And thou hast overthrown me, and my pride
Is broken down, for Enid sees my fall!'   590
And rising up he rode to Arthur's court,
And there the Queen forgave him easily.
°And, being young, he changed and came to loathe
His crime of traitor, slowly drew himself
Bright from his old dark life, and fell at last   595
In the great battle fighting for the King.

But when the °third day from the hunting-morn
Made a °low splendor in the world, and wings
Moved in her ivy, Enid, for she lay
With her fair head in the dim-yellow light,   600
Among the dancing shadows of the birds,
Woke and bethought her of her promise given
No later than last eve to Prince Geraint —
So bent he seem'd on going the third day,
He would not leave her till her promise given —   605
To ride with him this morning to the court,
And there be made known to the stately Queen,
And there be wedded with all ceremony.
At this she cast her eyes upon her dress,
And thought it never yet had look'd so mean.   610
For as a leaf in mid-November is

To what it was in mid-October, seem'd
The dress that now she look'd on to the dress
She look'd on ere the coming of Geraint.
And still she look'd, and still the terror grew   615
Of that strange bright and dreadful thing, a court,
All staring at her in her faded silk;
And softly to her own sweet heart she said:

'This noble prince who won our earldom back,
So splendid in his acts and his attire,   620
Sweet heaven, how much I shall discredit him!
Would he could tarry with us here awhile,
But being so beholden to the prince,
It were but little grace in any of us,
Bent as he seem'd on going this third day,   625
To seek a second favor at his hands.
Yet if he could but tarry a day or two,
Myself would work eye dim and finger lame
Far liefer than so much discredit him.'

And Enid fell in longing for a dress   630
All °branch'd and flower'd with gold, a costly gift
Of her good mother, given her on the night
Before her birthday, three sad years ago,
That night of fire, when Edyrn sack'd their house
And scatter'd all they had to all the winds;   635
For while the mother show'd it, and the two

Were turning and admiring it, the work
To both appear'd so costly, rose a cry
That Edyrn's men were on them, and they fled
With little save the jewels they had on,   640
Which being °sold and sold had bought them bread :
And Edyrn's men had caught them in their flight,
And placed them in this ruin ; and she wish'd
The prince had found her in her ancient home ;
Then let her fancy flit across the past,   645
And roam the goodly places that she knew ;
And last bethought her how she used to watch,
Near that old home, a pool of golden carp ;
And one was patch'd and blurr'd and lustreless
Among his burnish'd brethren of the pool ;   650
And half asleep she made comparison
Of that and these to her own faded self
And the gay court, and fell asleep again.
°And dreamt herself was such a faded form
Among her burnish'd sisters of the pool ;   655
But this was in the garden of a king,
And tho' she lay dark in the pool she knew
That all was bright ; that all about were birds
Of sunny plume in gilded trellis-work ;
That all the turf was rich in plots that look'd   660
Each like a garnet or °a turkis in it ;
And lords and ladies of the high court went
In silver tissue talking things of state ;

..nd children of the King in cloth of gold
Glanced at the doors or gambol'd down the walks; 665
And while she thought, 'They will not see me,' came
A stately queen whose name was Guinevere,
And all the children in their cloth of gold
Ran to her, crying, 'If we have fish at all
Let them be gold; and charge the gardeners now 670
To pick the faded creature from the pool,
And cast it on the °mixen that it die.'
And therewithal one came and seized on her,
And Enid started waking, with her heart
All overshadowed by the foolish dream, 675
And lo! it was her mother grasping her
To get her well awake; and in her hand
A suit of bright apparel, which she laid
Flat on the couch, and spoke exultingly:

'See here, my child, how fresh the colors look, 680
How fast they hold, like colors of a shell
That keeps the wear and polish of the wave.
Why not? It never yet was worn, I trow:
Look on it, child, and tell me if ye know it.'

And Enid look'd, but, all confused at first, 685
Could scarce divide it from her foolish dream :
Then suddenly she knew it and rejoiced,
And answer'd, 'Yea, I know it; your good gift,

So sadly lost on that unhappy night;
Your own good gift!'   'Yea, surely,' said the dame,
'And gladly given again this happy morn.   691
For when the jousts were ended yesterday,
Went Yniol thro' the town, and everywhere
He found the sack and plunder of our house
All scatter'd thro' the houses of the town,   695
And gave command that all which once was ours
Should now be ours again; and yester-eve,
While ye were talking sweetly with your prince,
Came one with this and laid it in my hand,
For love or fear, or seeking favor of us,   700
Because we have our earldom back again.
And yester-eve I would not tell you of it,
But kept it for a sweet surprise at morn.
Yea, truly is it not a sweet surprise?
For I myself unwillingly have worn   705
My faded suit, as you, my child, have yours,
And, howsoever patient. Yniol his.
Ah, dear, he took me from a goodly house,
With store of rich apparel, sumptuous fare, and page,
And maid, and squire, and seneschal,   710
And pastime both of hawk and hound, and all
That appertains to °noble maintenance.
Yea, and he brought me to a goodly house;
But since our fortune swerved from sun to shade,
And all thro' that young traitor, cruel need   715

Constrain'd us, but a better time has come;
So clothe yourself in this, that better fits
Our mended fortunes and a prince's bride:
For tho' ye won the prize of fairest fair,
And tho' I heard him call you fairest fair, 720
Let never maiden think, however fair,
She is not fairer in new clothes than old.
And should some great court-lady say, the prince
Hath pick'd a °ragged-robin from the hedge,
And like a madman brought her to the court, 725
Then were ye shamed, and, worse, might shame the prince
To whom we are beholden; but I know,
When my dear child is set forth at her best,
That neither court nor country, tho' they sought
Thro' all the provinces like °those of old 730
That lighted on Queen Esther, has her match.'

Here ceased the kindly mother out of breath,
And Enid listen'd brightening as she lay;
Then, as the white and glittering star of morn
Parts from a bank of snow, and by and by 735
Slips into golden cloud, the maiden rose,
And left her maiden couch, and robed herself,
Help'd by the mother's careful hand and eye,
Without a mirror, in the gorgeous gown;
Who, after, turn'd her daughter round, and said 740

She never yet had seen her half so fair;
And call'd her like that maiden in the tale,
Whom °Gwydion made by glamour out of flowers,
And sweeter than the °bride of Cassivelaun,
Flur, for whose love the Roman Cæsar first   745
Invaded Britain: ' But we beat him back,
As this great prince invaded us, and we,
Not beat him back, but welcomed him with joy.
And I can scarcely ride with you to court,
For old am I, and rough the ways and wild;   750
But Yniol goes, and I full oft shall dream
I see my princess as I see her now,
Clothed with my gift and gay among the gay.'

    But while the women thus rejoiced, Geraint
Woke where he slept in the high hall, and call'd   755
For Enid, and when Yniol made report
Of that good mother making Enid gay
In such apparel as might well beseem
His princess, or indeed the stately Queen,
He answer'd: 'Earl, entreat her by my love   760
Albeit I give no reason but my wish,
°That she ride with me in her faded silk.'
Yniol with that hard message went; it fell
°Like flaws in summer laying lusty corn:
For Enid, all abash'd she knew not why,   765
Dare not to glance at her good mother's face,

But silently, in all obedience,
Her mother silent too, nor helping her,
Laid from her limbs the costly-broider'd gift,
And robed them in her ancient suit again,   770
And so descended.   °Never man rejoiced
More than Geraint to greet her thus attired;
And glancing all at once as keenly at her
As careful robins eye the delver's toil,
Made her cheek burn and either eyelid fall,   775
But rested with her sweet face satisfied;
Then seeing cloud upon the mother's brow,
Her by both hands he caught, and sweetly said:

'O my new mother, be not wroth or grieved
At thy new son, for my petition to her.   780
When late I left Caerleon, our great Queen,
In words whose echo lasts, they were so sweet,
Made promise that, whatever bride I brought,
Herself would clothe her like the sun in heaven.
Thereafter, when I reach'd this ruin'd hall,   785
Beholding one so bright in dark estate,
I vow'd that, could I gain her, our fair Queen,
No hand but hers, should make your Enid burst
Sunlike from cloud — and likewise thought perhaps,
That service done so graciously would bind   790
The two together; fain I would the two
Should love each other: how can Enid find

A nobler friend ?   Another thought was mine :
I came among you here so suddenly
That tho' her gentle presence at the lists   795
Might well have served for proof that I was loved,
I doubted whether daughter's tenderness,
Or easy nature, might not let itself
Be moulded by your wishes for her weal ;
Or whether some false sense in her own self   800
Of my contrasting brightness overbore
Her fancy dwelling in this dusky hall ;
And such a sense might make her long for court
And all its perilous glories : and I thought,
That could I some way prove such force in her   805
Link'd with such love for me that at a word,
No reason given her, she could cast aside
A splendor dear to women, new to her,
And therefore dearer ; or if not so new,
Yet therefore tenfold dearer by the power   810
Of intermitted usage ; then I felt
That I could rest, a rock in ebbs and flows,
Fixt on her faith.   Now, therefore, I do rest,
°A prophet certain of my prophecy,
That never shadow of mistrust can cross   815
Between us.   Grant me pardon for my thoughts ;
And for my strange petition I will make
Amends hereafter by some °gaudy-day,
When your fair child shall wear your costly gift

Beside your own warm hearth, with, on her knees, 820
Who knows? another gift of the high God,
Which, maybe, shall have learn'd to lisp you thanks.'

He spoke: the mother smiled, but half in tears,
Then brought a mantle down and wrapt her in it,
And claspt and kiss'd her, and they rode away. 825

Now thrice that morning Guinevere had climb'd
The giant tower, from whose high crest, they say,
Man saw the goodly hills of Somerset,
And °white sails flying on the yellow sea;
But not to goodly hill or yellow sea 830
Look'd the fair Queen, but up the vale of Usk,
By the flat meadow, till she saw them come;
And then descending met them at the gates,
Embraced her with all welcome as a friend,
And did her honor as the prince's bride, 835
And clothed her for her bridals like the sun;
And all that week was old Caerleon gay,
For by the hands of Dubric, the high saint,
They twain were wedded with all ceremony.

And this was on the last year's Whitsuntide. 840
But Enid ever kept the faded silk,
Remembering how first he came on her
Drest in that dress, and how he loved her in it,

I

And all her foolish fears about the dress,
And all his journey toward her, as himself   845
Had told her, and their coming to the court.

   And now this morning when he said to her,
'Put on your worst and meanest dress,' she found
And took it, and array'd herself therein.

GERAINT AND ENID

°O PURBLIND race of miserable men,
How many among us at this very hour
Do °forge a lifelong trouble for ourselves,
By taking true for false, or false for true;
Here, thro' the feeble twilight of this world   5
Groping, how many, until we pass and reach
That other °where we see as we are seen.

So fared it with Geraint, who issuing forth
That morning, when they both had got to horse,
Perhaps because he loved her passionately,   10
And felt that tempest brooding round his heart
Which, if he spoke at all, would break perforce
Upon a head so dear in thunder, said:
'Not at my side.   I charge thee ride before,
Ever a good way on before; and this   15
I charge thee, on thy duty as a wife,
Whatever happens not to speak to me,
No, not a word!' and Enid was aghast;
And forth they rode, but scarce three paces on,
When crying out, °'Effeminate as I am,   20
I will not fight my way with gilded arms,

All shall be iron ; ' he loosed a mighty purse,
Hung at his belt, and hurl'd it toward the squire.
So the last sight that Enid had of home
Was all the marble threshold flashing, strown   2⸱
With gold and scatter'd coinage, and the squire
Chafing his shoulder : then he cried again,
'To the wilds !' and Enid leading down the tracks
Thro' which he bade her lead him on, they past
The °marches, and by bandit-haunted holds,   30
Gray swamps and pools, waste places of the hern,
And wildernesses, perilous paths, they rode.
Round was their pace at first, but slacken'd soon.
A stranger meeting them had surely thought,
They rode so slowly and they look'd so pale,   35
That each had suffer'd some exceeding wrong.
For he was ever saying to himself,
'O, I that wasted time to tend upon her,
To compass her with sweet observances,
To dress her beautifully and keep her true ' —   40
And there he broke the sentence in his heart
Abruptly, as a man upon his tongue
May break it when his passion masters him.
And she was ever praying the sweet heavens
To save her dear lord whole from any wound.   45
And ever in her mind she cast about
For that unnoticed failing in herself
Which made him look so cloudy and so cold ;

Till the °great plover's human whistle amazed
Her heart, and glancing round the waste she fear'd 50
In every wavering break an ambuscade:
Then thought again, ° 'If there be such in me,
I might amend it by the grace of Heaven,
If he would only speak and tell me of it.'

But when the fourth part of the day was gone, 55
Then Enid was aware of three tall knights
On horseback, wholly arm'd, behind a rock
In shadow, waiting for them, caitiffs all;
And heard one crying to his fellow, 'Look,
Here comes a laggard hanging down his head, 60
Who seems no bolder than a beaten hound;
Come, we will slay him and will have his horse
And armor, and his damsel shall be ours.'

Then Enid ponder'd in her heart, and said:
'I will go back a little to my lord, 65
And I will tell him all their caitiff talk;
For, be he wroth even to slaying me,
Far liefer by his dear hand had I die
Than that my lord should suffer loss or shame.'

Then she went back some paces of return, 70
Met his full frown timidly firm, and said:
'My lord, I saw three bandits by the rock
Waiting to fall on you, and heard them boast

That they would slay you, and possess your horse
And armor, and your damsel should be theirs.'   75

  He made a wrathful answer : ° 'Did I wish
Your warning or your silence ? one command
I laid upon you, not to speak to me,
And thus ye keep it !   Well then, look — for now,
Whether ye wish me victory or defeat,   80
Long for my life, or hunger for my death,
Yourself shall see my vigor is not lost.'

  Then Enid waited pale and sorrowful,
And down upon him bare the bandit three.
And at the midmost charging, Prince Geraint   85
Drave the long spear a °cubit thro' his breast
And out beyond; and then against his brace
Of comrades, each of whom had broken on him
A lance that splinter'd like an icicle,
Swung from his brand a windy buffet out   90
Once, twice, to right, to left, and stunn'd the twain
Or slew them, and dismounting, like a man
That skins the wild beast after slaying him,
Stript from the °three dead wolves of woman born
The three gay suits of armor which they wore,   95
And let the bodies lie, but bound the suits
Of armor on their horses, each on each,
And tied the bridle-reins of all the three

Together, and said to her, 'Drive them on
Before you;' and she drove them thro' the waste.   100

   He follow'd nearer: °ruth began to work
Against his anger in him, while he watch'd
The being he loved best in all the world,
With difficulty in mild obedience
Driving them on: he fain had spoken to her,   105
And loosed in words of sudden fire the wrath
And smoulder'd wrong that burnt him all within;
But evermore it seem'd an easier thing
At once without remorse to strike her dead
Than to cry 'Halt,' and to her own bright face   110
Accuse her of the least immodesty:
And thus tongue-tied, it made him wroth the more
That she *could* speak whom his own ear had heard
Call herself false; and suffering thus he made
Minutes an age: but in scarce longer time   115
Than at °Caerleon the full-tided Usk,
Before he turn to fall seaward again,
Pauses, did Enid, keeping watch, behold
In the first °shallow shade of a deep wood
Before a gloom of °stubborn-shafted oaks,   120
Three other horsemen waiting, wholly arm'd
Whereof one seem'd far larger than her lord,
And °shook her pulses, crying, 'Look, a prize!
Three horses and three goodly suits of arms,

And all in charge of whom ?   a girl : °set on.'   125
'Nay,' said the second, 'yonder comes a knight.'
The third, 'A craven ; how he hangs his head !'
The giant answer'd merrily, 'Yea, but one ?
Wait here, and when he passes fall upon him !'

    And Enid ponder'd in her heart and said: 130
'I will abide the coming of my lord,
And I will tell him all their villany.
My lord is weary with the fight before,
And they will fall upon him unawares.
I needs must disobey him for his good ;   135
How should I dare obey him to his harm ?
Needs must I speak, and tho' he kill me for it,
I save a life dearer to me than mine.'

    And she abode his coming, and said to him
With timid firmness, 'Have I leave to speak ? '   140
He said, ' Ye take it, speaking,' and she spoke :

    'There lurk three villains yonder in the wood,
And each of them is wholly arm'd, and one
Is larger-limb'd than you are, and they say
That they will fall upon you while ye pass.'   145

    To which he flung a wrathful answer back :
'And if there were an hundred in the wood,

And every man were larger-limb'd than I,
And all at once should sally out upon me,
I swear it would not ruffle me so much   150
As you that °not obey me.   Stand aside,
And if I fall, cleave to the better man.'

And Enid stood aside to wait the event,
Not dare to watch the combat, only breathe
°Short fits of prayer, at every stroke a breath.   155
And he she dreaded most bare down upon him.
Aim'd at the helm, his lance °err'd; but Geraint's,
A little in the late encounter strain'd,
Struck thro' the bulky bandit's °corselet home,
And then brake short, and down his enemy roll'd,   160
And there lay still; as he that tells the tale
Saw once a great piece of a promontory,
That had a sapling growing on it, slide
From the long shore-cliff's °windy walls to the beach,
And there lie still, and yet the sapling grew: 165
So lay the man transfixt.   His craven pair
Of comrades making slowlier at the prince,
When now they saw their bulwark fallen, stood;
On whom the victor, to confound them more,
Spurr'd with his terrible war-cry; for as one,   170
°That listens near a torrent mountain-brook,
All thro' the crash of the near cataract hears
The drumming thunder of the huger fall

At distance, were the soldiers wont to hear
His voice in battle, and be kindled by it,   175
And foemen scared, like that false pair who turn'd
Flying, but, overtaken, died the death
Themselves had wrought on many an innocent.

Thereon Geraint, dismounting, pick'd the lance
That pleased him best, and drew from those dead
     wolves   180
Their three gay suits of armor, each from each,
And bound them on their horses, each on each,
And tied the bridle-reins of all the three
Together, and said to her, 'Drive them on
Before you,' and she drove them thro' the wood.   185

He follow'd nearer still: the pain she had
To keep them in the wild ways of the wood,
Two sets of three laden with jingling arms,
Together, served a little to °disedge
The sharpness of that pain about her heart: 190
And they themselves, like creatures gently born
But into bad hands fallen, and now so long
By bandits groom'd, prick'd their light ears, and felt
Her low firm voice and tender government.

So thro' the green gloom of the wood they past,   195
And issuing under open heavens beheld

A little town with towers, upon a rock,
And close beneath, a °meadow gemlike chased
In the brown wild, and mowers mowing in it;
And down a rocky pathway from the place   200
There came a fair-hair'd youth, that in his hand
Bare °victual for the mowers; and Geraint
Had ruth again on Enid looking pale:
Then, moving downward to the meadow ground,
He, when the fair-hair'd youth came by him, said, 205
'Friend, let her eat; the damsel is so faint.'
'Yea, willingly,' replied the youth; 'and thou
My lord, eat also, tho' the fare is coarse,
And only meet for mowers;' then set down
His basket, and dismounting on the sward   210
They let the horses graze, and ate themselves.
And Enid took a little delicately,
Less having stomach for it than desire
To close with her lord's pleasure; but Geraint
Ate all the mowers' victuals unawares,   215
And when he found all empty was amazed;
And 'Boy,' said he, 'I have eaten all, but take
A horse and arms for °guerdon; choose the best.'
He reddening in extremity of delight,
'My lord, you overpay me fifty-fold.'   220
'Ye will be all the wealthier,' cried the prince.
'I take it as free gift, then,' said the boy,
'Not guerdon; for myself can easily,

While your good damsel rests, return and fetch
Fresh victual for these mowers of our earl ;   225
For these are his, and all the field is his,
And I myself am his ; and I will tell him
How great a man thou art : he loves to know
When men of mark are in his territory ;
And he will have thee to his palace here   230
And serve thee costlier than with mowers' fare.

Then said Geraint : 'I wish no better fare :
I never ate with angrier appetite
Than when I left your mowers dinnerless.
And into no earl's palace will I go.   235
I know, God knows, too much of palaces !
And if he want me, let him come to me.
But hire us some fair chamber for the night,
And stalling for the horses, and return
With victuals for these men, and let us know.'   240

' Yea, my kind lord,' said the glad youth, and went,
Held his head high, and thought himself a knight,
And up the rocky pathway disappear'd,
Leading the horse, and they were left alone.

But when the prince had brought his °errant eyes 245
Home from the rock, sideways he let them glance
At Enid, where she droopt : his own °false doom,

That shadow of mistrust should never cross
Betwixt them, came upon him, and he sigh'd;
Then with another °humorous ruth remark'd   250
The lusty mowers laboring dinnerless,
And watch'd the sun blaze on the turning scythe,
And after nodded sleepily in the heat.
But she, remembering her old ruin'd hall,
And all the windy clamor of the daws   255
About her hollow turret, pluck'd the grass
There growing longest by the meadow's edge,
And into many a °listless annulet,
Now over, now beneath her marriage ring,
Wove and unwove it, till the boy return'd   260
And told them of a chamber, and they went;
Where, after saying to her, 'If ye will,
Call for the woman of the house,' to which
She answer'd, 'Thanks, my lord;' the two remain'd
Apart by all the chamber's width, and mute   265
As creatures voiceless thro' the fault of birth,
Or two wild men °supporters of a shield,
Painted, who stare at open space, nor glance
The one at other, parted by the shield.

On a sudden, many a voice along the street,   270
And heel against the pavement echoing, burst
Their drowse; and either started while the door,
Push'd from without, drave backward to the wall,

And midmost of a rout of roisterers,
Femininely fair and dissolutely pale,   275
Her suitor in old years before Geraint
Enter'd, the wild lord of the place, °Limours.
He moving up with pliant courtliness
Greeted Geraint full face, but stealthily,
In the mid-warmth of welcome and graspt hand,   280
Found Enid with the corner of his eye,
And knew her sitting sad and solitary.
Then cried Geraint for wine and goodly cheer
To feed the sudden guest, and sumptuously
According to his fashion, bade the host   285
Call in what men soever were his friends,
And feast with these in honor of their earl;
'And care not for the cost; the cost is mine.'

    And wine and food were brought, and Earl Limours
Drank till he jested with all ease, and told   290
Free tales, and °took the word and play'd upon it,
And made it of two colors; for his talk,
When wine and free companions kindled him,
Was wont to glance and sparkle like a gem
Of fifty facets; thus he moved the prince   295
To laughter and his comrades to applause.
Then, when the prince was merry, ask'd Limours,
'Your leave, my lord, to cross the room, and speak
To your good damsel there who sits apart,

And seems so lonely?' °'My free leave,' he said; 300
'Get her to speak: she doth not speak to me.'
Then rose Limours, and looking at his feet,
Like him who tries the bridge he fears may fail,
Crost and came near, lifted adoring eyes,
Bow'd to her side and utter'd whisperingly : 305

'Enid, the °pilot star of my lone life,
Enid, my early and my only love,
Enid, the loss of whom hath turn'd me wild —
What chance is this? how is it I see you here?
Ye are in my power at last, are in my power. 310
Yet fear me not: I call mine own self wild,
But keep a touch of sweet civility
Here in the heart of waste and wilderness.
I thought, but that your father came between
In former days you saw me favorably. 315
And if it were so do not keep it back:
Make me a little happier: let me know it:
Owe you me nothing for a life half-lost?
Yea, yea, the whole dear debt of all you are.
And, Enid, you and he, I see with joy, 320
Ye sit apart, you do not speak to him,
You come with no attendance, page or maid,
To serve you — doth he love you as of old?
For, call it °lovers' quarrels, yet I know
Tho' men may °bicker with the things they love, 325

They would not make them laughable in all eyes,
Not while they loved them; and your wretched dress,
A wretched insult on you, dumbly speaks
Your story, that this man loves you no °more.
Your beauty is not beauty to him now: 330
A common chance — right well I know it — pall'd —
For I know men: nor will ye win him back,
For the man's love once gone never returns.
But here is one who loves you as of old;
With more exceeding passion than of old: 335
Good, speak the word: my followers ring him round:
He sits unarm'd; I hold a finger up;
They understand: nay, I do not mean blood;
Nor need ye look so scared at what I say.
My malice is no deeper than a moat,   340
No stronger than a wall: there is the °keep;
He shall not cross us more; speak but the word:
Or speak it not; but then by Him that made me
The one true lover whom you ever own'd,
I will make use of all the power I have.   345
O pardon me! the madness of that hour
When first I parted from thee moves me yet.'

    At this the tender sound of his own voice
And sweet self-pity, or the fancy of it,
Made his eyes moist; but Enid fear'd his eyes,   350
Moist as they were, wine-heated from the feast,

And answered with such craft as women use,
Guilty or guiltless, to stave off a chance
That breaks upon them perilously, and said:

'Earl, if you love me as in former years,   355
And do not practise on me, come with morn,
And snatch me from him as by violence;
Leave me to-night: I am weary to the death.'

Low at leave-taking, with his brandish'd plume
Brushing his instep, bow'd the all-amorous earl,   360
And the stout prince bade him a loud good-night.
He moving homeward babbled to his men,
How Enid never loved a man but him,
Nor cared a °broken egg-shell for her lord.

But Enid left alone with Prince Geraint,   365
Debating his command of silence given,
And that she now perforce must violate it,
Held commune with herself, and while she held
He fell asleep, and Enid had no heart
To wake him, but hung o'er him, wholly pleased   370
To find him yet unwounded after fight,
And hear him breathing low and equally.
Anon she rose and, stepping lightly, heap'd
The pieces of his armor in one place,
All to be there against a sudden need;   375
Then dozed awhile herself, but, overtoil'd

K

By that day's grief and travel, evermore
Seem'd catching at a rootless thorn, and then
Went slipping down horrible precipices,
And strongly striking out her limbs awoke;   380
Then thought she heard the wild earl at the door,
With all his °rout of random followers,
Sound on a dreadful trumpet, summoning her;
Which was the red cock shouting to the light,
As the gray dawn stole o'er the dewy world   385
And glimmer'd on his armor in the room.
And once again she rose to look at it,
But touch'd it unawares: jangling, the casque
Fell, and he started up and stared at her.
Then breaking his command of silence given,   390
She told him all that Earl Limours had said,
Except the passage that he loved her not;
Nor left untold the craft herself had used,
But ended with apology so sweet,
Low-spoken, and of so few words, and seem'd   395
So justified by that necessity,
That tho' he thought, 'Was it for him she wept
In Devon?' he but gave a wrathful groan,
Saying, 'Your sweet faces make good fellows fools
And traitors.   Call the host and bid him bring   400
Charger and palfrey.'   So she glided out
Among the heavy breathings of the house,
And like a household spirit at the walls

Beat, till she woke the sleepers, and return'd;
Then tending her rough lord, tho' all unask'd, 405
In silence, did him service as a squire;
Till issuing arm'd he found the host and cried,
'Thy reckoning, friend?' and ere he learnt it,
   'Take
Five horses and their armors;' and the host,
°Suddenly honest, answer'd in amaze, 410
'My lord, I scarce have spent the worth of one!'
'Ye will be all the wealthier,' said the prince,
And then to Enid, 'Forward! and to-day
I charge you, Enid, more especially,
What thing soever ye may hear, or see, 415
Or fancy — tho' I count it of small use
To charge you — that ye speak not but obey.'

And Enid answer'd: 'Yea, my lord, I know
Your wish and would obey; but, riding first,
I hear the violent threats you do not hear, 420
I see the danger which you cannot see:
Then not to give you warning, that seems hard,
Almost beyond me; yet I would obey.'

'Yea so,' said he, 'do it: be not too wise;
Seeing that ye are wedded to a man,
Not all mismated with a yawning clown, 425
But one with arms to guard his head and yours,

With eyes to find you out however far,
And ears to hear you even in his dreams.'

    With that he turn'd and look'd as keenly at her   43⁀
°As careful robins eye the delver's toil;
And that within her which a wanton fool
Or hasty judger would have call'd her guilt
Made her cheek burn and either eyelid fall.
And Geraint look'd and was not satisfied.   435

    Then forward by a way which, beaten broad,
Led from the territory of false Limours
To the waste earldom of another earl,
Doorm, whom his shaking vassals call'd the Bull,
Went Enid with her sullen follower on.   440
Once she look'd back, and when she saw him ride
More near by many a rood than yestermorn,
It wellnigh made her cheerful; till Geraint,
Waving an angry hand as who should say,
'Ye watch me,' sadden'd all her heart again.   445
But while the sun yet beat a dewy blade,
The sound of many a heavily-galloping hoof
Smote on her ear, and turning round she saw
Dust, and the points of lances °bicker in it.
Then, not to disobey her lord's behest,   450
And yet to give him warning, for he rode
As if he heard not, moving back she held

Her finger up, and pointed to the dust.
At which the warrior in his obstinacy,
Because she kept the letter of his word,
Was in a manner pleased, and turning stood. 455
And in the moment after, wild Limours,
Borne on a black horse, like a thunder-cloud
Whose skirts are loosen'd by the breaking storm,
Half ridden off with by the thing he rode, 460
And all in passion uttering a °dry shriek,
Dash'd on Geraint, who closed with him, and bore
Down by the length of lance and arm beyond
The crupper, and so left him stunn'd or dead,
And overthrew the next that follow'd him, 465
And blindly rush'd on all the rout behind.
But at the flash and motion of the man
They vanish'd panic-stricken, like a shoal
Of darting fish, that on a summer morn
Adown the °crystal dykes at Camelot 470
Come slipping o'er their shadows on the sand,
But if a man who stands upon the brink
But lift a shining hand against the sun,
There is not left the twinkle of a fin
Betwixt the °cressy islets white in flower; 475
So, scared but at the motion of the man,
Fled all the °boon companions of the earl,
And left him lying in the public way;
So vanish friendships only made in wine.

Then like a stormy sunlight smiled Geraint,   480
Who saw the chargers of the two that fell
Start from their fallen lords and wildly fly,
Mixt with the flyers.   'Horse and man,' he said,
'All of one mind and all right-honest friends!
°Not a hoof left: and I methinks till now   485
Was honest — paid with horses and with arms;
I cannot steal or plunder, no, nor beg:
And so what say ye, shall we strip him there,
Your lover? has your palfrey heart enough
To bear his armor? °shall we fast or dine?   490
No? — then do thou, being right honest, pray
That we may meet the horsemen of Earl Doòrm;
I too would still be honest.'   Thus he said;
And sadly gazing on her bridle-reins,
And answering not one word, she led the way.   495

But as a man to whom a dreadful loss
Falls in a far land and he knows it not,
But coming back he learns it, and the loss
So pains him that he °sickens nigh to death;
So fared it with Geraint, who, being prick'd   500
In combat with the follower of Limours,
Bled underneath his armor secretly,
And so rode on, nor told his gentle wife
What ail'd him, hardly knowing it himself,
Till his eye darken'd and his helmet wagg'd;   505

And at a sudden swerving of the road,
Tho' happily down on a bank of grass,
The prince, without a word, from his horse fell.

   And Enid heard the clashing of his fall,
Suddenly came, and at his side all pale　　　　　510
Dismounting loosed the fastenings of his arms,
Nor let her true hand falter, nor blue eye
Moisten, till she had lighted on his wound,
And tearing off her veil of faded silk
Had bared her forehead to the blistering sun,　515
And swathed the hurt that drain'd her dear lord's life.
Then, after all was done that hand could do,
She rested, and her desolation came
Upon her, and she wept beside the way.
   And many past, but none regarded her,　　　520
For in that realm of lawless turbulence
A woman weeping for her murder'd mate
Was cared as much for as a °summer shower.
One took him for a victim of Earl Doorm,
Nor dared to waste a °perilous pity on him:　525
Another hurrying past, a man-at-arms,
Rode on a mission to the bandit earl;
Half whistling and half singing a coarse song,
He drove the dust against her veilless eyes:
Another, flying from the wrath of Doorm　　　530
Before an ever-fancied arrow, made

The long way °smoke beneath him in his fear ;
At which her palfrey whinnying lifted heel,
And scour'd into the coppices and was lost,
While the great charger stood, grieved like a man.   535

   But at the point of noon the huge Earl Doorm,
Broad-faced with under-fringe of russet beard,
Bound on a foray, rolling eyes of prey,
Came riding with a hundred lances up ;
But ere he came, like one that hails a ship,   540
Cried out with a big voice, ' What, is he dead ? '
' No, no, not dead ! ' she answer'd in all haste.
' Would some of your kind people take him up,
And bear him hence out of this cruel sun ?
Most sure am I, quite sure, he is not dead.'   545

   Then said Earl Doorm : ' Well, if he be not dead,
Why wail ye for him thus ? ye seem a child.
And be he dead, I count you for a fool ;
Your wailing will not quicken him : dead or not,
Ye mar a comely face with °idiot tears.   550
Yet, since the face is comely — some of you,
Here, take him up, and bear him to our hall :
And if he live, we will have him of our band ;
And if he die, why earth has earth enough
To hide him.   See ye take the charger too,   555
A noble one.'

He spake and past away,
But left two brawny spearmen, who advanced,
Each growling like a dog, when his good bone
Seems to be pluck'd at by the village boys
Who love to vex him eating, and he fears   560
To lose his bone, and lays his foot upon it,
Gnawing and growling: so the ruffians growl'd,
Fearing to lose, and all for a dead man,
Their chance of booty from the morning's raid,
Yet raised and laid him on a °litter-bier,   565
Such as they brought upon their forays out
For those that might be wounded; laid him on it
All in the hollow of his shield, and took
And bore him to the naked hall of Doorm —
His gentle charger following him unled —   570
And cast him and the bier in which he lay
Down on an oaken °settle in the hall,
And then departed, hot in haste to join
Their luckier mates, but growling as before,
And cursing their lost time, and the dead man,   575
And their own earl, and their own souls and her.
They might as well have blest her: she was deaf
To blessing or to cursing save from one.

So for long hours sat Enid by her lord
There in the naked hall, propping his head,   580
And chafing his pale hands, and calling to him,

Till at the last he waken'd from his swoon,
And found his own dear bride propping his head,
And chafing his faint hands, and calling to him;
And felt the warm tears falling on his face,   585
And said to his own heart, 'She weeps for me;'
And yet lay still, and feign'd himself as dead,
That he might prove her to the uttermost,
And say to his own heart, 'She weeps for me.'

But in the falling afternoon return'd   590
The huge Earl Doorm with plunder to the hall.
His lusty spearmen follow'd him with noise:
Each hurling down a heap of things that rang
Against the pavement, cast his lance aside,
And doff'd his helm; and then there flutter'd in,   595
Half-bold, half-frightened, with dilated eyes,
A tribe of women, dress'd in many hues,
And mingled with the spearmen; and Earl Doorm
Struck with a knife's haft hard against the board,
And call'd for flesh and wine to feed his °spears.   600
And men brought in whole hogs and quarter beeves,
And all the hall was dim with steam of flesh;
And none spake word, but all sat down at once,
And ate with tumult in the naked hall,
Feeding like horses when you hear them feed;   605
Till Enid shrank far back into herself,
To shun the wild ways of the lawless tribe.

But when Earl Doorm had eaten all he would,
He roll'd his eyes about the hall, and found
A damsel drooping in a corner of it.   610
Then he remember'd her, and how she wept;
And out of her there came a power upon him;
And rising on the sudden he said: 'Eat!
I never yet beheld a thing so pale.
God's curse, it makes me mad to see you weep.   615
Eat! Look yourself. Good luck had your good man,
For were I dead who is it would weep for me?
Sweet lady, never since I first drew breath
Have I beheld a lily like yourself.
And so there lived some color in your cheek,   620
There is not one among my gentlewomen
Were fit to wear your slipper for a glove.
But listen to me, and by me be ruled,
And I will do the thing I have not done,
For ye shall share my earldom with me, girl,   625
And we will live like two birds in one nest,
And I will fetch you forage from all fields,
For I compel all creatures to my will.'

He spoke: the brawny spearman let his cheek   629
Bulge with the unswallow'd piece, and turning stared;
While some, whose souls the °old serpent long had drawn
Down, °as the worm draws in the wither'd leaf
And makes it earth, hiss'd each at other's ear

What shall not be recorded — women they,
Women, or what had been those °gracious things,   635
But now desired the humbling of their best,
Yea, would have help'd him to it; and all at once
They hated her, who took no thought of them,
But answer'd in a low voice, her meek head yet
Drooping, 'I pray you of your courtesy,   640
He being as he is, to let me be.'

She spake so low he hardly heard her speak,
But like a mighty patron, satisfied
With what himself had done so graciously,
Assumed that she had thank'd him, adding, 'Yea,   645
Eat and be glad, for I account you mine.'

She answer'd meekly, 'How should I be glad
Henceforth in all the world at anything,
Until my lord arise and look upon me?'

Here the huge earl cried out upon her talk,   650
As all but empty heart and weariness
And sickly nothing; suddenly seized on her,
And bare her by main violence to the board,
And thrust the dish before her, crying, 'Eat.'

'No, no,' said Enid, vext, 'I will not eat   655
Till yonder man upon the bier arise,

And eat with me.' 'Drink, then,' he answer'd. 'Here!'—
And fill'd a horn with wine and held it to her, —
'Lo! I, myself, when flush'd with fight, or hot,
God's curse, with anger — often I myself,   660
Before I well have drunken, scarce can eat:
Drink therefore, and the wine will change your will.'

 'Not so,' she cried, ' by Heaven, I will not drink
Till my dear lord arise and bid me do it,
And drink with me; and if he rise no more,   665
I will not look at wine until I die.'

 At this he turn'd all red and paced his hall,
Now gnaw'd his under, now his upper lip,
And coming up close to her, said at last:
'Girl, for I see ye scorn my courtesies,   670
Take warning: yonder man is surely dead;
And I compel all creatures to my will.
Not eat nor drink? And wherefore wail for one
Who put your beauty to this flout and scorn
By dressing it in rags? Amazed am I,   675
Beholding how ye butt against my wish,
That I forbear you thus: cross me no more.
At least put off to please me this poor gown,
This silken rag, this beggar-woman's °weed:
I love that beauty should go beautifully;   680
For see ye not my gentlewomen here,

How gay, how suited to the house of one
Who loves that beauty should go beautifully?
Rise therefore: robe yourself in this: obey.'

He spoke, and one among his gentlewomen   685
Display'd a splendid silk of foreign loom,
Where like a ° shoaling sea the lovely blue
Play'd into green, and thicker down the front
With jewels than the sward with drops of dew,
When all night long a cloud clings to the hill,   690
And with the dawn ascending lets the day
Strike where it clung: so thickly shone the gems.

But Enid answer'd, harder to be moved
Than hardest tyrants in their day of power,
With lifelong injuries burning unavenged,   695
And now their hour has come; and Enid said:

'In this poor gown my dear lord found me first,
And loved me serving in my father's hall;
In this poor gown I rode with him to court,
And there the Queen array'd me like the sun;   700
In this poor gown he bade me clothe myself,
When now we rode upon this fatal quest
Of honor, where no honor can be gain'd;
And this poor gown I will not cast aside
Until himself arise a living man,   705

And bid me cast it. I have grief enough:
Pray you be gentle, pray you let me be:
I never loved, can never love but him:
Yea, God, I pray you of your gentleness,
He being as he is, to let me be.' 710

Then strode the brute earl up and down his hall,
And took his russet beard between his teeth;
Last, coming up quite close, and in his mood
Crying, 'I count it of no more avail,
Dame, to be gentle than ungentle with you; 715
Take my salute,' unknightly with flat hand,
However lightly, smote her on the cheek.

Then Enid, in her utter helplessness,
And since she thought, 'He had not dared to do it,
Except he surely knew my lord was dead,' 720
Sent forth a sudden sharp and bitter cry,
As of a wild thing taken in the trap,
Which sees the trapper coming thro' the wood.

This heard Geraint, and grasping at his sword, —
It lay beside him in the hollow shield, — 725
Made but a single bound, and with a sweep of it
° Shore thro' the swarthy neck, and like a ball
The russet-bearded head roll'd on the floor.
So died Earl Doorm by him he counted dead.

And all the men and women in the hall   730
Rose when they saw the dead man rise, and fled
Yelling as from a spectre, and the two
Were left alone together, and he said:

'Enid, I have used you worse than that dead man,
Done you more wrong: we both have undergone   735
That trouble which has left me thrice your own:
Henceforward I will rather die than doubt.
And here I lay this penance on myself,
Not, tho' mine own ears heard you yestermorn —
You thought me sleeping, but I heard you say,   740
I heard you say, that you were no true wife:
I swear I will not ask your meaning in it:
I do believe yourself against yourself,
And will henceforward rather die than doubt.'

    And Enid could not say one tender word,   745
She felt so blunt and stupid at the heart:
She only pray'd him, 'Fly, they will return
And slay you; fly, your charger is without,
My palfrey lost.'   'Then, Enid, shall you ride
Behind me.'   'Yea,' said Enid, 'let us go.'   750
And moving out they found the stately horse,
Who now no more a vassal to the thief,
But free to stretch his limbs in lawful fight,
Neigh'd with all gladness as they came, and stoop'd

With a low whinny toward the pair : and she   755
Kiss'd the white star upon his noble front,
Glad also ; then Geraint upon the horse
Mounted, and reach'd a hand, and on his foot
She set her own and climb'd ; he turn'd his face
And kiss'd her climbing, and she cast her arms   760
About him, and at once they rode away.

°And never yet, since high in Paradise
O'er the °four rivers the first roses blew,
Came purer pleasure unto mortal kind
Than lived thro' her who in that perilous hour   765
Put hand to hand beneath her husband's heart,
And felt him hers again : she did not weep,
But o'er her meek eyes came a °happy mist
Like that which kept the heart of Eden green
Before the useful trouble of the rain :   770
Yet not so misty were her meek blue eyes
As not to see before them on the path,
Right in the gateway of the bandit hold,
A knight of Arthur's court, who laid his lance
In rest and made as if to fall upon him.   775
Then, fearing for his hurt and loss of blood,
She, with her mind all full of what had chanced,
Shriek'd to the stranger, ' Slay not a dead man ! '
' The voice of Enid,' said the knight ; but she,
Beholding it was Edyrn, son of Nudd,   780

L

Was moved so much the more, and shriek'd again,
'O cousin, slay not him who gave you life.'
And Edyrn moving frankly forward spake:
'My lord Geraint, I greet you with all love;
I took you for a bandit knight of Doorm;   785
And fear not, Enid, I should fall upon him,
Who love you, prince, with something of the love
Wherewith we love the Heaven that chastens us.
For once, when I was up so high in pride
That I was halfway down the slope to hell,   790
°By overthrowing me you threw me higher
Now, made a knight of Arthur's Table Round,
And since I knew this earl when I myself
Was half a bandit in my lawless hour,
I come the mouthpiece of our King to Doorm —   795
The King is close behind me — bidding him
Disband himself, and scatter all his powers,
Submit, and hear the judgment of the King.'

'He hears the judgment of the King of kings,'
Cried the wan prince; 'and lo, the powers of Doorm   800
Are scatter'd!' and he pointed to the field,
Where, huddled here and there on mound and knoll,
Were men and women staring and aghast,
While some yet fled; and then he plainlier told
How the huge earl lay slain within his hall.   805
But when the knight besought him, 'Follow me,

Prince, to the camp, and in the King's own ear
Speak what has chanced; ye surely have endured
Strange chances here alone;' that other flush'd,
And hung his head, and halted in reply,   810
Fearing the mild face of the blameless King,
And after madness acted question ask'd:
Till Edyrn crying, 'If ye will not go
To Arthur, then will Arthur come to you,'
'Enough,' he said, 'I follow,' and they went.   815
But Enid in their going had two fears,
One from the bandit scatter'd in the field,
And one from Edyrn. Every now and then,
When Edyrn rein'd his charger at her side,
She shrank a little. In a °hollow land,   820
From which old fires have broken, men may fear
Fresh fire and ruin. He, perceiving, said:

'Fair and dear cousin, you that most had cause
To fear me, fear no longer, I am changed.
Yourself were first the blameless cause to make   825
My nature's prideful sparkle in the blood
Break into furious flame; being repulsed
By Yniol and yourself, I schemed and wrought
Until I overturn'd him; then set up —
°With one main purpose ever at my heart —   830
My haughty jousts, and took a paramour;
Did her mock-honor as the fairest fair,

And, toppling over all antagonism,
So wax'd in pride that I believed myself
°Unconquerable, for I was wellnigh mad :   835
And, but for my main purpose in these jousts,
I should have slain your father, seized yourself.
I lived in hope that sometime you would come
To these my lists with him whom best you loved,
And there, poor cousin, with your meek blue eyes, 840
The truest eyes that °ever answer'd Heaven,
Behold me overturn and trample on him.
Then, had you cried, or knelt, or pray'd to me,
I should not less have kill'd him.   And you came, —
But once you came, — and with your own true 845
    eyes
Beheld the man you loved — I speak as one
Speaks of a service done him — overthrow
My proud self, and my purpose three years old,
And set his foot upon me, and give me life.
There was I broken down; there was I saved :   850
Tho' thence I rode all-shamed, hating the life
He gave me, meaning to be rid of it.
And all the penance the Queen laid upon me
Was but to rest awhile within her court ;
Where first as sullen as a beast new-caged,   855
And waiting to be treated like a wolf,
Because I knew my deeds were known, I found,
Instead of scornful pity or pure scorn,

Such fine reserve and noble reticence,
Manners so kind, yet stately, such a grace   860
Of tenderest courtesy, that I began
To glance behind me at my former life,
And find that it had been the wolf's indeed:
And oft I talk'd with Dubric, the high saint,
Who, with mild heat of holy oratory,   865
Subdued me somewhat to that gentleness
Which, when it weds with manhood, makes a man.
And you were often there about the Queen,
But saw me not, or mark'd not if you saw;
Nor did I care or dare to speak with you,   870
But kept myself aloof till I was changed;
And fear not, cousin; I am changed indeed.'

   He spoke, and Enid easily believed,
Like simple noble natures, credulous
Of what they long for, good in friend or foe,   875
There most in those who most have done them ill.
And when they reach'd the camp the King himself
Advanced to greet them, and beholding her
Tho' pale, yet happy, ask'd her not a word,
But went apart with Edyrn, whom he held   880
In converse for a little, and return'd,
And, gravely smiling, lifted her from horse,
And kiss'd her with all pureness, brother-like,
And show'd an empty tent allotted her,

And glancing for a minute, till he saw her   885
Pass into it, turn'd to the prince, and said:

'Prince, when of late ye pray'd me for my leave
To move to your own land and there defend
Your marches, I was prick'd with some reproof,
As one that let foul wrong stagnate and be,   890
By having look'd too much thro' alien eyes,
And wrought too long with delegated °hands,
Not used mine own: but now behold me come
To cleanse this common sewer of all my realm,
With Edyrn and with others: have ye look'd   895
At Edyrn? have ye seen how nobly changed?
This work of his is great and wonderful.
His very face with change of heart is changed.
The world will not believe a man repents:
And this wise world of ours is mainly right.   900
Full seldom doth a man repent, or use
Both grace and will to pick the °vicious quitch
Of blood and custom wholly out of him,
And make all clean, and plant himself afresh.
Edyrn has done it, weeding all his heart   905
As I will weed this land before I go.
I, therefore, made him of our Table Round,
Not rashly, but have proved him every way
One of our noblest, our most valorous,
Sanest and most obedient: and indeed   910

This work of Edyrn, wrought upon himself
After a life of violence, seems to me
A thousand-fold more great and wonderful
Than if some knight of mine, risking his life,
My subject with my subjects under him, 915
Should make an onslaught single on a realm
Of robbers, tho' he slew them one by one,
And were himself nigh wounded to the death.'

So spake the King; low bow'd the prince, and felt
His work was neither great nor wonderful, 920
And past to Enid's tent; and thither came
The King's own leech to look into his hurt;
And Enid tended on him there; and there
Her constant motion round him, and the breath
Of her sweet tendence hovering over him, 925
Fill'd all the genial courses of his blood
With deeper and with ever deeper love,
As the Southwest that blowing °Bala lake
Fills all the sacred Dee.   So past the days.

But while Geraint lay healing of his hurt, 930
The blameless King went forth and cast his eyes
On each of all whom Uther left in charge
Long since, to guard the justice of the King:
He look'd and found them wanting; and as now
Men weed the °White Horse on the Berkshire hills, 935

To keep him bright and clean as heretofore,
He rooted out the slothful officer
Or guilty, which for bribe had wink'd at wrong,
And in their chairs set up a stronger race
With hearts and hands, and sent a thousand men   940
To till the wastes, and moving everywhere
Clear'd the dark places and let in the law,
And broke the bandit holds and cleansed the land.

Then, when Geraint was whole again, they past
With Arthur to Caerleon upon Usk.   945
There the great Queen once more embraced her friend
And clothed her in apparel like the day.
And tho' Geraint could never take again
That comfort from their converse which he took
Before the Queen's fair name was breathed upon,   950
He rested well content that all was well.
Thence after tarrying for a space they rode,
And fifty knights rode with them to the shores
Of Severn, and they past to their own land.
And there he kept the justice of the King   955
So vigorously yet mildly that all hearts
Applauded, and the °spiteful whisper died:
And being ever foremost in the chase,
And victor at the tilt and tournament,
They call'd him the great prince and man of men.   960
But Enid, whom her ladies loved to call

Enid the Fair, a grateful people named
Enid the Good; and in their halls arose
The cry of children, Enids and Geraints
Of times to be; nor did he doubt her more.   965
But rested in her fealty till he crown'd
A happy life with a fair death, and fell
Against the heathen of the Northern Sea
In battle, °fighting for the blameless King.

LANCELOT AND ELAINE

°ELAINE the fair, Elaine the lovable,
Elaine, the °lily maid of Astolat,
High in her chamber up a tower to the east
Guarded the °sacred shield of Lancelot;
Which first she placed where morning's earliest ray   5
Might strike it, and awake her with the gleam;
Then fearing rust or soilure fashion'd for it
A case of silk, and braided thereupon
All the devices blazon'd on the shield
In their own tinct, and added, of her wit   10
A border fantasy of branch and flower,
And yellow-throated nestling in her nest.
Nor rested thus content, but day by day,
Leaving her household and good father, climb'd
That eastern tower, and entering barr'd her door,   15
Stript off the case, and read the naked shield,
Now guess'd a hidden meaning in his arms,
Now made a pretty history to herself
Of every dint a sword had beaten in it,
And every scratch a lance had made upon it,   20
Conjecturing when and where; this cut is fresh;
154

That ten years back; this dealt him at °Caerlyle;
That at Caerleon; this at °Camelot:
And ah, God's mercy, what a stroke was there!
And here a thrust that might have kill'd, but God   25
Broke the strong lance, and roll'd his enemy down,
And saved him: so she °lived in fantasy.

How came the lily maid by that good shield
Of Lancelot, she that knew not even his name?
He left it with her, when he rode to tilt   30
For the great diamond in the <u>diamond jousts</u>,
Which Arthur had ordain'd, and by that name
Had named them, since a <u>diamond</u> was the <u>prize</u>.

For Arthur, long before they crown'd him king,
Roving the trackless realms of °Lyonnesse,   35
Had found a glen, gray boulder and black °tarn.
A horror lived about the <u>tarn</u>, and clave
Like its own mists to all the mountain side:
For here °two brothers, one a king, had met
And fought together; but their names were lost;   40
And each had slain his brother at a blow;
And down they fell and made the glen abhorr'd:
And there they lay till all their bones were bleach'd,
And lichen'd into color with the crags:
And he that once was king had on a crown   45
Of diamonds, one in front and four aside.

And Arthur came, and laboring up the pass,
All in a misty moonshine, unawares
Had trodden that crown'd skeleton, and the skull
Brake from the nape, and from the skull the crown   50
Roll'd into light, and turning on its rims
Fled like a glittering rivulet to the tarn:
And down the shingly scaur he plunged, and caught,
And set it on his head, and in his heart
Heard murmurs, 'Lo, thou likewise shalt be king.'   55

   Thereafter, when a king, he had the gems
Pluck'd from the crown, and show'd them to his
      knights
Saying: 'These jewels, whereupon I chanced
Divinely, are the kingdom's, not the King's —
For public use: henceforward let there be,   60
Once every year, a joust for one of these:
For so by nine years' proof we needs must learn
Which is our mightiest, and ourselves shall grow
In use of arms and manhood, till we drive
The heathen, who, some say, shall rule the land   65
Hereafter, which God hinder!'   Thus he spoke:
And eight years past, eight jousts had been, and
      still
Had Lancelot won the diamond of the year,
With purpose to present them to the Queen
When all were won; but, meaning all at once   70

To snare her royal fancy with a boon
Worth half her realm, had never spoken word.

Now for the central diamond and the last
And largest, Arthur, holding then his court
Hard on the river nigh the place which now
Is °this world's hugest, let proclaim a joust   75
At Camelot, and when the time drew nigh
Spake — for she had been sick — to Guinevere:
'Are you so sick, my Queen, you cannot move
To these fair jousts?' 'Yea, lord,' she said, 'ye
    know it.'   80
'Then will ye miss,' he answer'd, 'the great deeds
Of Lancelot, and his prowess in the lists,
A sight ye love to look on.' And the Queen
Lifted her eyes, and they dwelt languidly
On Lancelot, where he stood beside the King.   85
He, thinking that he read her meaning there,
'Stay with me, I am sick; my love is more
Than many diamonds,' yielded; and a heart
Love-loyal to the least wish of the Queen —
However much he yearn'd to make complete   90
The tale of diamonds for his destined boon —
Urged him to speak against the truth, and say,
'Sir King, mine ancient wound is hardly whole,
And lets me from the saddle;' and the King
Glanced °first at him, then her, and went his way.   95
No sooner gone than suddenly she began:

You are

" To blame, my lord Sir Lancelot, much to blame!
Why go ye not to these fair jousts? the knights
Are half of them our enemies, and the crowd
Will murmur, " Lo the shameless ones, who take   100
Their pastime now the trustful King is gone!'"
Then Lancelot, °vext at having lied in vain: *said*
' Are ye so wise? ye were not once so wise,
My Queen, that summer when ye loved me first.
Then of the crowd ye took no more account   105
Than of the °myriad cricket of the mead,
When its own voice clings to each blade of grass,
And every voice is nothing.   As to knights,
Them surely can I silence with all ease.
But now my royal worship is allow'd ~~accepted &~~ *approved*   110
Of all men: many a bard, without offence,
Has link'd our names together in his lay,
Lancelot, the flower of bravery, Guinevere,
The pearl of beauty; and our knights at feast
Have pledged us in this union, while the King   115
Would listen smiling.   How then? is there more?
Has Arthur spoken aught? or would yourself,
Now weary of my service and devoir,
Henceforth be truer to your faultless lord?'

    She broke into a little scornful laugh: 120
' Arthur, my lord, Arthur, °the faultless King,
That passionate perfection, my good lord —

But who can gaze upon the sun in heaven?
He never spake word of reproach to me,
He never had a glimpse of mine untruth,   125
He cares not for me: only here to-day
There gleamed a vague suspicion in his eyes:
Some meddling rogue has tamper'd with him — else
Rapt in this fancy of his Table Round,
And swearing men to °vows impossible,   130
To make them like himself; but, friend, to me
He is all fault who hath no fault at all:
For who loves me must have a touch of earth;
The low sun makes the color: I am yours,
Not Arthur's, as ye know, save by the bond.   135
And therefore hear my words: go to the jousts:
The tiny-trumpeting gnat can break our dream
When sweetest; and the °vermin voices here
May buzz so loud — we scorn them, but they sting.'

Then answer'd Lancelot, the chief of knights: 140
'And with what face, after my pretext made,
Shall I appear, O Queen, at Camelot, I
Before a king who honors his own word
As if it were his °God's?'

Arthur's simplicity   'Yea,' said the Queen,
'A moral child without the craft to rule,   145
Else had he not lost me: but listen to me,

If I must find you wit: we hear it said
That men go down before your spear at a touch,
But knowing you are Lancelot; your great name,
This conquers: hide it therefore; go unknown: 150
Win! by this kiss you will: and our true King
Will then allow your pretext, O my knight,
As for all glory; for to speak him true,
Ye know right well, how meek soe'er he seem,
No keener hunter after glory breathes.   155
He loves it in his knights more than himself;
'They prove to him his work: win and return.'

Then got Sir Lancelot suddenly to horse,
Wroth at himself.   Not willing to be known,
He left the barren-beaten thoroughfare,   160
Chose the green path that show'd the rarer foot,
And there among the solitary downs,
Full often lost in fancy, lost his way;
Till as he traced a faintly-shadow'd track,
That all in loops and links among the dales   165
Ran to the Castle of Astolat, he saw
Fired from the west, far on a hill, the towers.
Thither he made, and blew the gateway horn.
Then came an old, dumb, myriad-wrinkled man,
Who let him into lodging and disarm'd.   170
And Lancelot marvell'd at the wordless man;
And issuing found the Lord of Astolat

With two strong sons, Sir Torre and Sir Lavaine,
Moving to meet him in the castle court;
And close behind them stept the lily maid   175
°Elaine, his daughter: mother of the house
There was not.   Some light jest among them rose
With laughter dying down as the great knight
Approach'd them; then the Lord of Astolat: *said*
'Whence comest thou, my guest, and by what name 180
°Livest between the lips? for by thy state
And presence I might guess thee chief of those,
After the King, who eat in Arthur's halls.
Him have I seen: the rest, his Table Round,
Known as they are, to me they are unknown.'   185

Then answer'd Lancelot, the chief of knights:
'Known am I, and of Arthur's hall, and known,
What I by mere mischance have brought, my shield.
But since I go to joust as one unknown
At Camelot for the diamond, ask me not;   190
Hereafter ye shall know me — and the shield —
I pray you lend me one, if such you have,
Blank, or at least with some device not mine.'

Then said the Lord of Astolat: 'Here is Torre's:
Hurt in his first tilt was my son, Sir Torre;   195
And so, God wot, his shield is blank enough.
His ye can have.'   Then added plain Sir Torre,

M

'Yea, since I cannot use it, ye may have it.'
Here laugh'd the father saying: 'Fie, Sir Churl,
Is that an answer for a noble knight?   200
Allow him! but °Lavaine, my younger here,
He is so full of lustihood, he will ride,
Joust for it, and win, and bring it in an hour,
And set it in this damsel's golden hair,
To make her thrice as wilful as before.'   205

'Nay, father, nay, good father, shame me not
Before this noble knight,' said young Lavaine,
'For nothing.   Surely I but play'd on Torre:
He seem'd so sullen, vext he could not go:
A jest, no more! for, knight, the maiden dreamt   210
That some one put this diamond in her hand,
And that it was too slippery to be held,
And slipt and fell into some pool or stream,
The castle-well, belike; and then I said
That *if* I went and *if* I fought and won it—   215
But all was jest and joke among ourselves—
Then must she keep it safelier.   All was jest.
But, father, give me leave, and if he will,
To ride to Camelot with this noble knight:
Win shall I not, but do my best to win;   220
Young as I am, yet would I do my best.'

'So ye will grace me,' answer'd Lancelot,
Smiling a moment, ' with your fellowship

O'er these waste downs whereon I lost myself,
Then were I glad of you as guide and friend :   225
And you shall win this diamond, — as I hear,
It is a fair large diamond, — if ye may,
And yield it to this maiden, if ye will.'
'A fair large diamond,' added plain Sir Torre,
'Such be for queens, and not for simple maids.'   230
Then she, who held her eyes upon the ground,
Elaine, and heard her name so tost about,
Flush'd slightly at the slight disparagement
Before the stranger knight, who, looking at her,
Full courtly, yet not falsely, thus return'd :   235
'If what is fair be but for what is fair,
And only queens are to be counted so,
Rash were my judgment then, who deem this maid
Might wear as fair a jewel as is on earth,
Not violating the bond of like to like.'   240
  He spoke and ceased : the lily maid Elaine,
Won by the mellow voice before she look'd,
Lifted her eyes and read his lineaments.
The great and guilty love he bare the Queen,
In battle with the love he bare his lord,   245
°Had marr'd his face, and mark'd it ere his time.
Another sinning on such heights with one,
The flower of all the west and all the world,
Had been the sleeker for it ; but in him
His mood was often like a fiend, and rose   250

And drove him into wastes and solitudes
For agony, who was yet a living soul.
Marr'd as he was, he seem'd the goodliest man
That ever among ladies ate in hall,
And noblest, when she lifted up her eyes.　　255
However marr'd, of more than twice her years,
Seam'd with an ancient sword-cut on the °cheek,
And bruised and bronzed, she lifted up her eyes
And loved him, with that love which was her doom.

Then the great knight, the darling of the court,　260
Loved of the loveliest, into that rude hall
Stept with all grace, and not with half disdain
Hid under grace, as in a smaller time,
But kindly man moving among his kind:
Whom they with meats and vintage of their best　265
And talk and minstrel melody entertain'd.
And much they ask'd of court and Table Round,
And ever well and readily answer'd he;
But Lancelot, when they °glanced at Guinevere,
Suddenly speaking of the wordless man,　　270
Heard from the baron that, ten years before,
The heathen caught and reft him of his tongue.
'He learnt and warn'd me of their fierce design
Against my house, and him they caught and maim'd;
But I, my sons, and little daughter fled　　275
From bonds or death, and dwelt among the woods

By the great river in a boatman's hut.
Dull days were those, till our good Arthur broke
The Pagan yet once more on °Badon hill.'

'O there, great lord, doubtless,' Lavaine said, °rapt
By all the sweet and sudden passion of youth   281
Toward greatness in its elder, 'you have fought.
O, tell us — for we live apart — you know
Of Arthur's glorious wars.'   And Lancelot spoke
And answer'd him at full, as having been   285
With Arthur in the fight which all day long
Rang by the white mouth of °the violent Glem;
And in the four loud battles by the shore
Of Duglas; that on Bassa; then the war
That thunder'd in and out the gloomy skirts   290
Of Celidon the forest; and again
By Castle Gurnion, where the glorious King
Had on his cuirass worn our Lady's Head,
Carved of one emerald centred in a sun
Of silver rays, that lighten'd as he breathed;   295
And at Caerleon had he helped his lord,
When the strong neighings of the wild White Horse
Set every gilded parapet shuddering;
And up in Agned-Cathregonion too,
And down the waste sand-shores of Trath Treroit,   300
Where many a heathen fell; 'and on the mount
Of Badon I myself beheld the King

Charge at the head of all his Table Round,
And all his legion crying Christ and him,
And brake them; and I saw him, after, stand   305
High on a heap of slain, from spur to plume
Red as the rising sun with heathen blood,
And seeing me, with a great voice he cried,
" They are broken, they are broken! " for the King,
However mild he seems at home, nor cares   310
For triumph in our mimic wars, the jousts —
For if his own knight cast him down, he laughs,
Saying his knights are better men than he —
Yet in this heathen war the °fire of God
Fills him: I never saw his like; there lives   315
No greater leader.'

                    While he utter'd this,
Low to her own heart said the lily maid,
' Save your great self, fair lord; ' and when he fell
From talk of war to traits of pleasantry —
Being mirthful he, but in a stately kind —   320
She still took note that when the living smile
Died from his lips, across him came a cloud
Of melancholy severe, from which again,
Whenever in her hovering to and fro
The lily maid had striven °to make him cheer,   325
There brake a sudden-beaming tenderness
Of manners and of nature: and she thought

That all was nature, all, perchance, for her.
And all night long his face before her lived,
As when a painter, poring on a face,   330
Divinely thro' all hindrance finds the man
Behind it, and so paints him that his face,
The shape and color of a mind and life,
Lives for his children, ever at its best
And fullest; so the face before her lived,   335
Dark-splendid, speaking in the silence, full
Of noble things, and held her from her sleep,
Till °rathe she rose, half-cheated in the thought
She needs must bid farewell to sweet Lavaine.
First as in fear, step after step, she stole   340
Down the long tower-stairs, hesitating:
Anon, she heard Sir Lancelot cry in the court,
'This shield, my friend, where is it?' and Lavaine
Past inward, as she came from out the tower.
There to his proud horse Lancelot turn'd, and smooth'd
The glossy shoulder, humming to himself.   346
Half-envious of the flattering hand, she drew
Nearer and stood.   He look'd, and, more amazed
Than if seven man had set upon him, saw
The maiden standing in the dewy light.   350
He had not dream'd she was so beautiful.
Then came on him a sort of sacred fear,
For silent, tho' he greeted her, she stood
'Rapt on his face as if it were a god's.

Suddenly flash'd on her a wild desire   355
That he should wear her favor at the tilt.
She braved a riotous heart in asking for it.
'Fair lord, whose name I know not — noble it is
I well believe, the noblest — will you wear
My favor at this tourney?' 'Nay,' said he,   360
'Fair lady, since I never yet have worn
Favor of any lady in the lists.
Such is my wont, as those who know me know.'
'Yea, so,' she answer'd; 'then in wearing mine
Needs must be lesser likelihood, noble lord,   365
That those who know should know you.' And he turn'd
Her counsel up and down within his mind,
And found it true, and answer'd: 'True, my child.
Well, I will wear it: fetch it out to me:
What is it?' and she told him, 'A red sleeve   370
Broider'd with pearls,' and brought it: then he bound
Her token on his helmet, with a smile
Saying, 'I never yet have done so much
For any maiden living,' and the blood
Sprang to her face and fill'd her with delight;   375
But left her the paler when Lavaine
Returning brought the yet un-blazon'd shield,
His brother's; which he gave to Lancelot,
Who parted with his own to fair Elaine:
'Do me this grace, my child, to have my shield   380
In keeping till I come.' 'A grace to me,'

She answer'd, 'twice to-day.   I am your squire!'
Whereat Lavaine said laughingly: 'Lily maid,
For fear our people call you lily maid
In earnest, let me bring your color back;   385
Once, twice, and thrice: now get you hence to bed:'
So kiss'd her, and Sir Lancelot his own hand,
And thus they moved away: she staid a minute,
Then made a sudden step to the gate, and there —
Her bright hair blown about the serious face   390
Yet rosy-kindled with her brother's kiss —
Paused by the gateway, standing near the shield
In silence, while she watch'd their arms far-off
Sparkle, until they dipt below the downs.
Then to her tower she climb'd and took the shield, 395
There kept it, and so lived in fantasy.

    Meanwhile the new companions past away
Far o'er the long backs of the bushless downs,
To where Sir Lancelot knew there lived a knight
Not far from Camelot, now for forty years   400
°A hermit, who had pray'd, labor'd and pray'd,
And ever laboring had scoop'd himself
In the white rock a chapel and a hall
Of massive columns, like a shore-cliff cave,
And cells and chambers: all were fair and dry;   405
The green °light from the meadows underneath
Struck up and lived along the milky roofs;

And in the meadows tremulous aspen-trees
And poplars made a °noise of falling showers.
And thither wending there that night they bode.   410

But when the next day broke from underground,
And shot red fire and shadows thro' the cave
They rose, heard mass, broke fast, and rode away.
Then Lancelot saying, 'Hear, but hold my name
Hidden, you ride with Lancelot of the Lake,'   415
Abash'd Lavaine, whose instant reverence,
Dearer to true young hearts than their own praise,
But left him leave to stammer, 'Is it indeed?'
And after muttering, 'The great Lancelot,'
At last he got his breath and answer'd: 'One,   420
One have I seen — that other, our liege lord,
The dread °Pendragon, Britain's King of kings,
Of whom the people talk mysteriously,
He will be there — then were I stricken blind
That minute, I might say that I had seen.'   425

So spake Lavaine, and when they reach'd the lists
By Camelot in the meadow, let his eyes
Run thro' the peopled gallery which half round
°Lay like a rainbow fallen upon the grass,
Until they found the clear-faced King, who sat   430
Robed in red samite, easily to be known,
Since to his crown the golden dragon clung,

And down his robe the dragon writhed in gold,
And from the carven-work behind him crept
Two dragons gilded, sloping down to make   435
Arms for his chair, while all the rest of them
Thro' knots and loops and folds innumerable
Fled ever thro' the woodwork, till they found
The new design wherein they lost themselves,
Yet with °all ease, so tender was the work: 440
And, in the costly canopy o'er him set
Blazed the last diamond of the °nameless king.

    Then Lancelot answer'd young Lavaine and said:
'Me you call great: mine is the firmer seat,
The truer lance: but there is many a youth   445
Now °crescent, who will come to all I am
And overcome it: and in me there dwells
No greatness, save it be some far-off touch
Of greatness to know well I am not great:
There is the man.' And Lavaine gaped upon him   450
As on a thing miraculous, and anon
The trumpets blew; and then did either side,
They that assail'd, and they that °held the lists,
Set lance in rest, strike spur, suddenly move,
Meet in the midst, and there so furiously   455
Shock that a man afar-off might well perceive,
If any man that day were left afield,
The hard earth shake, and a low thunder of arms.

And Lancelot °bode a little, till he saw
Which were the weaker; then he hurl'd into it   460
Against the stronger: little need to speak
Of Lancelot in his glory!   King, duke, earl,
Count. baron — whom he smote, he overthrew.

But in the field were Lancelot's kith and kin,
Ranged with the Table Round that held the lists,   465
Strong men, and wrathful that a stranger knight
Should do and almost overdo the deeds
Of Lancelot; and one said to the other, ' Lo!
What is he?   I do not mean the force alone —
The grace and versatility of the man!   470
Is it not Lancelot?'   ' When has Lancelot worn
Favor of any lady in the lists?
Not such his wont, as we that know him know.'
' How then? who then?' a fury seized them all,
A fiery family passion for the name   475
Of Lancelot, and a glory one with theirs.
They couch'd their spears and prick'd their steeds, and
        thus,
Their plumes driven backward by the wind they made
In moving, all together down upon him
Bare, °as a wild wave in the wide North Sea,   480
Green-glimmering toward the summit, bears, with all
Its stormy crests that smoke against the skies,
Down on the bark, and overbears the bark

And him that helms it; so they overbore
Sir Lancelot and his charger, and a spear   485
Down-glancing lamed the charger, and a spear
Prick'd sharply his own cuirass, and the head
Pierced thro' his side, and there snapt and remain'd

Then Sir Lavaine did well and worshipfully:
He bore a knight of old repute to the earth,   490
And brought his horse to Lancelot where he lay.
He up the side, sweating with agony, got,
But thought to do while he might yet endure,
And being lustily holpen by the rest,
His party, — tho' it seem'd half-miracle   495
To those he fought with, — drave his kith and kin,
And all the Table Round that held the lists,
Back to the barrier; then the trumpets blew
Proclaiming his the prize who wore the sleeve
Of scarlet and the pearls; and all the knights,   500
His party, cried, 'Advance and take thy prize
The diamond;' but he answer'd: 'Diamond me
No diamonds! for God's love, a little air!
Prize me no prizes, for my prize is death!
Hence will I, and I charge you, follow me not.'   505

He spoke, and vanish'd suddenly from the field
With young Lavaine into the poplar grove.
There from his charger down he slid, and sat,

Gasping to Sir Lavaine, 'Draw the lance-head.'
'Ah, my sweet lord Sir Lancelot,' said Lavaine,   510
'I dread me, if I draw it, you will die.'
But he, 'I die already with it : draw —
Draw,' — and Lavaine drew, and Sir Lancelot gave
A marvellous great shriek and ghastly groan,
And half his blood burst forth, and down he sank   515
For the pure pain, and wholly swoon'd away.
Then came the hermit out and bare him in,
There stanch'd his wound ; and there, in daily doubt
Whether to live or die, for many a week
Hid from the wild world's rumor by the grove   520
Of poplars with their noise of falling showers,
And ever-tremulous aspen-trees, he lay.

But on that day when Lancelot fled the lists,
His party, knights of utmost North and West,
Lords of waste marshes, kings of desolate isles,   525
Came round their great Pendragon, saying to him,
'Lo, Sire, our knight, thro' whom we won the day,
Hath gone sore wounded, and hath left his prize
Untaken, crying that his prize is death.'
'Heaven hinder,' said the King, 'that such an one, 530
So great a knight as we have seen to-day —
He seem'd to me another Lancelot —
Yea, twenty times I thought him Lancelot —
He must not pass uncared for.   Wherefore rise,

°O Gawain, and ride forth and find the knight.   535
Wounded and wearied, needs must he be near.
I charge you that you get at once to horse.
And, knights and kings, there breathes not one of you
Will deem this prize of ours is rashly given:
His prowess was too wondrous. We will do him   540
No customary honor: since the knight
Came not to us, of us to claim the prize,
Ourselves will send it after. Rise and take
This diamond, and deliver it, and return,
And bring us where he is, and how he fares,   545
And cease not from your quest until ye find.'

So saying, from the carven flower above,
To which it made a °restless heart, he took
And gave the diamond: then from where he sat
At Arthur's right, with smiling face arose,   550
With smiling face and frowning heart, a prince
In the mid might and flourish of his May,
Gawain, surnamed the Courteous, fair and strong.
And after Lancelot, Tristram, and Geraint,
And Gareth, a good knight, but therewithal   555
°Sir Modred's brother, and the child of Lot,
Nor often loyal to his word, and now
Wroth that the King's command to sally forth
In quest of whom he knew not, made him leave
The banquet and concourse of knights and kings.   560

So all in wrath he got his horse and went;
While Arthur to the banquet, dark in mood,
Past, thinking, 'Is it Lancelot who hath come
Despite the wound he spake of, all for gain
Of glory, and hath added wound to wound,   565
And ridden away to die?'   So fear'd the King,
And, after two days' °tarriance there, return'd.
Then when he saw the Queen, embracing ask'd,
'Love, are you yet so sick?' 'Nay, lord,' she said.
'And where is Lancelot?'   Then the Queen amazed,
'Was he not with you? won he not your prize?'   571
'Nay, but one like him.' 'Why, that like was he.'
And when the King demanded how she knew,
Said: 'Lord, no sooner had ye parted from us
Than Lancelot told me of a common talk   575
That men went down before his spear at a touch,
But knowing he was Lancelot; his great name
Conquer'd; and therefore would he hide his name
From all men, even the King, and to this end
Had made the pretext of a hindering wound,   580
That he might joust unknown of all, and learn
If his old prowess were in aught decay'd;
And added, "°Our true Arthur, when he learns,
Will well allow my pretext, as for gain
Of purer glory."'

Then replied the King: 585
‘Far lovelier in our Lancelot had it been,
In lieu of idly dallying with the truth,
To have trusted me as he hath trusted thee.
Surely his King and most familiar friend
Might well have kept his secret. True, indeed,   590
Albeit I know my knights fantastical,
°So fine a fear in our large Lancelot
Must needs have moved my laughter: now remains
But little cause for laughter: his own kin —
Ill news, my Queen, for all who love him, this! —   595
His kith and kin, not knowing, set upon him;
So that he went sore wounded from the field.
Yet good news too; for goodly hopes are mine
That Lancelot is no more a lonely heart.
He wore, against his wont, upon his helm   600
A sleeve of scarlet, broider’d with great pearls,
Some gentle maiden’s gift.’

‘Yea, lord,’ she said,
‘Thy hopes are mine,’ and saying that, she choked,
And sharply turn’d about to hide her face,
Past to her chamber and there flung herself   605
Down on the great King’s couch, and writhed
    upon it,
And clench’d her fingers till they bit the palm,
And shriek’d out ‘°Traitor!’ to the unhearing wall,

N

Then flash'd into wild tears, and rose again,
And moved about her palace, proud and pale.   610

   Gawain the while thro' all the region round
Rode with his diamond, wearied of the quest,
Touch'd at all points except the poplar grove
And came at last, tho' late, to Astolat;
Whom glittering in enamell'd arms the maid   615
Glanced at, and cried, ' What news from Camelot, lord ?
What of the knight with the red sleeve ? '   ' He won.'
' I knew it,' she said.   ' But parted from the jousts
Hurt in the side; ' whereat she caught her breath ;
Thro' her own side she felt the sharp lance go ;   620
Thereon she smote her hand; wellnigh she swoon'd :
And, while he gazed wonderingly at her, came
The Lord of Astolat out, to whom the prince
Reported who he was, and on what quest
Sent, that he bore the prize and could not find   625
The victor, but had ridden at random round
To seek him, and had wearied of the search.
To whom the Lord of Astolat: ' Bide with us,
And ride no more at random, noble prince !
Here was the knight and here he left a shield ;   630
This will he send or come for: furthermore,
Our son is with him; we shall hear anon,
Needs must we hear.'   To this the courteous prince
Accorded with his wonted courtesy,

Courtesy with a touch of traitor in it,   635
And staid; and cast his eyes on fair Elaine;
Where could be found face daintier? then her shape
From forehead down to foot, perfect — again
From foot to forehead exquisitely turn'd:
'Well — if I bide, lo! this wild flower for me!'   640
And oft they met among the garden yews,
And there he set himself to play upon her
With sallying wit, free flashes from a height
Above her, graces of the court, and songs,
Sighs, and low smiles, and golden eloquence   645
And amorous adulation, till the maid
Rebell'd against it, saying to him: 'Prince,
O loyal nephew of our noble King,
Why ask you not to see the shield he left,
Whence you might learn his name? Why slight your
    King,   650
And lose the quest he sent you on, and prove
No surer than our falcon yesterday,
Who lost the hern we slipt her at, and went
To all the winds?' 'Nay by mine head,' said he,
'I lose it, as we lose the lark in heaven,   655
O damsel, in the light of your blue eyes;
But an ye will it let me see the shield.'
And when the shield was brought, and Gawain saw
Sir Lancelot's azure lions, crown'd with gold,
Ramp in the field, he smote his thigh, and mock'd: 660

'Right was the King! our Lancelot! that true man!'
'And right was I,' she answer'd merrily, 'I,
Who dream'd my knight the greatest knight of all.'
'And if I dream'd,' said Gawain, 'that you love
This greatest knight, your pardon! lo, ye know it!   665
Speak therefore: shall I waste myself in vain?'
Full simple was her answer: 'What know I?
My brethren have been all my fellowship;
And I, when often they have talk'd of love,
Wish'd it had been my mother, for they talk'd,   670
Meseem'd, of what they knew not; so myself —
I know not if I know what true love is,
But if I know, then, if I love not him,
I know there is none other I can love.'
'Yea, by God's death,' said he, 'ye love him well,   675
But would not, knew ye what all others know,
And whom he loves.'   'So be it,' cried Elaine,
And lifted her fair face and moved away:
But he pursued her, calling, 'Stay a little!
One golden minute's grace! he wore your sleeve: 680
Would he break faith with one I may not name?
Must our true man change like a leaf at last?
Nay — like enow: why then, far be it from me
To cross our mighty Lancelot in his loves!
And, damsel, for I deem you know full well   685
Where your great knight is hidden, let me leave
My quest with you; the diamond also: here!

For if you love, it will be sweet to give it;
And if he love, it will be sweet to have it
From your own hand; and whether he love or not, 690
A diamond is a diamond.   Fare you well
A thousand times!—a thousand times farewell!
Yet, if he love, and his love hold, we two
May meet at court hereafter: there, I think,
So ye will learn the courtesies of the court, 695
We two shall know each other.'

                              Then he gave
And slightly kiss'd the hand to which he gave,
The diamond, and all wearied of the quest
Leapt on his horse, and carolling as he went
A true-love ballad, lightly rode away. 700

   Thence to the court he past; there told the
      King
What the King knew, 'Sir Lancelot is the knight.'
And added, 'Sire, my liege, so much I learnt;
But fail'd to find him tho' I rode all round
The region: but I lighted on the maid 705
Whose sleeve he wore; she loves him; and to
      her,
Deeming °our courtesy is the truest law,
I gave the diamond: she will render it;
For by mine head she knows his hiding-place.'

The seldom-frowning King frown'd, and replied, 710
'Too courteous truly! ye shall go no more
On quest of mine, seeing that ye forget
Obedience is the courtesy due to kings.'

He spake and parted.   Wroth, but all in awe,
For twenty strokes of the blood, without a word, 715
Linger'd that other, staring after him;
Then shook his hair, strode off, and buzz'd abroad
About the maid of Astolat, and her love.
All ears were prick'd at once, all tongues were loosed:
'The maid of Astolat loves Sir Lancelot, 720
Sir Lancelot loves the maid of Astolat.'
Some read the King's face, some the Queen's, and all
Had marvel what the maid might be, but most
Predoom'd her as unworthy.   One old dame
Came suddenly on the Queen with the sharp news. 725
She, that had heard the noise of it before,
But sorrowing Lancelot should have stoop'd so low,
°Marr'd her friend's aim with pale tranquillity.
So ran the tale like fire about the court.
Fire in dry stubble a nine-days' wonder flared: 730
Till even the knights at banquet twice or thrice
Forgot to drink to Lancelot and the Queen,
And pledging Lancelot and the lily maid
Smiled at each other, while the Queen, who sat
With lips severely placid, felt the knot 735

Climb in her throat, and with her feet unseen
Crush'd the wild passion out against the floor
Beneath the banquet, where the meats became
As wormwood, and she hated all who pledged.

But far away the maid in Astolat,   740
Her guiltless rival, she that ever kept
The one-day-seen Sir Lancelot in her heart,
Crept to her father, while he mused alone,
Sat on his knee, stroked his gray face and said:
'Father, you call me wilful, and the fault   745
Is yours who let me have my will, and now,
Sweet father, will you let me lose my wits?'
'Nay,' said he, 'surely.'   'Wherefore, let me hence,'
She answer'd, 'and find out our dear Lavaine.'
'Ye will not lose your wits for dear Lavaine: 750
Bide,' answer'd he: 'we needs must hear anon
Of him, and of that other.'   'Ay,' she said,
'And of that other, for I needs must hence
And find that other, wheresoe'er he be,
And with my own hand give his diamond to him,   755
Lest I be found as faithless in the quest
As yon proud prince who left the quest to me.
Sweet father, I behold him in my dreams
Gaunt as it were the skeleton of himself,
Death-pale, for the lack of gentle maiden's aid.   760
The gentler-born the maiden, the more bound,
My father, to be sweet and serviceable

To noble knights in sickness, as ye know,
When these have worn their tokens: let me hence,
I pray you.'   Then her father nodding said: 765
'Ay, ay, the diamond: wit ye well, my child,
Right fain were I to learn this knight were whole,
Being our greatest: yea, and you must give it —
And sure I think this fruit is hung too high
For any mouth to gape for save a queen's —   770
Nay, I mean nothing: so then, get you gone,
Being so very wilful you must go.'

   Lightly, her suit allow'd, she slipt away,
And while she made her ready for her ride
Her father's latest word humm'd in her ear,   775
'Being so very wilful you must go,'
And changed itself and echo'd in her heart,
'Being so very wilful you must die.'
But she was happy enough and shook it off,
As we shake off the bee that buzzes at us;   780
And in her heart she answer'd it and said,
'What matter, so I help him back to life?'
Then far away with good Sir Torre for guide
Rode o'er the long backs of the bushless downs
To Camelot, and before the city gates   785
Came on her brother with a happy face
Making a roan horse caper and curvet
For pleasure all about a field of flowers;

Whom when she saw, 'Lavaine,' she cried, 'Lavaine,
How fares my lord Sir Lancelot?' He amazed,   790
'Torre and Elaine! why here? Sir Lancelot!
How know ye my lord's name is Lancelot?'
But when the maid had told him all her tale,
Then turn'd Sir Torre, and being in his moods
Left them, and under the strange-statued gate,   795
Where Arthur's wars were render'd mystically,
Past up the still rich city to his kin,
His own far blood, which dwelt at Camelot;
And her, Lavaine across the poplar grove
Led to the caves: there first she saw the casque   800
Of Lancelot on the wall: her scarlet sleeve,
Tho' carved and cut, and half the pearls away,
Stream'd from it still; and in her heart she laugh'd,
Because he had not loosed it from his helm,
But meant once more perchance to tourney in it.   805
And when they gain'd the cell wherein he slept,
His °battle-writhen arms and mighty hands
Lay naked on the wolf-skin, and a dream
Of dragging down his enemy made them move.
Then she that saw him lying unsleek, unshorn,   810
Gaunt as it were the skeleton of himself,
Utter'd a little tender dolorous cry.
The sound not wonted in a place so still
Woke the sick knight, and while he roll'd his eyes
Yet blank from sleep, she started to him, saying,   815

'Your prize the diamond sent you by the King.'
His eyes glisten'd: she fancied, 'Is it for me?'
And when the maid had told him all the tale
Of king and prince, the diamond sent, the quest
Assign'd to her not worthy of it, she knelt   820
Full lowly by the corners of his bed,
And laid the diamond in his open hand.
Her face was near, and as we kiss the child
That does the task assign'd, he kiss'd her face.
At once she slipt like water to the floor.   825
'Alas,' he said, 'your ride hath wearied you.
Rest must you have.'   'No rest for me,' she said;
'Nay, for near you, fair lord, I am at rest.'
What might she mean by that? his large black eyes,
Yet larger thro' his leanness, dwelt upon her,   830
Till all her heart's sad secret blazed itself
In the heart's colors on her simple face;
And Lancelot look'd and was perplext in mind,
And being weak in body said no more,
But did not love the color; woman's love,   835
Save one, he not regarded, and so turn'd
Sighing, and feign'd a sleep until he slept.

Then rose Elaine and glided thro' the fields,
And past beneath the weirdly-sculptured gates
Far up the dim rich city to her kin;   840
There bode the night: but woke with dawn, and past

Down thro' the dim rich city to the fields,
Thence to the cave.   So day by day she past
In either twilight ghost-like to and fro
Gliding, and every day she tended him,   845
And likewise many a night; and Lancelot
Would, tho' he call'd his wound a little hurt
Whereof he should be quickly whole, at times
Brain-feverous in his heat and agony, seem
Uncourteous, even he: but the meek maid   850
Sweetly forebore him ever, being to him
Meeker than any child to a rough nurse,
Milder than any mother to a sick child,
And never woman yet, since man's first fall,
Did kindlier unto man, but her deep love   855
Upbore her; till the hermit, skill'd in all
The simples and the science of that time,
Told him that her fine care had saved his life
And the sick man forgot her simple blush,
Would call her friend and sister, sweet Elaine,   860
Would listen for her coming and regret
Her parting step, and held her tenderly,
And loved her with all love except the love
Of man and woman when they love their best,
Closest and sweetest, and had died the death   865
In any knightly fashion for her sake.
And peradventure had he seen her first
She might have made this and that other world

Another world for the sick man; but now
The shackles of an old love straiten'd him,   370
°His honor rooted in dishonor stood,
And faith unfaithful kept him falsely true.

　　Yet the great knight in his mid-sickness made
Full many a holy vow and pure resolve.
These, as but born of sickness, could not live ;   875
For when the blood ran lustier in him again,
Full often the bright image of one face,
Making a treacherous quiet in his heart,
Dispersed his resolution like a cloud.
Then if the maiden, while that ghostly grace   880
Beam'd on his fancy, spoke, he answer'd not,
Or short and coldly, and she knew right well
°What the rough sickness meant, but what this meant
She knew not, and the sorrow dimm'd her sight,
And drave her ere her time across the fields   885
Far into the rich city, where alone
She murmur'd, ' Vain, in vain : it cannot be.
He will not love me : how then ? must I die ? '
Then as a little helpless innocent bird,
That has but one plain passage of few notes,   890
Will sing the simple passage o'er and o'er
For all an April morning, till the ear
Wearies to hear it, so the simple maid
Went half the night repeating, ' Must I die ? '

And now to right she turn'd, and now to left, 895
And found no ease in turning or in rest ;
And 'Him or death,' she mutter'd, 'death or him,'
Again and like a °burthen, 'Him or death.'

But when Sir Lancelot's deadly hurt was whole,
To Astolat returning rode the three. 900
There morn by morn, arraying her sweet self
In that wherein she deem'd she look'd her best,
She came before Sir Lancelot, for she thought,
'If I be loved, these are my festal robes,
If not, the °victim's flowers before he fall.' 905
And Lancelot ever prest upon the maid
That she should ask some goodly gift of him
For her own self or hers : 'and do not shun
To speak the wish most near to your true heart ;
Such service have ye done me that I make 910
My will of yours, and prince and lord am I
In mine own land, and what I will I can.'
Then like a ghost she lifted up her face,
But like a ghost without the power to speak.
And Lancelot saw that she withheld her wish, 915
And bode among them yet a little space
Till he should learn it ; and one morn it chanced
He found her in among the garden yews,
And said, 'Delay no longer, speak your wish,
Seeing I go to-day :' then out she brake: 920

'Going ? and we shall never see you more.
And I must die for want of one bold word.'
'Speak : °that I live to hear,' he said, ' is yours.'
°Then suddenly and passionately she spoke :
'I have gone mad.   I love you: let me die.'   925
'Ah, sister,' answer'd Lancelot, 'what is this ? '
And innocently extending her white arms,
'Your love,' she said, ' your love — to be your wife.'
And Lancelot answer'd, ' Had I chosen to wed,
I had been wedded earlier, sweet Elaine ;   930
But now there never will be wife of mine.'
'No, no,' she cried, 'I care not to be wife,
But to be with you still, to see your face,
To serve you, and to follow you thro' the world.'
And Lancelot answer'd : ' Nay, the world, the world,
All ear and eye, with such a stupid heart   936
To interpret ear and eye, and such a tongue
To blare its own interpretation — nay,
Full ill then should I °quit your brother's love,
And your good father's kindness.'   And she said   940
'Not to be with you, not to see your face —
Alas for me then, my good days are done !'
'Nay, noble maid,' he answer'd, ' ten times nay.
This is not love, but love's first flash in youth,
Most common : yea, I know it of mine own self ;   945
And you yourself will smile at your own self !
Hereafter, when you yield your flower of life

To one more fitly yours, not thrice your age.
And then will I, for true you are and sweet
Beyond mine old belief in womanhood,   950
More specially should your good knight be poor,
Endow you with broad land and territory
Even to the °half my realm beyond the seas,
So that would make you happy: furthermore,
Even to the death, as tho' ye were my blood,   955
In all your quarrels will I be your knight.
This will I do, dear damsel, for your sake,
And more than this I cannot.'

                    While he spoke
She neither blush'd nor shook, but deathly-pale
Stood grasping what was nearest, then replied,   960
'Of all this will I nothing'; and so fell,
And thus they bore her swooning to her tower.

    Then spake, to whom thro' those black walls of yew
Their talk had pierced, her father: 'Ay, a flash,
I fear me, that will strike my blossom dead.   965
Too courteous are ye, fair Lord Lancelot.
I pray you, use some rough discourtesy
To blunt or break her passion.'

                    Lancelot said,
'That were °against me: what I can I will;'
And there that day remain'd, and toward even   970

Sent for his shield : full meekly rose the maid,
Stript off the case, and gave the naked shield ;
Then, when she heard his horse upon the stones,
Unclasping flung the casement back, and look'd
Down on his helm, from which her sleeve had gone.
And Lancelot knew the little clinking sound ;   976
And she by °tact of love was well aware
That Lancelot knew that she was looking at him.
And yet he glanced not up, nor waved his hand,
Nor bade farewell, but sadly rode away.   980
This was the one discourtesy that he used.

So in her tower alone the maiden sat :
His very shield was gone ; only the case,
Her own poor work, her empty labor, left.
But still she heard him, still his picture form'd   985
And grew between her and the pictured wall.
Then came her father, saying in low tones,
'Have comfort,' whom she greeted quietly.
Then came her brethren saying, ' Peace to thee,
Sweet sister,' whom she answer'd with all calm.   990
But when they left her to herself again,
Death, like a friend's voice from a distant field
Approaching thro' the darkness, call'd ; the owls
Wailing had power upon her, and she mixt
Her fancies with the sallow-rifted glooms   995
Of evening and the moanings of the wind.

And in those °days she made a little song,
And call'd her song 'The Song of Love and Death,'
And sang it: sweetly could she make and sing.

'Sweet is true love tho' given in vain, in vain;   1000
And sweet is death who puts an end to pain:
I know not which is sweeter, no, not I.

'Love, art thou sweet? then bitter death must be:
Love, thou art bitter; sweet is death to me.
O Love, if death be sweeter, let me die.   1005

'Sweet love, that seems not made to fade away;
Sweet death, that seems to make us loveless clay:
I know not which is sweeter, no, not I.

'I fain would follow love, if that could be;
I needs must follow death, who calls for me;   1010
Call and I follow, I follow! let me die.'

High with the last line scaled her voice, and this,
All in a fiery dawning wild with wind
That shook her tower, the brothers heard, and
    thought
With shuddering, 'Hark the °Phantom of the house
That ever shrieks before a death,' and call'd   1016
The father, and all three in hurry and fear

o

Ran to her, and lo ! the blood-red light of dawn
Flared on her face, she shrilling, 'Let me die !'

As when we dwell upon a word we know,　　　　1020
Repeating, till the word we know so well
Becomes a wonder, and we know not why,
So dwelt the father on her face, and thought,
'Is this Elaine ?' till back the maiden fell,
Then gave a languid hand to each, and lay,　　　1025
Speaking a still good-morrow with her eyes.
At last she said : 'Sweet brothers, yesternight
I seem'd a curious little maid again,
As happy as when we dwelt among the woods,
And when ye used to take me with the flood　　　1030
Up the great river in the boatman's boat.
Only ye would not pass beyond the cape
That had the poplar on it : there ye fixt
Your limit, oft returning with the tide.
And yet I cried because ye would not pass　　　1035
Beyond it, and far up the shining flood
Until we found the palace of the King.
And yet ye would not ; but this night I dream'd.
That I was all alone upon the flood,
And then I said, "Now shall I have my will :"　　1040
And there I woke, but still the wish remain'd.
So let me hence that I may pass at last
Beyond the poplar and far up the flood,

Until I find the palace of the King.
There will I enter in among them all,   1045
And no man there will dare to mock at me;
But there the fine Gawain will wonder at me,
And there the great °Sir Lancelot muse at me;
Gawain, who bade a thousand farewells to me,
Lancelot, who coldly went, nor bade me one: 1050
And there the King will know me and my love,
And there the Queen herself will pity me,
And all the gentle court will welcome me,
And after my long voyage I shall rest!'

'Peace,' said her father, 'O my child, ye seem   1055
Light-headed, for what force is yours to go
So far, being sick? and wherefore would ye look
On this proud fellow again, who scorns us all?'

Then the rough Torre began to heave and move,
And bluster into stormy sobs and say: 1060
'I never loved him: an I meet with him,
I care not howsoever great he be,
Then will I strike at him and strike him down;
Give me good fortune, I will strike him dead,
For this discomfort he hath done the house.'   1065

To whom the gentle sister made reply:
'Fret not yourself, dear brother, nor be·wroth,
Seeing it is no more Sir Lancelot's fault

Not to love me than it is mine to love
Him of all men who seems to me the highest.'   1070

  'Highest?' the father answer'd, echoing 'highest?'—
He meant to break the passion in her — 'nay,
Daughter, I know not what you call the highest;
But this I know, for all the people know it,
He loves the Queen, and in an open shame: 1075
And she returns his love in open shame;
If this be high, what is it to be low?'

  Then spake the lily maid of Astolat:
'Sweet father, all too faint and sick am I
For anger: these are slanders; never yet   1080
Was noble man but made ignoble talk.
He makes no friend who never made a foe.
But now it is my glory to have loved
One peerless, without stain: so let me pass,
My father, howsoe'er I seem to you,   1085
Not all unhappy, having loved God's best
And greatest, tho' my love had no return:
Yet, seeing you desire your child to live,
Thanks, but you work against your own desire;
For if I could believe the things you say   1090
I should but die the sooner; wherefore cease,
Sweet father, and bid call the °ghostly man
Hither, and let me °shrive me clean and die.'

So when the ghostly man had come and gone,
She, with a face bright as for sin forgiven,   1095
Besought Lavaine to write as she devised
A letter, word for word; and when he ask'd,
'Is it for Lancelot, is it for my dear lord?
Then will I bear it gladly;' she replied,
'For Lancelot and the Queen and all the world,   1100
But I myself must bear it.'   Then he wrote
The letter she devised; which being writ
And folded, 'O sweet father, tender and true,
Deny me not,' she said — 'ye never yet
Denied my fancies — this, however strange,   1105
My latest: lay the letter in my hand
A little ere I die, and close the hand
Upon it; I shall guard it even in death.
And when the heat has gone from out my heart,
Then take the little bed on which I died   1110
For Lancelot's love, and deck it like the Queen's
For richness, and me also like the Queen
In all I have of rich, and lay me on it.
And let there be prepared a chariot-bier   1115
To take me to the river, and a barge
Be ready on the river, clothed in black.
I go in state to court, to meet the Queen.
There surely I shall speak for mine own self,
And none of you can speak for me so well.
And therefore let our dumb old man alone   1120

Go with me; he can steer and row, and he
Will guide me to that palace, to the doors.'

She ceased: her father promised; whereupon
She grew so cheerful that they deem'd her death
Was rather in the fantasy than the blood.   1125
But ten slow mornings past, and on the eleventh
Her father laid the letter in her hand,
And closed the hand upon it, and she died.
So that day there was dole in Astolat.

But when the next sun brake from underground, 1130
Then, those two brethren slowly with bent brows
Accompanying, the sad chariot-bier
Past like a shadow thro' the field, that shone
Full-summer, °to that stream whereon the barge,
Pall'd all its length in blackest samite, lay.   1135
There sat the lifelong creature of the house,
Loyal, the dumb old servitor, on deck,
Winking his eyes, and twisted all his face.
So those two brethren from the chariot took
°And on the black decks laid her in her bed   1140
Set in her hand a lily, o'er her hung
The silken case with braided blazonings,
And kiss'd her quiet brows, and saying to her,
'Sister, farewell forever,' and again,
'Farewell, sweet sister,' parted all in tears.   1145
Then rose the dumb old servitor, and the dead,

Oar'd by the dumb, went upward with the flood —
In her right hand the lily, in her left
The letter — all her bright hair streaming down —
And all the coverlid was cloth of gold   1150
Drawn to her waist, and she herself in white
All but her face, and that clear-featured face
Was lovely, for she did not seem as dead,
But fast asleep, and lay as tho' she smiled.

    That day Sir Lancelot at the palace craved   1155
Audience of Guinevere, to give at last
The price of half a realm, his costly gift,
Half-won and hardly won with bruise and blow,
With deaths of others, and almost his own,
The nine-years-fought-for diamonds; for he saw   1160
One of her house, and sent him to the Queen
Bearing his wish, whereto the Queen agreed
With such and so unmoved a majesty
She might have seem'd her statue, but that he,
Low-drooping till he wellnigh kiss'd her feet   1165
For loyal awe, saw with a sidelong eye
The shadow of some piece of pointed lace,
In the Queen's shadow, vibrate on the walls,
And parted, laughing in his courtly heart.

    All in an °oriel on the summer side,   1170
Vine-clad, of Arthur's palace toward the stream,
They met, and Lancelot kneeling utter'd : ' Queen,

Lady, my liege, in whom I have my joy,
Take, what I had not won except for you,
These jewels, and make me happy, making them   1175
An armlet for the roundest arm on earth,
Or necklace for a neck to which the swan's
Is °tawnier than her cygnet's : these are words ;
Your beauty is your beauty, and I sin
In speaking, yet O, grant my worship of it   1180
Words, as we grant grief tears.   Such sin in words,
Perchance, we both can pardon ; but, my Queen,
I hear of rumors flying thro' your court.
Our bond, as not the bond of man and wife,
Should have in it an absoluter trust   1185
To make up that defect : let rumors be :
When did not rumors fly ? these, as I trust
That you trust me in your own nobleness,
I may not well believe that you believe.'

While thus he spoke, half turn'd away, the Queen 1190
Brake from the vast oriel-embowering vine
Leaf after leaf, and tore, and cast them off,
Till all the place whereon she stood was green ;
Then, when he ceased, in one cold passive hand
Received at once and laid aside the gems   1195
There on a table near her, and replied :

  ' It may be I am quicker of belief
Than you believe me, °Lancelot of the Lake.

Our bond is not the bond of man and wife.
This good is in it, whatsoe'er of ill,   1200
It can be broken easier.   I for you
This many a year have done despite and wrong
To one whom ever in my heart of hearts
I did acknowledge nobler.   What are these ?
Diamonds for me ! they had been thrice their worth 1205
Being your gift, had you not lost your own.
To loyal hearts the value of all gifts
Must vary as the giver's.   Not for me !
°For her ! for your new fancy.   Only this
Grant me, I pray you: have your joys apart.   1210
I doubt not that, however changed you keep
So much of what is graceful : and myself
Would shun to break those bonds of courtesy
In which as Arthur's Queen I move and rule ;
So cannot speak my mind.   An end to this !   1215
A strange one ! yet I take it with Amen.
So pray you, add my diamonds to her °pearls ;
Deck her with these ; tell her, she shines me down :
An armlet for an arm to which the Queen's
Is haggard, or a necklace for a neck   1220
O, as much fairer — as a faith once fair
Was richer than these diamonds— hers not mine —
Nay, by the mother of our Lord himself,
Or hers or mine, mine now to work my will —
She shall not have them.'

Saying which she seized,
And, thro' the casement standing wide for heat,   1226
Flung them, and down they flash'd, and smote the
    stream.
Then from the smitten surface flash'd, as it were,
Diamonds to meet them, and they past away.
Then while Sir Lancelot leant, in half disdain   1230
At love, life, all things, on the window ledge,
Close underneath his eyes, and right across
Where these had fallen, °slowly past the barge
Whereon the lily maid of Astolat
Lay smiling, like a star in blackest night.   1235

But the wild Queen, who saw not, burst away
To weep and wail in secret; and the barge,
On to the palace-doorway sliding, paused.
There two stood arm'd, and kept the door; to whom,
All up the marble stair, tier over tier,   1240
Were added mouths that gaped, and eyes that
    ask'd,
'What is it?' but that oarsman's haggard face,
As hard and still as is °the face that men
Shape to their fancy's eye from broken rocks
On some cliff-side, appall'd them, and they said: 1245
'He is enchanted, cannot speak — and she,
Look how she sleeps — the Fairy Queen, so fair!
Yea, but how pale! what are they? flesh and blood?

Or come to take the King to Fairyland?
For some do hold our Arthur cannot die,   1250
But that he passes into Fairyland.'

While thus they babbled of the King, the King
Came girt with knights: then turned the tongueless
    man
From the half-face to the full eye, and rose
And pointed to the damsel and the doors.   1255
So Arthur bade the meek °Sir Percivale
And pure °Sir Galahad to uplift the maid;
And reverently they bore her into hall.
Then came the fine Gawain and wonder'd at her,
And Lancelot later came and mused at her,   1260
And last the Queen herself, and pitied her;
But Arthur spied the letter in her hand,
Stoopt, took, brake seal, and read it; this was all:

°' Most noble lord, Sir Lancelot of the Lake,
I, sometime call'd the maid of Astolat,   1265
Come, for you left me taking no farewell,
Hither, to take my last farewell of you.
I loved you and my love had no return,
And therefore my true love has been my death.
And therefore to our Lady Guinevere,   1270
And to all other ladies, I make moan:
Pray for my soul, and yield me burial.

Pray for my soul thou too, Sir Lancelot,
As thou art a knight peerless.'

                      Thus he read;
And ever in the reading lords and dames   1275
Wept, looking often from his face who read
To hers which lay so silent, and at times,
So touch'd were they, half-thinking that her lips
Who had devised the letter moved again.

    Then freely spoke Sir Lancelot to them all: 1280
' My lord liege Arthur, and all ye that hear,
Know that for this most gentle maiden's death
Right heavy am I; for good she was and true,
But loved me with a love beyond all love
In women, whomsoever I have known.   1285
Yet to be loved makes not to love again;
Not at my years, however it hold in youth.
I swear by truth and knighthood that I gave
No cause, not willingly, for such a love.
To this I call my friends in testimony,   1290
Her brethren, and her father, who himself
Besought me to be plain and blunt, and use,
To break her passion, some discourtesy
Against my nature: what I could, I did.
I left her and I bade her no farewell;   1295
Tho' had I dreamt the damsel would have died,

I might have put my wits to some rough use,
And help'd her from herself.'

              Then said the Queen —
°Sea was her wrath, yet working after storm :
' Ye might at least have done her so much grace,   1300
Fair lord, as would have help'd her from her death.'
He raised his head, their eyes met and hers fell,
He adding :

       ' Queen, she would not be content
Save that I wedded her, which could not be.
Then might she follow me thro' the world, she ask'd ; 1305
It could not be. I told her that her love
Was but the flash of youth, would darken down,
To rise hereafter in a stiller flame
Toward one more worthy of her — then would I,
More specially were he she wedded poor,   1310
Estate them with large land and territory
In mine own realm beyond the narrow seas,
To keep them in all joyance : more than this
I could not ; this she would not, and she died.'

  He pausing, Arthur answer'd : ' O my knight,   1315
It will be to thy worship, as my knight,
And mine, as head of all our Table Round,
To see that she be buried worshipfully.'

So toward that °shrine which then in all the realm
Was richest, Arthur leading, slowly went   1320
The marshall'd Order of their Table Round,
And Lancelot sad beyond his wont, to see
The maiden buried, not as one unknown,
Nor meanly, but with gorgeous obsequies,
And mass, and rolling music, like a queen.   1325
And when the knights had laid her comely head
Low in the dust of half-forgotten kings,
Then Arthur spake among them : ' Let her tomb
Be costly, and her image thereupon,
And let the shield of Lancelot at her feet   1330
Be carven, and her lily in her hand.
And let the story of her dolorous voyage
For all true hearts be blazon'd on her tomb
In letters gold and azure !' which was wrought
Thereafter; but when now the lords and dames   1335
And people, from the high door streaming, brake
Disorderly, as homeward each, the Queen,
Who mark'd Sir Lancelot where he moved apart,
Drew near, and sigh'd in passing, ' Lancelot,
Forgive me ; mine was jealousy in love.'   1340
He answer'd with his eyes upon the ground,
' That is love's curse; pass on, my Queen, for-
      given.'
But Arthur, who beheld his cloudy brows,
Approach'd him, and with full affection said:

'Lancelot, my Lancelot, thou in whom I have   1345
Most joy and most °affiance, for I know
What thou hast been in battle by my side,
And many a time have watch'd thee at the tilt
Strike down the lusty and long practised knight
And let the younger and unskill'd go by   1350
To win his honor and to make his name,
And loved thy courtesies and thee, a man
Made to be loved; but now I would to God,
Seeing the homeless trouble in thine eyes,
Thou couldst have loved this maiden, shaped, it seems,
By God for thee alone, and from her face,   1356
If one may judge the living by the dead,
Delicately pure and marvellously fair,
Who might have brought thee, now a lonely man
Wifeless and heirless, noble issue, sons   1360
Born to the glory of thy name and fame,
My knight, the great Sir Lancelot of the Lake.'

Then answer'd Lancelot: 'Fair she was, my King,
Pure, as you ever wish your knights to be.
To doubt her fairness were to want an eye,   1365
To doubt her pureness were to want a heart —
Yea, to be loved, if what is worthy love
Could bind him, but free love will not be bound.'

'Free love, so bound, were freest,' said the King.
'Let love be free; free love is for the best: 1370

And, after heaven, on our dull side of death,
What should be best, if not so pure a love
Clothed in so pure a loveliness ? yet thee
She fail'd to bind, tho' being, as I think,
°Unbound as yet, and gentle, as I know.'   1375

And Lancelot answer'd nothing, but he went,
And at the inrunning of a little brook
Sat by the river in a cove, and watch'd
The high reed wave, and lifted up his eyes
And saw the barge that brought her moving down, 1380
Far-off, a blot upon the stream, and said
Low in himself : ' Ah, simple heart and sweet,
Ye loved me, damsel, surely with a love
Far tenderer than my Queen's.   Pray for thy soul ?
Ay, that will I.   Farewell too — now at last —   1385
Farewell, fair lily.   "Jealousy in love ? "
Not rather dead love's harsh heir, jealous pride ?
Queen, if I grant the jealousy as of love,
May not your crescent fear for name and fame
Speak, as it waxes, of a love that wanes ?   1390
Why did the King dwell on my name to me ?
Mine own name shames me, seeming a reproach,
Lancelot, whom the Lady of the Lake
Caught from his mother's arms — the wondrous one
Who passes thro' the vision of the night —   1395
She chanted snatches of mysterious hymns

Heard on the winding waters, eve and morn
She kiss'd me saying, "Thou art fair, my child,
As a king's son," and often in her arms
She bare me, pacing on the dusky mere.   1400
Would she had drown'd me in it, where'er it be!
For what am I? what profits me my name
Of greatest knight? I fought for it, and have it:
Pleasure to have it, none; to lose it, pain:
Now grown a part of me: but what use in it?   1405
To make men worse by making my sin known?
Or sin seem less, the sinner seeming great?
°Alas for Arthur's greatest knight, a man
Not after Arthur's heart! I needs must break
These bonds that so defame me: not without   1410
She wills it: would I, if she will'd it? nay,
Who knows? but if I would not, then may God,
I pray him, send a sudden angel down
To seize me by the hair and bear me far,
And fling me deep in that forgotten mere,   1415
Among the tumbled fragments of the hills.'

    So groan'd Sir Lancelot in remorseful pain,
°Not knowing he should die a holy man.

THE HOLY GRAIL

FROM noiseful arms, and acts of prowess done
In tournament or tilt, °Sir Percivale,
Whom Arthur and his knighthood call'd the Pure,
Had past into the °silent life of prayer,
Praise, fast, and alms; and leaving for the °cowl   5
The helmet in an abbey far away
From Camelot, there, and not long after, died.

And one, a fellow-monk among the rest,
Ambrosius, loved him much beyond the rest,
And honor'd him, and wrought into his heart   10
A way by love that waken'd love within,
To answer that which came: and as they sat
Beneath a °world-old yew-tree, darkening half
The cloisters, on a gustful April morn
That puff'd the swaying branches into °smoke   15
Above them, ere the summer when he died,
The monk Ambrosius question'd Percivale:

'O brother, I have seen this yew-tree °smoke
Spring after spring, for half a hundred years;
For never have I known the world without.   20

Nor even stray'd beyond °the pale : but thee,
When first thou camest — such a courtesy
Spake thro' the limbs and in the voice — I knew
For one of those who eat in Arthur's hall ;
For good ye are and bad, and like to coins,   25
Some true, some light, but every one of you
Stamped with the image of the King ; and now
Tell me, what drove thee from the Table Round,
My brother ? was it earthly passion crost ? '

°' Nay,' said the knight ; 'for no such passion mine.
But the sweet vision of the °Holy Grail   31
Drove me from all vainglories, rivalries,
And earthly heats that spring and sparkle out
Among us in the jousts, while women watch
Who wins, who falls ; and waste the spiritual
        strength   35
Within us, better offer'd up to Heaven.'

    To whom the monk : 'The Holy Grail ! — I trust
We are °green in Heaven's eyes ; but here too much
We moulder — as to things without I mean —
Yet one of your own knights, a guest of ours,   40
Told us of this in our °refectory,
But spake with such a sadness and so low
We heard not half of what he said.   What is it ?
The phantom of a cup that comes and goes ? '

'Nay, monk! what phantom?' answer'd Percivale.
The cup, the cup itself, from which our Lord   46
Drank at the last sad supper with his own.
This, from the blessed land of °Aromat —
After the °day of darkness, when the dead
Went wandering o'er Moriah — the good saint   50
Arimathæan Joseph, journeying brought
To °Glastonbury, where the winter thorn
Blossoms at Christmas, mindful of our Lord.
And there awhile it bode; and if a man
Could touch or see it, he was heal'd at once,   55
By faith, of all his ills.   But then the times
Grew to such evil that the holy cup
Was caught away to heaven, and disappear'd.'

To whom the monk: 'From our old books I know
That Joseph came of old to Glastonbury,   60
And there the heathen Prince, °Arviragus,
Gave him an isle of marsh whereon to build;
And there he built with °wattles from the marsh
A little lonely church in days of yore,
For so they say, these books of ours, but seem   65
Mute of this miracle, far as I have read.
But who first saw the holy thing to-day?'

'A woman,' answer'd Percivale, 'a nun,
And one no further off in blood from me

°Than sister ; and if ever holy maid 70
With knees of adoration wore the stone,
A holy maid ; tho' never maiden glow'd,
But that was in her earlier maidenhood,
With such a fervent flame of human love,
Which, being rudely blunted, glanced and shot 75
Only to holy things ; to prayer and praise
She gave herself, to fast and alms.   And yet,
Nun as she was, the scandal of the Court,
Sin against Arthur and the Table Round,
And the strange sound of an adulterous race, 80
Across the iron grating of her cell
Beat, and she pray'd and fasted all the more.

   ' And he to whom she told her sins, or what
Her all but utter whiteness held for sin,
A man wellnigh a hundred winters old, 85
Spake often with her of the Holy Grail,
A legend handed down thro' five or six,
And each of these a hundred winters old,
From our Lord's time.   And when King Arthur made
His Table Round, and all men's hearts became 90
Clean for a season, surely he had thought
That now the Holy Grail would come again ;
But sin broke out.   Ah, Christ, that it would come,
And heal the world of all their wickedness !
" O Father ! " ask'd the maiden, " might it come 95

To me by prayer and fastings ? "   " Nay," said he,
" I know not, for thy heart is pure as snow."
And so she pray'd and fasted, till the sun
Shone, and the wind blew, thro' her, and I thought
She might have risen and floated when I saw her.   100

' For on a day she sent to speak with me.
And when she came to speak, behold her eyes
Beyond my knowing of them, beautiful,
Beyond all knowing of them, wonderful,
Beautiful in the light of holiness !   105
And " O my brother Percivale," she said,
°" Sweet brother, I have seen the Holy Grail :
For, waked at dead of night, I heard a sound
As of a silver horn from o'er the hills
Blown, and I thought, ' It is not Arthur's use   110
To hunt by moonlight ; ' and the slender sound
As from a distance beyond distance grew
Coming upon me — O never harp nor horn,
Nor aught we blow with breath, or touch with hand,
Was like that music as it came ; and then   115
Stream'd thro' my cell a cold and silver beam,
And down the long beam stole the Holy Grail,
°Rose-red with beatings in it, as if alive,
Till all the white walls of my cells were dyed
With rosy colors leaping on the wall ;   120
And then the music faded, and the Grail

Past, and the beam decay'd, and from the walls
The rosy quiverings died into the night.
So now the Holy Thing is here again
Among us, brother, fast thou too and pray,   125
And tell thy brother knights to fast and pray,
That so perchance the vision may be seen
By thee and those, and all the world be heal'd."

   ' Then leaving the pale nun, I spake of this
To all men ; and myself fasted and pray'd   130
Always, and many among us many a week
Fasted and pray'd even to the uttermost,
Expectant of the wonder that would be.

   ' And one there was among us, ever moved
Among us in white armor, °Galahad.   135
" God make thee good as thou art beautiful ! "
Said Arthur, when he dubbed him knight ; and none
In so young youth was ever made a knight
Till Galahad ; and this Galahad, when he heard
My sister's vision, filled me with amaze ;   140
His eyes became so like her own, they seem'd
Hers, and himself her brother more than I.

   ' Sister or brother none had he ; but some
Call'd him a son of Lancelot, and some said
Begotten by enchantment — chatterers they,   145

Like birds of passage piping up and down,
That gape for flies — we know not whence they come,
For when was Lancelot wanderingly lewd ?

'But she, the wan sweet maiden, shore away
Clean from her forehead all that wealth of hair   ,a
Which made a silken mat-work for her feet ;
And out of this she plaited broad and long
A strong sword-belt, and wove with silver thread
And crimson in the belt a strange device,
A crimson grail within a silver beam ;   155
And saw the bright boy-knight and bound it on
    him,
Saying : " My knight, my love, my knight of heaven,
O thou, my love, whose love is one with mine,
I, maiden, round thee, maiden, bind my belt.
Go forth, for thou shalt see what I have seen,   160
And break thro' all, till one °will crown thee king
Far in the spiritual city : " and as she spake
She sent the deathless passion in her eyes
Thro' him, and made him hers, and laid her mind
On him, and °he believed in her belief.   165

'Then came a year of miracle : O brother,
In our great hall there stood a °vacant chair,
Fashion'd by Merlin ere he °past away,
And carven with strange figures ; and in and out

The figures, like a serpent, ran a scroll   170
Of letters in a tongue no man could read.
And Merlin call'd it " the Siege Perilous,"
Perilous for good and ill; " for there," he said,
" No man could sit but he should lose himself: "
And once by misadvertence Merlin sat   175
In his own chair, and so was lost; but he,
Galahad, when he heard of Merlin's doom,
Cried, " If I lose myself, I save myself! "

  ' Then on a summer night it came to pass,
While the great banquet lay along the hall,   180
That Galahad would sit down in Merlin's chair.

  ' And all at once, as there we sat, we heard
A cracking and a riving of the roofs,
And rending, and a blast, and overhead
Thunder, and in the thunder was a cry.   185
And in the blast there smote along the hall
A beam of light seven times more clear than day;
And down the long beam stole the Holy Grail
All over cover'd with a luminous cloud,
And none might see who bare it, and it past.   190
But every knight beheld his fellow's face
As in a glory, and all the knights arose,
And staring each at other iike dumb men
Stood, till I found a voice and sware a vow.

'I sware a vow before them all, that I,   195
Because I had not seen the Grail, would ride
A twelvemonth and a day in quest of it,
Until I found and saw it, as the nun
My sister saw it; and Galahad sware the vow,
And good Sir Bors, our Lancelot's cousin, sware,   200
And Lancelot sware, and many among the knights,
And Gawain sware, and louder than the rest.'

Then spake the monk Ambrosius, asking him,
'What said the King?   Did Arthur take the vow?'

'Nay, for my lord,' said Percivale, 'the King   205
Was not in hall: for early that same day,
Scaped thro' a cavern from a bandit hold,
An outraged maiden sprang into the hall
Crying on help: for all her shining hair
Was smear'd with earth, and either milky arm   210
Red-rent with hooks of bramble, and all she wore
Torn as a sail that leaves the rope is torn
In tempest: °so the King arose and went
To smoke the scandalous hive of those wild bees
That made such honey in his realm.   Howbeit   215
Some little of this marvel he too saw,
Returning o'er the plain that then began
To darken under Camelot; whence the King
Look'd up, calling aloud, "Lo, there! the roofs

Of our great hall are roll'd in thunder-smoke!   220
Pray Heaven, they be not smitten by the bolt!"
For dear to Arthur was that hall of ours,
As having there so oft with all his knights
Feasted, and as the stateliest under heaven.

  'O brother, had you known our mighty hall,   225
Which Merlin built for Arthur long ago!
For all the sacred mount of Camelot,
And all the dim rich city, roof by roof,
Tower after tower, spire beyond spire,
By grove, and garden-lawn, and rushing brook,   230
Climbs to the mighty hall that Merlin built.
°And four great zones of sculpture, set betwixt
With many a mystic symbol, gird the hall:
And in the lowest beasts are slaying men,
And in the second men are slaying beasts,   235
And on the third are warriors, perfect men,
And on the fourth are men with growing wings,
And over all one statue in the °mould
Of Arthur, made by Merlin, with a crown,
And peak'd wings pointed to the Northern Star.   240
And eastward fronts the statue, and the crown
And both the wings are made of gold, and flame
At sunrise till the people in far fields,
Wasted so often by the heathen hordes,
Behold it, crying, "We have still a king."   245

'And, brother, had you known our hall within,
Broader and higher than any in all the lands!
Where twelve great windows blazon Arthur's wars,
And all the light that falls upon the board
Streams thro' the twelve great battles of our King. 250
Nay, one there is, and at the eastern end,
Wealthy with wandering lines of mount and mere,
°Where Arthur finds the brand Excalibur.
And also one to the west, and °counter to it,
And blank: and who shall blazon it? when and how? —
O, there, perchance, when all our wars are done,   256
The brand Excalibur will be cast away!

'So to this hill full quickly rode the King,
In horror lest the work by Merlin wrought,
Dreamlike, should on the sudden vanish, wrapt   260
In unremorseful folds of rolling fire.
And in he rode, and up I glanced, and saw
The golden dragon sparkling over all;
°And many of those who burnt the hold, their arms
Hack'd, and their foreheads grimed with smoke and
        sear'd,   265
Follow'd, and in among bright faces, ours,
Full of the vision, prest: and then the King
Spake to me, being nearest, "Percivale," —
Because the hall was all in tumult — some
Vowing, and some protesting, — "what is this?"   270

'O brother, when I told him what had chanced,
My sister's vision and the rest, his face
°Darken'd, as I have seen it more than once,
When some brave deed seem'd to be done in vain,
Darken; and "Woe is me, my knights," he cried,   275
"Had I been here, ye had not sworn the vow."
Bold was mine answer, "Had thyself been here,
My King, thou wouldst have sworn."   "Yea, yea,"
        said he,
"Art thou so bold and hast not seen the Grail?"

'"Nay, lord, I heard the sound, I saw the light,   280
But since I did not see the holy thing,
I sware a vow to follow it till I saw."

'Then when he ask'd us, knight by knight, if any
Had seen it, all their answers were as one:
"Nay, lord, and therefore have we sworn our vows."   285

'"Lo, now," said Arthur, "have ye seen a cloud?
What go ye into the wilderness to see?"

'Then Galahad on the sudden, and in a voice
Shrilling along the hall to Arthur, call'd,
"But I, Sir Arthur, saw the Holy Grail,   290
I saw the Holy Grail and heard a cry —
'O Galahad, and O Galahad, follow me.'"

'"Ah, Galahad, Galahad," said the King, "for such
As thou art is the vision, not for these.
Thy holy nun and thou have seen a sign —   295
Holier is none, my Percivale, than she —
A sign to maim this Order which I made
But ye that follow but the leader's bell," —
Brother, the King was hard upon his knights, —
°"Taliessin is our fullest throat of song,   300
And one hath sung and all the dumb will sing.
Lancelot is Lancelot, and hath overborne
Five knights at once, and every younger knight,
Unproven, holds himself as Lancelot,
Till overborne by one, he learns — and ye,   305
What are ye? Galahads? no, nor Percivales" —
For thus it pleased the King to range me close
After Sir Galahad; — "nay," said he, "but men
With strength and will to right the wrong'd, of power
To lay the sudden heads of violence flat,   310
Knights that in twelve great battles splash'd and dyed
The strong White Horse in his own heathen blood —
But one hath seen, and all the blind will see.
Go, since your vows are sacred, being made:
Yet — for ye know the cries of all my realm   315
Pass thro' this hall — how often, O my knights,
Your places being vacant at my side,
This chance of noble deeds will come and go
Unchallenged, while ye follow wandering fires

Lost in the quagmire! Many of you, yea most,   320
Return no more : ye think I show myself
Too dark a prophet : come now, let us meet
The morrow morn once more in one full field
Of gracious pastime, that once more the King,
Before ye leave him for this quest, may count   325
The yet-unbroken strength of all his knights,
Rejoicing in that Order which he made."

   ' So when the sun broke next from underground,
All the great table of our Arthur closed
And clash'd in such a tourney and so full,   330
So many lances broken — never yet
Had Camelot seen the like since Arthur came ;
And I myself and Galahad, for a strength
Was in us from the vision, overthrew
So many knights that all the people cried,   335
And almost burst the barriers in their heat,
Shouting, "Sir Galahad and Sir Percivale !"

   ' But when the next day brake from underground —
O brother, had you known our Camelot,
Built by old kings, age after age, so old   340
The King himself had fears that it would fall,
So strange, and rich, and dim ; for where the roofs
Totter'd toward each other in the sky,
Met foreheads all along the street of those

Who watch'd us pass; and lower, and where the long
Rich galleries, lady-laden, weigh'd the necks   346
Of dragons clinging to the crazy walls,
Thicker than drops from thunder, showers of flowers
Fell as we past; and men and boys astride
°On wyvern, lion, dragon, griffin, swan,   350
At all the corners, named us each by name,
Calling " God speed ! " but in the ways below
The knights and ladies wept, and rich and poor
Wept, and the King himself could hardly speak
For grief, and all in middle street the Queen,   355
Who rode by Lancelot, wail'd and shriek'd aloud,
" This madness has come on us for our sins."
So to the °Gate of the Three Queens we came,
Where Arthur's wars are render'd mystically,
And thence departed every one his way.   360

    °' And I was lifted up in heart, and thought
Of all my late-shown prowess in the lists,
How my strong lance had beaten down the knights,
So many and famous names; and never yet
Had heaven appear'd so blue, nor earth so green,   365
For all my blood danced in me, and I knew
That I should light upon the Holy Grail.

    'Thereafter, the dark warning of our King,
That most of us would follow wandering fires,

Came like a driving gloom across my mind. 370
Then every evil word I had spoken once,
And every evil thought I had thought of old,
And every evil deed I ever did,
Awoke and cried, "This quest is not for thee."
And lifting up mine eyes, I found myself 375
Alone, and in a land of sand and thorns,
And I was thirsty even unto death;
And I, too, cried, "This quest is not for thee."

' And on I rode, and when I thought my thirst
Would slay me, saw deep lawns, and then a brook, 380
With one sharp rapid, where the crisping white
Play'd ever back upon the sloping wave
And took both ear and eye; and o'er the brook
Were apple-trees, and apples by the brook
Fallen, and on the lawns. "I will rest here," 385
I said, "I am not worthy of the quest;"
But even while I drank the brook, and ate
The goodly apples, all these things at once
Fell into dust, and I was left alone
And thirsting in a land of sand and thorns. 390

' And then behold a woman at a door
Spinning; and fair the house whereby she sat,
And kind the woman's eyes and innocent,
And all her bearing gracious; and she rose

Q

Opening her arms to meet me, as who should say,   395
"Rest here;" but when I touch'd her, lo! she, too,
Fell into dust and nothing, and the house
Became no better than a broken shed,
And in it a dead babe; and also this
Fell into dust, and I was left alone.   400

'And on I rode, and greater was my thirst.
Then flash'd a yellow gleam across the world,
And where it smote the plowshare in the field
The plowman left his plowing and fell down
Before it; where it glitter'd on her pail   405
The milkmaid left her milking, and fell down
Before it, and I knew not why, but thought
"The sun is rising," tho' the sun had risen.
Then was I aware of one that on me moved
In golden armor with a crown of gold   410
About a casque all jewels, and his horse
In golden armor jewelled everywhere:
And on the splendor came, flashing me blind,
And seem'd to me the lord of all the world,
Being so huge.   But when I thought he meant   415
To crush me, moving on me, lo! he, too,
Open'd his arms to embrace me as he came,
And up I went and touch'd him, and he, too,
Fell into dust, and I was left alone
And wearying in a land of sand and thorns.   420

'And I rode on and found a mighty hill,
And on the top a city wall'd : the spires
Prick'd with incredible pinnacles into heaven.
And by the gateway stirr'd a crowd ; and these
Cried to me climbing, " Welcome, Percivale !   425
Thou mightiest and thou purest among men !"
And glad was I and clomb, but found at top
No man, or any voice.   And thence I past
Far thro' a ruinous city, and I saw
That man had once dwelt there; but there I
      found   430
Only one man of an exceeding age.
" Where is that goodly company," said I,
" That so cried out upon me ?" and he had
Scarce any voice to answer, and yet gasp'd,
" Whence and what art thou ?" and even as he
      spoke   435
Fell into dust and disappear'd, and I
Was left alone once more and cried in grief,
" Lo, if I find the Holy Grail itself
And touch it, it will crumble into dust !"

'And thence I dropt into a lowly vale,   440
Low as the hill was high, and where the vale
Was lowest found a chapel, and thereby
A holy hermit in a hermitage,
To whom I told my phantoms, and he said:

' " O son, thou hast not true humility,   445
The highest virtue, mother of them all;
For when the Lord of all things made Himself
Naked of glory for his mortal change,
' Take thou my robe,' °she said, ' for all is thine,'
And all her form shone forth with sudden light   450
So that the angels were amazed, and she
Follow'd Him down, and like a flying star
Led on the gray-hair'd wisdom of the east;
But her thou hast not known: for what is this
Thou thoughtest of thy prowess and thy sins?   455
Thou hast not lost thyself to save thyself
As Galahad."   When the hermit made an end,
In silver armor suddenly Galahad shone
Before us, and against the chapel door
Laid lance and enter'd, and we knelt in prayer.   460
And there the hermit slaked my burning thirst,
And at the °sacring of the mass I saw
The holy elements alone; but he,
" Saw ye no more?   I, Galahad, saw the Grail,
The Holy Grail, descend upon the shrine: 465
I saw °the fiery face as of a child
That smote itself into the bread and went;
And hither am I come; and never yet
Hath what thy sister taught me first to see,
This holy thing, fail'd from my side, nor come   470
Cover'd, but moving with me night and day,

Fainter by day, but always in the night
Blood-red, and sliding down the blacken'd marsh
Blood-red, and on the naked mountain top
Blood-red, and in the sleeping mere below   475
Blood-red.   And in the strength of this I rode,
Shattering all evil customs everywhere,
And past thro' °Pagan realms, and made them mine,
And clash'd with Pagan hordes, and bore them down,
And broke thro' all, and in the strength of this   480
Come victor.   But my time is hard at hand,
And hence I go; and one will crown me king
Far in the spiritual city; and come thou, too,
For thou shalt see the vision when I go."

‘ While thus he spake, his eye, dwelling on mine, 485
Drew me, with power upon me, till I grew
One with him, to believe as he believed.
Then when the day began to wane, we went.

°‘ There rose a hill that none but man could climb,
Scarr'd with a hundred wintry water-courses —   490
Storm at the top, and when we gain'd it, storm
Round us and death; for every moment glanced
His silver arms and gloom'd: so quick and thick
The lightnings here and there to left and right
Struck, till the dry old trunks about us, dead,   495
Yea, rotten with a hundred years of death,

Sprang into fire : and at the base we found
On either hand, as far as eye could see,
A great black swamp and of an evil smell,
Part black, part whiten'd with the bones of men,   500
Not to be crost, save that some ancient king
Had built a way, where, link'd with many a bridge,
A thousand piers ran into the great Sea.
And Galahad fled along them bridge by bridge,
And every bridge as quickly as he crost   505
Sprang into fire and vanish'd, tho' I yearn'd
To follow ; and thrice above him all the heavens
Open'd and blazed with thunder such as seem'd
Shoutings of all the sons of God : and first
At once I saw him far on the great Sea,   510
In silver-shining armor starry-clear ;
And o'er his head the Holy Vessel hung
Clothed in white samite or a luminous cloud.
And with exceeding swiftness ran the boat,
If boat it were — I saw not whence it came.   515
And when the heavens open'd and blazed again
Roaring, I saw him like a silver star —
And had he set the sail, or had the boat
Become a living creature clad with wings?
And o'er his head the Holy Vessel hung   520
Redder than any rose, a joy to me,
For now I knew the veil had been withdrawn.
Then in a moment when they blazed again

Opening, I saw the least of little stars
Down on the waste, and straight beyond the star   525
°I saw the spiritual city and all her spires
And gateways in a glory like one pearl —
No larger, tho' the goal of all the saints —
Strike from the sea; and from the star there shot
A rose-red sparkle to the city, and there   530
Dwelt, and I knew it was the Holy Grail,
Which never eyes on earth again shall see.
Then fell the floods of heaven drowning the deep,
And how my feet recrost the deathful ridge
No memory in me lives; but that I touch'd   535
The chapel-doors at dawn I know; and thence
Taking my war-horse from the holy man,
Glad that no phantom vext me more, return'd
To whence I came, the gate of Arthur's wars.'

' O brother,' ask'd Ambrosius, — ' for in sooth   540
These ancient books — and they would win thee — teem,
Only I find not there this Holy Grail,
With miracles and marvels like to these,
Not all unlike; which oftentime I read,
Who read but on my °breviary with ease,   545
Till my head swims, and then go forth and pass
Down to the little °thorpe that lies so close,
And almost plaster'd like a martin's nest
To these old walls — and mingle with our folk;

And knowing every honest face of theirs   550
As well as ever shepherd knew his sheep,
And every homely secret in their hearts,
Delight myself with gossip and old wives,
And ills and aches, and teethings, lyings-in,
And mirthful sayings, children of the place,   555
That have no meaning half a league away ;
Or lulling random squabbles when they rise,
Chafferings and chatterings at the °market-cross,
Rejoice, °small man, in this small world of mine,
Yea, even in their hens and in their eggs —   560
O brother, saving this Sir Galahad,
Came ye on none but phantoms in your quest,
No man, no woman ? '

             Then Sir Percivale :
' All men, to one so bound by such a vow,
And women were as phantoms.   O, my brother,   565
Why wilt thou shame me to confess to thee
How far I falter'd from my quest and vow ?
For after I had lain so many nights,
A bed-mate of the snail and eft and snake,
In grass and burdock, I was changed to wan   570
And meagre, and the vision had not come ;
And then I chanced upon a goodly town
With one great dwelling in the middle of it.
Thither I made, there was I disarm'd

By maidens each as fair as any flower;   575
But when they led me into the hall, behold,
The princess of that° castle was the one,
Brother, and that one only, who had ever
Made my heart leap; for when I moved of old
A slender page about her father's hall,   580
And she a slender maiden, all my heart
Went after her with longing, yet we twain
Had never kiss'd a kiss or vow'd a vow.
And now I came upon her once again,
And one had wedded her, and he was dead,   585
And all his land and wealth and state were hers.
And while I tarried, every day she set
A banquet richer than the day before
By me, for all her longing and her will
Was toward me as of old, till one fair morn,   590
I walking to and fro beside a stream
That flash'd across her orchard underneath
Her castle-walls, she stole upon my walk,
And calling me the greatest of all knights,
Embraced me, and so kiss'd me the first time,   595
And gave herself and all her wealth to me.
Then I remember'd Arthur's warning word,
That most of us would follow wandering fires,
And the quest faded in my heart.   Anon,
The °heads of all her people drew to me,   600
With supplication both of knees and tongue:

"We have heard of thee: thou art our greatest knight,
Our Lady says it, and we well believe:
Wed thou our Lady, and rule over us,
And thou shalt be as Arthur in our land."   605
O me, my brother! but one night my vow
Burnt me within, so that I rose and fled,
But wail'd and wept, and hated mine own self,
And even the holy quest, and all but her;
Then after I was join'd with Galahad   610
Cared not for her nor anything upon earth.'

Then said the monk: 'Poor men, °when yule is cold,
Must be content to sit by little fires.
And this am I, so that ye care for me
Ever so little; yea, and blest be Heaven   615
That brought thee here to this poor house of ours
Where all the brethren are so hard, to warm
My cold heart with a friend; but O the pity
To find thine own first love once more — to hold,
Hold her a wealthy bride within thine arms,   620
Or all but hold, and then — cast her aside,
Foregoing all her sweetness, like a weed!
For we that want the warmth of double life,
We that are plagued with dreams of something sweet
Beyond all sweetness in a life so rich, —   625
Ah, blessed Lord, I speak too earthly-wise,
Seeing I never stray'd beyond the cell,

But live like an old badger in his earth,
With earth about him everywhere, despite
All fast and penance.   Saw ye none beside,   630
None of your knights?'

                              'Yea, so,' said Percivale:
'One night my pathway swerving east, I saw
°The pelican on the casque of our Sir Bors
All in the middle of the rising moon,
And toward him spurr'd, and hail'd him, and he me,
And each made joy of either; then he ask'd: 636
"Where is he? hast thou seen him — Lancelot? —
      Once,"
Said good Sir Bors, " he dash'd across me — mad,
And °maddening what he rode; and when I cried,
'Ridest thou then so hotly on a quest   640
So holy?' Lancelot shouted, 'Stay me not!
I have been the sluggard, and I ride apace,
For now there is a °lion in the way!'
So vanish'd."

                              'Then Sir Bors had ridden on
Softly, and sorrowing for our Lancelot,   645
Because °his former madness, once the talk
And scandal of our table, had return'd;
For Lancelot's kith and kin so worship him
That ill to him is ill to them, to Bors

Beyond the rest: he well had been content   650
Not to have seen, so Lancelot might have seen,
The Holy Cup of healing; and, indeed,
Being so clouded with his grief and love,
Small heart was his after the holy quest;
If God would send the vision, well; if not,   655
The quest and he were in the hands of Heaven.

'And then, with small adventure met, Sir Bors
Rode to the lonest tract of all the realm,
And found a people there among their crags,
Our race and blood, a remnant that were left   660
°Paynim amid their circles, and the stones
They pitch up straight to heaven; and their wise men
Were strong in that old magic which can trace
The wandering of the stars, and scoff'd at him
And this high quest as at a simple thing,   665
Told him he follow'd — almost Arthur's words —
A mocking fire: "what other fire than he
Whereby the blood beats, and the blossom blows,
And the sea rolls, and all the world is warm'd?"
And when his answer chafed them, the rough crowd,
Hearing he had a difference with their priests,   671
Seized him, and bound and plunged him into a cell
Of great piled stones; and lying bounden there
In darkness thro' innumerable hours
He heard the °hollow-ringing heavens sweep   675

Over him till by miracle — what else ? —
Heavy as it was a great stone slipt and fell,
Such as no wind could move; and thro' the gap
Glimmer'd the streaming scud: then came a night
Still as the day was loud, and through the gap   680
°The seven clear stars of Arthur's Table Round —
For, brother, so one night, because they roll
Thro' such a round in heaven, we named the stars,
Rejoicing in ourselves and in our King —
And these, like bright eyes of familiar friends,   685
In on him shone: "And then to me, to me,"
Said good Sir Bors, "beyond all hopes of mine,
Who scarce had pray'd or ask'd it for myself —
Across the seven clear stars — O grace to me ! —
In color like the fingers of a hand   690
Before a burning taper, the sweet Grail
Glided and past, and close upon it peal'd
A sharp quick thunder." Afterwards, a maid,
Who kept our holy faith among her kin
In secret, entering, loosed and let him go.'   695

    To whom the monk : 'And I remember now
That pelican on the casque: Sir Bors it was
Who spake so low and sadly at our board ;
And mighty reverent at our grace was he :
A square-set man and honest; and his eyes,   700
An outdoor sign of all the warmth within,

Smiled with his lips — a smile beneath a cloud,
But heaven had meant it for a sunny one:
Ay, ay, Sir Bors, who else ?   But when ye reach'd
The city, found ye all your knights return'd,   705
Or was there sooth in Arthur's prophecy,
Tell me, and what said each, and what the King?'

Then answer'd Percivale: 'And that can I,
Brother, and truly ; since the living words
Of so great men as Lancelot and our King   710
Pass not from door to door and out again,
But sit within the house.   O, when we reach'd
The city, our horses stumbling as they trode
On °heaps of ruin, hornless unicorns,
Crack'd basilisks, and splinter'd cockatrices,   715
And shatter'd talbots, which had left the stones
Raw that they fell from, brought us to the hall.

'And there sat Arthur on the dais-throne,
And those that had gone out upon the quest,
Wasted and worn, and but a tithe of them,   720
And those that had not, stood before the King,
Who, when he saw me, rose and bade me °hail,
Saying: "A welfare in thine eyes reproves
Our fear of some disastrous chance for thee
On hill or plain, at sea or flooding ford.   725
So fierce a gale made havoc here of late

Among the strange devices of our kings,
Yea, shook this newer, stronger hall of ours,
And from the statue Merlin moulded for us
Half-wrench'd a golden wing; but now — the quest, 730
This vision — hast thou seen the Holy Cup,
That Joseph brought of old to Glastonbury ? "

'So when I told him all thyself hast heard,
Ambrosius, and my fresh but fixt resolve
To pass away into the quiet life, 735
He answer'd not, but, sharply turning, ask'd
Of Gawain, ° " Gawain, was this quest for thee ? "

'" Nay, lord," said Gawain, "not for such as I.
Therefore I communed with a saintly man,
Who made me sure the quest was not for me; 740
For I was much a-wearied of the quest,
But found a silk pavilion in a field,
And merry maidens in it; and then this gale
Tore my pavilion from the tenting pin,
And blew my merry maidens all about 745
With all discomfort; yea, and but for this,
My twelvemonth and a day were pleasant to me."

'He ceased; and Arthur turn'd to whom at first
He saw not, for Sir Bors, on entering, push'd
Athwart the throng to Lancelot, caught his hand, 750

Held it, and there, half-hidden by him, stood,
Until the King espied him, saying to him,
" Hail, Bors! if ever loyal man and true
Could see it, thou hast seen the Grail; " and Bors,
" Ask me not, for I may not speak of it: 755
I saw it; " and the tears were in his eyes.

'Then there remain'd but Lancelot, for the rest
Spake but of sundry perils in the storm;
Perhaps, like° him of Cana in Holy Writ,
Our Arthur kept his best until the last;   760
" Thou, too, my Lancelot," ask'd the King, "my friend,
Our mightiest, hath this quest avail'd for thee? "

'" Our mightiest! " answer'd Lancelot, with a groan;
" O King! " — and when he paused methought I spied
A dying fire of madness in his eyes —   765
" O King, my friend, if friend of thine I be,
Happier are those that welter in their sin,
Swine in the mud, that cannot see for slime,
Slime of the ditch; but in me lived a sin
So strange, of such a kind, that all of pure,   770
Noble, and knightly in me twined and clung
Round that one sin, until the wholesome flower
And poisonous grew together, each as each,
Not to be pluck'd asunder; and when thy knights
Sware, I sware with them only in the hope   775

That could I touch or see the Holy Grail
They might be pluck'd asunder. Then I spake
To one most holy saint, who wept and said
That, save they could be pluck'd asunder, all
My quest were but in vain; to whom I vow'd   780
That I would work according as he will'd.
And forth I went, and while I yearn'd and strove
To tear the twain asunder in my heart,
My madness came upon me as of old,
And whipt me into waste fields far away.   785
There was I beaten down by little men,
Mean knights, to whom the moving of my sword
And shadow of my spear had been enow
To scare them from me once; and then I came
All in my folly to the naked shore,   790
Wide flats, where nothing but coarse grasses grew;
But such a blast, my king, began to blow,
So loud a blast along the shore and sea,
Ye could not hear the waters for the blast,
Tho' heapt in mounds and ridges all the sea   795
Drove like a cataract, and all the sand
Swept like a river, and the clouded heavens
Were shaken with the motion and the sound.
And °blackening in the sea-foam sway'd a boat,
Half-swallow'd in it, anchor'd with a chain;   800
And in my madness to myself I said,
'I will embark and I will lose myself,

R

And in the great sea wash away my sin.'
I burst the chain, I sprang into the boat.
Seven days I drove along the dreary deep,   805
And with me drove the moon and all the stars;
And the wind fell, and on the seventh night
I heard the shingle grinding in the surge,
And felt the boat shock earth, and looking up,
Behold, the enchanted towers of °Carbonek,   810
A castle like a rock upon a rock,
With chasm-like portals open to the sea,
And steps that met the breaker!   There was none
Stood near it but a lion on each side
That kept the entry, and the moon was full.   815
Then from the boat I leapt, and up the stairs,
There drew my sword.   With sudden-flaring manes
Those two great beasts rose upright like a man,
Each gript a shoulder, and I stood between,
And, when I would have smitten them, heard a voice,
' Doubt not, go forward; if thou doubt, the beasts   821
Will tear thee piecemeal.'   Then with violence
The sword was dash'd from out my hand, and fell.
And up into the sounding hall I past;
But nothing in the sounding hall I saw,   825
No bench nor table, painting on the wall
Or shield of knight, only the rounding moon
Thro' the tall oriel on the rolling sea.
But always in the quiet house I heard,

Clear as a lark, high o'er me as a lark,　　　　830
A sweet voice singing in the topmost tower
To the eastward.　Up I climb'd a thousand steps
With pain; as in a dream I seem'd to climb
For ever: at the last I reach'd a door,
A light was in the °crannies, and I heard,　　　835
' Glory and joy and honor to our Lord
And to the Holy Vessel of the Grail !'
Then in my madness I essay'd the door;
It gave, and thro' a stormy glare, a heat
As from a seven-times-heated furnace, I,　　　840
Blasted and burnt, and blinded as I was,
With such a fierceness that I swoon'd away —
O, yet methought I saw the Holy Grail,
°All pall'd in crimson samite, and around
Great angels, awful shapes, and wings and eyes!　845
And but for all my madness and my sin,
And then my swooning, I had sworn I saw
That which I saw ; but what I saw was veil'd
And cover'd, and this quest was not for me."

' So speaking, and here ceasing, Lancelot left　85c
The hall long silent, till Sir Gawain — nay,
Brother, I need not tell thee foolish words, —
A reckless and irreverent knight was he,
Now bolden'd by the silence of his king, —
Well, I will tell thee: " O King, my liege," he said,

"Hath Gawain fail'd in any quest of thine?   856
When have I stinted stroke in foughten field?
But as for thine, my good friend Percivale,
Thy holy nun and thou have driven men mad,
Yea, made our mightiest madder than our least.   860
But by mine eyes and by mine ears I swear,
I will be °deafer than the blue-eyed cat,
And thrice as blind as any noonday owl,
To holy virgins in their ecstasies,
Henceforward."

          '"Deafer," said the blameless King,
"Gawain, and blinder unto holy things,   866
Hope not to make thyself by idle vows,
Being too blind to have desire to see.
But if indeed there came a sign from heaven,
Blessed are Bors, Lancelot, and Percivale,   870
For those have seen according to their sight.
For every fiery prophet in old times,
And all the sacred madness of the bard,
When God made music thro' them, could but speak
His music by the framework and the chord;   875
And as ye saw it ye have spoken truth.

          '"Nay — but thou errest, Lancelot: never yet
Could all of true and noble in knight and man
Twine round one sin, whatever it might be,

With such a closeness but apart there grew,   880
Save that he were the swine thou spakest of,
Some root of knighthood and pure nobleness:
Whereto see thou, that it may bear its flower.

  ' " And spake I not too truly, O my knights?
Was I too dark a prophet when I said   885
To those who went upon the Holy Quest,
That most of them would follow wandering fires,
Lost in the quagmire ? — lost to me and gone,
And left me gazing at a barren board,
And a lean Order — scarce return'd a tithe —   890
And out of those to whom the vision came
My greatest hardly will believe he saw.
Another hath beheld it afar off,
And, leaving human wrongs to right themselves,
Cares but to pass into the silent life.   895
And one hath had the vision face to face,
And now his chair desires him here in vain,
However they may crown him otherwhere.

  ' " And some among you held that if the King
Had seen the sight he would have sworn the vow ;
Not easily, °seeing that the King must guard   901
That which he rules, and is but as the hind
To whom a space of land is given to plow,
Who may not wander from the allotted field

Before his work be done, but being done,   905
Let visions of the night or of the day
Come as they will; and many a time they come,
Until this earth he walks on seems not earth,
This light that strikes his eyeball is not light,
This air that smites his forehead is not air   910
But vision — yea, his very hand and foot —
In moments when he feels he cannot die,
And knows himself no vision to himself,
Nor the high God a vision, nor that One
Who rose again : ye have seen what ye have seen."   915

'So spake the King: I knew not all he meant.'

THE LAST TOURNAMENT

DAGONET, the fool, whom Gawain in his mood
Had made mock-knight of Arthur's Table Round,
At Camelot, high above the yellowing woods,
Danced like a wither'd leaf before the hall.
And toward him from the hall, with harp in hand,   5
And from the crown thereof a °carcanet
Of ruby swaying to and fro, the prize
Of °Tristram in the jousts of yesterday,
Came Tristram, saying, 'Why skip ye so, Sir Fool?'

For Arthur and Sir Lancelot riding once,   10
Far down beneath a winding wall of rock
Heard a child wail.   A stump of oak half-dead,
From roots like some black coil of carven snakes,
Clutch'd at the crag, and started thro' mid air
Bearing an eagle's nest; and thro' the tree   15
Rush'd ever a rainy wind, and thro' the wind
Pierced ever a child's cry: and crag and tree
Scaling, Sir Lancelot from the perilous nest,
This ruby necklace thrice around her neck,
And all unscarr'd from beak or talon, brought   20
A maiden babe, which Arthur pitying took,

Then gave it to his Queen to rear.   The Queen,
But coldly acquiescing, in her white arms
Received, and after loved it tenderly,
And named it °Nestling; so forgot herself   25
A moment, and her cares; till that young life
Being smitten in mid heaven with mortal cold
Past from her, and in time the carcanet
Vext her with plaintive memories of the child:
So she, delivering it to Arthur, said,   30
'Take thou the jewels of this dead innocence,
And make them, an thou wilt, a tourney-prize.'

　　To whom the King, 'Peace to thine eagle-borne
Dead nestling, and this honor after death,
Following thy will! but, O my Queen, I muse   35
Why ye not wear on arm, or neck, or zone
Those diamonds that I rescued from the tarn,
And Lancelot won, methought, for thee to wear.'

　　'Would rather you had let them fall,' she cried,
'Plunge and be lost — ill-fated as they were,   40
A bitterness to me! — ye look amazed,
Not knowing they were lost as soon as given —
Slid from my hands when I was leaning out
Above the river — that unhappy child
Past in her barge; but rosier luck will go   45
With these rich jewels, seeing that they came

Not from the skeleton of a brother-slayer,
But the sweet body of a maiden babe.
Perchance — who knows? — the purest of thy knights
May win them for the purest of my maids.'   50

She ended, and the cry of a great jousts
With trumpet-blowings ran on all the ways
From Camelot in among the faded fields
To furthest towers; and everywhere the knights
Arm'd for a day of glory before the King.   55

But on the hither side of that loud morn
Into the hall stagger'd, his visage ribb'd
From ear to ear with dogwhip-weals, his nose
Bridge-broken, one eye out, and one hand off,
And one with shatter'd fingers dangling lame,   60
A churl, to whom indignantly the King:

'My churl, for whom Christ died, what evil beast
Hath drawn his claws athwart thy face? or fiend?
Man was it who marr'd heaven's image in thee thus?'

Then, sputtering thro' the hedge of splinter'd
    teeth,   65
Yet strangers to the tongue, and with blunt stump
°Pitch-blacken'd sawing the air, said the maim'd churl:
'He took them and he drave them to his tower —

Some hold he was a table-knight of thine —
A hundred goodly ones — the Red Knight, he —   70
Lord, I was tending swine, and the Red Knight
Brake in upon me and drave them to his tower;
And when I call'd upon thy name as one
That doest right by gentle and by churl,
Maim'd me and maul'd, and would outright have slain,
Save that he sware me to a message, saying: 76
" Tell thou the King and all his liars that I
Have founded my Round Table in the North,
And whatsoever his own knights have sworn
My knights have sworn the counter to it — and say 80
My tower is full of harlots, like his court,
But mine are worthier, seeing they profess
To be none other than themselves — and say
My knights are all adulterers like his own,
But mine are truer, seeing they profess   85
To be none other ; and say his hour is come,
The heathen are upon him, his long lance
Broken, and his Excalibur a straw.'''

    Then Arthur turn'd to Kay the seneschal:
'Take thou my churl, and tend him °curiously   90
Like a king's heir, till all his hurts be whole.
The heathen — but that ever-climbing wave,
Hurl'd back again so often in empty foam,
Hath lain for years at rest — and renegades,

Thieves, bandits, leavings of confusion, whom   95
The wholesome realm is purged of otherwhere,
Friends, thro' your manhood and your fealty, — now
Make their last °head like Satan in the North.
My younger knights, new-made, in whom your flower
Waits to be solid fruit of golden deeds,   100
Move with me toward their quelling, which achieved,
The loneliest ways are safe from shore to shore.
But thou, Sir Lancelot, sitting in my place
Enchair'd to-morrow, arbitrate the field ;
For wherefore shouldst thou care to mingle with it,   105
Only to yield my Queen her own again ?
Speak, Lancelot, thou art silent : is it well ?'

Thereto Sir Lancelot answer'd : 'It is well ;
Yet better if the King abide, and leave
The leading of his younger knights to me.   110
Else, for the King has will'd it, it is well.'

Then Arthur rose and Lancelot follow'd him,
And while they stood without the doors, the King
Turn'd to him saying : °' Is it then so well ?
Or mine the blame that oft I seem as he   115
Of whom was written, °" A sound is in his ears " ?
The foot that loiters, bidden go, — the glance
That only seems half-loyal to command, —
A manner somewhat fallen from reverence —

Or have I dream'd the bearing of our knights   120
Tells of a manhood ever less and lower?
Or whence the fear lest this my realm, uprear'd,
By noble deeds at one with noble vows,
From flat confusion and brute violences,
Reel back into the beast, and be no more?'   125

 He spoke, and taking °all his younger knights,
Down the slope city rode, and sharply turn'd
North by the gate. °In her high bower the Queen,
Working a tapestry, lifted up her head,
Watch'd her lord pass, and knew not that she
  sigh'd.   130
Then ran across her memory the strange rhyme
Of bygone Merlin, 'Where is he who knows?
From the great deep to the great deep he goes.'

 But when the morning of a tournament,
By these in earnest those in mockery call'd   135
The °Tournament of the Dead Innocence,
Brake with a wet wind blowing, Lancelot,
Round whose sick head all night, like birds of
  prey,
The words of Arthur flying shriek'd, arose,
And down a streetway hung with folds of pure   140
White samite, and by fountains running wine,
Where children sat in white with cups of gold,

Moved to the lists, and there, with slow sad steps
Ascending, fill'd his double-dragon'd chair.

He glanced and saw the stately galleries,   145
Dame, damsel, each thro' worship of their Queen
White-robed in honor of the stainless child,
And some with scatter'd jewels, like a bank
Of maiden snow mingled with sparks of fire.
He look'd but once, and vail'd his eyes again.   150

The sudden trumpet sounded as in a dream
To ears but half-awakened, then one low roll
Of autumn thunder, and the jousts began;
And ever the wind blew, and yellowing leaf,
And gloom and gleam, and shower and shorn plume   155
Went down it.   Sighing weariedly, as one
Who sits and gazes on a faded fire,
When all the goodlier guests are past away,
Sat their great umpire looking o'er the lists.
He saw the laws that ruled the tournament   160
Broken, but spake not; once, a knight cast down
Before his throne of arbitration cursed
The dead babe and the follies of the King;
And once the laces of a helmet crack'd,
And show'd him, like a vermin in its hole,   165
Modred, a narrow face: anon he heard
The voice that billow'd round the barriers roar

An ocean-sounding welcome to one knight,
But newly-enter'd, taller than the rest,
And armor'd all in forest green, whereon   170
There tript a hundred tiny silver deer,
And wearing but a holly-spray for crest,
With ever-scattering berries, and on shield
A spear, °a harp, a bugle — Tristram — late
From over-seas in Brittany return'd,   175
And marriage with a princess of that realm,
Isolt the White — °Sir Tristram of the Woods —
Whom Lancelot knew, had held sometime with pain
His own against him, and now yearn'd to shake
The burthen off his heart in one full shock   180
With Tristram even to death.   His strong hands gript
And dinted the gilt dragons right and left,
Until he groan'd for wrath — so many of those
That ware their ladies' colors on the casque
Drew from before Sir Tristram to the bounds,   185
And there with gibes and flickering mockeries
Stood, while he mutter'd, 'Craven crests !   O shame !
What faith have these in whom they sware to love ?
The glory of our Round Table is no more.'

So Tristram won, and Lancelot gave, the gems,   190
Not speaking other word than, 'Hast thou won ?
Art thou the purest, brother?   See, the hand
Wherewith thou takest this °is red !' to whom

Tristram, half plagued by Lancelot's languorous mood,
Made answer: 'Ay, but wherefore toss me this   195
Like a dry bone cast to some hungry hound?
Let be thy fair Queen's fantasy.   Strength of heart
And might of limb, but mainly use and skill,
Are winners in this pastime of our King.
My hand — belike the lance hath dript upon it —   200
No blood of mine, I trow; but O chief knight,
Right arm of Arthur in the battle-field,
Great brother, thou nor I have made the world;
Be happy in thy fair Queen as I in mine.'

And Tristram round the gallery made his horse   205
°Caracole; then bow'd his homage, bluntly saying,
'Fair damsels, each to him who worships each
Sole Queen of Beauty and of love, behold
This day my Queen of Beauty is not here.'
And most of these were mute, some anger'd, one   210
Murmuring, 'All courtesy is dead,' and one,
'The glory of our Round Table is no more.'

°Then fell thick rain, plume droopt and mantle hung,
And pettish cries awoke, and the wan day
Went glooming down in wet and weariness;   215
But under her black brows a swarthy one
Laugh'd shrilly, crying: 'Praise the patient saints,
Our one white day of Innocence hath past,

Tho' somewhat draggled at the skirt.   So be it.
The snowdrop only, flowering thro' the year,   220
Would make the world as blank as winter-tide.
Come — let us gladden their sad eyes, our Queen's
And Lancelot's, at this night's solemnity
With all the kindlier colors of the field.'

So dame and damsel glitter'd at the feast   225
Variously gay, °for he that tells the tale
Liken'd them, saying, as when an hour of cold
Falls on the mountain in midsummer snows,
And all the purple slopes of mountain flowers
Pass under white, till the warm hour returns   230
With veer of wind and all are flowers again,
So dame and damsel cast the simple white,
And glowing in all colors, the live grass,
°Rose-Campion, bluebell, kingcup, poppy, glanced
About the revels, and with mirth so loud   235
Beyond all use, that, half-amazed, the Queen,
And wroth at Tristram and the lawless jousts,
Brake up their sports, then slowly to her bower
Parted, and in her bosom pain was lord.

°And little Dagonet on the morrow morn,   240
High over all the yellowing autumn-tide,
Danced like a wither'd leaf before the hall.
Then **Tristram** saying, ' Why skip ye so, Sir Fool ? '

Wheel'd round on either heel, Dagonet replied,
'Belike for lack of wiser company; 245
Or being fool, and seeing too much wit
Makes the world rotten, why, belike I skip
To know myself the wisest knight of all.'
'Ay, fool,' said Tristram, 'but 't is eating dry
To dance without a catch, a roundelay 250
To dance to.' Then he twangled on his harp,
And while he twangled little Dagonet stood
Quiet as any water-sodden log
Stay'd in the wandering warble of a brook;
But when the twangling ended, skipt again; 255
And being ask'd, 'Why skipt ye not, Sir Fool?'
Made answer, 'I had liefer twenty years
Skip to the °broken music of my brains
Than any broken music thou canst make.'
Then Tristram, waiting for the quip to come, 260
'Good now, what music have I broken, fool?'
And little Dagonet, skipping, 'Arthur, the King's;
For when thou playest that air with Queen Isolt,
Thou makest broken music with thy bride,
Her daintier namesake down in Brittany — 265
And so thou breakest Arthur's music too.'
'Save for that broken music in thy brains,
Sir Fool,' said Tristram, 'I would break thy head.
Fool, I came late, the heathen wars were o'er,
The life had flown, we sware but by the shell — 270

s

I am but a fool to reason with a fool —
Come, thou art crabb'd and sour; but lean me down,
Sir Dagonet, one of thy long asses' ears,
And harken if my music be not true.

  ' " Free love — free field — we love but while we may :
The woods are hush'd, their music is no more ;   276
The leaf is dead, the yearning past away.
New leaf, new life — the days of frost are o'er ;
New life, new love, to suit the newer day ;
New loves are sweet as those that went before :   280
Free love — free field — we love but while we may."

  ' Ye might have moved slow-measure to my tune,
Not stood stock-still.   I made it in the woods,
And heard it ring as true as tested gold.'

  But Dagonet with one foot poised in his hand :   285
' Friend, did ye mark that fountain yesterday,
Made to run wine ? — but this had run itself
All out like a long life to a sour end —
And them that round it sat with golden cups
To hand the wine to whosoever came —   290
The twelve small °damosels white as Innocence,
In honor of poor Innocence the babe,
Who left the gems which Innocence the Queen
Lent to the King, and Innocence the King

Gave for a prize — and one of those white slips   295
Handed her cup and piped, the pretty one,
" Drink, drink, Sir Fool," and thereupon I drank,
Spat — pish — the cup was gold, the draught was mud.'

And Tristram: ' Was it muddier than thy gibes ?
Is all the laughter gone dead out of thee ? —   300
Not marking how the knighthood mock thee, fool —
"Fear God : honor the King — his one true knight —
Sole follower of the vows " —for here be they
Who knew thee swine enow before I came,
°Smuttier than blasted grain : but when the King   305
Had made thee fool, thy vanity so shot up
It frighted all free fool from out thy heart;
Which left thee less than fool, and less than swine,
A naked aught — yet swine I hold thee still,
For I have flung thee pearls and find thee swine.'   310

And little Dagonet mincing with his feet:
' Knight, an ye fling those rubies round my neck
In lieu of hers, I'll hold thou hast some touch
Of music, since I care not for thy pearls.
Swine ?   I have wallow'd, I have wash'd — the world
                                   315
Is flesh and shadow — I have had my day.
The dirty nurse, Experience, in her kind
Hath foul'd me — an I wallow'd, then I wash'd —

I have had my day and my philosophies —
And thank the Lord I am King Arthur's fool.　　320
Swine, say ye? swine, goats, asses, rams, and geese
Troop'd round a °Paynim harper once, who thrumm'd
On such a wire as musically as thou
Some such fine song — but never a king's fool.'

And Tristram, 'Then were swine, goats, asses,
　　geese　　　　　　　　　　　　　　　　　325
The wiser fools, seeing thy Paynim bard
Had such a mastery of his mystery
That he could harp his wife up out of hell.'

Then Dagonet, turning on the ball of his foot,
'And whither harp'st thou thine? down! and thy-
　　self　　　　　　　　　　　　　　　　　330
Down! and two more: a helpful harper thou,
That harpest downward! Dost thou know the star
We call the Harp of Arthur up in heaven?'

And Tristram, 'Ay, Sir Fool, for when our King
Was victor wellnigh day by day, the knights,　　335
Glorying in each new glory, set his name
High on all hills and in the signs of heaven.'

And Dagonet answer'd: 'Ay, and when the land
Was freed, and the Queen false, ye set yourself
To babble about him, all to show your wit —　　340

And whether he were king by courtesy,
Or king by right — and so went harping down
°The black king's highway, got so far and grew
So witty that ye play'd at ducks and drakes
With Arthur's vows on the great lake of fire.   345
Tuwhoo! do ye see it? do ye see the star?'

'Nay, fool,' said Tristram, 'not in open day.'
And Dagonet; 'Nay, nor will; I see it and hear.
It makes a silent music up in heaven,
And I and Arthur and the angels hear,   350
And then we skip.' 'Lo, fool,' he said, 'ye talk
Fool's treason: is the King thy brother fool?'
Then little Dagonet clapt his hands and shrill'd:
'Ay, ay, my brother fool, the king of fools!
Conceits himself as God that he can make   355
Figs out of thistles, silk from bristles, milk
From °burning spurge, honey from hornet-combs,
And men from beasts — Long live the king of fools!'

And down the city Dagonet danced away;
But thro' the slowly-mellowing avenues   360
And solitary passes of the wood
Rode Tristram toward Lyonnesse and the west.
Before him fled the face of Queen Isolt
With ruby-circled neck, but evermore
Past, as a rustle or twitter in the wood   365

Made dull his inner, keen his outer eye
For all that walk'd, or crept, or perch'd, or flew.
Anon the face, as, when a gust hath blown,
Unruffling waters re-collect the shape
Of one that in them sees himself, return'd;   370
But at the °slot or fewmets of a deer,
Or even a fallen feather, vanish'd again.

   So on for all that day from °lawn to lawn
Thro' many a league-long bower he rode.   At length
A lodge of intertwisted beechen-boughs,   375
Furze-cramm'd and bracken-rooft, the which himself
Built for a summer day with Queen Isolt
Against a shower, dark in the golden grove
Appearing, sent his fancy back to where
She lived a moon in that low lodge with him;   380
Till Mark her lord had past, the Cornish King,
With six or seven, when Tristram was away,
And snatch'd her thence, yet, dreading worse than
      shame
Her warrior Tristram, spake not any word
But bode his hour, devising wretchedness.   385

   And now that desert lodge to Tristram lookt
So sweet that, halting, in he past and sank
Down on a drift of foliage random-blown;
But could not rest for musing how to smooth

And sleek his marriage over to the queen. 390
Perchance in lone Tintagil far from all
The °tonguesters of the court she had not heard.
But then what folly had sent him over-seas
After she left him lonely here ? a name ?
Was it the name of one in Brittany, 395
Isolt, the daughter of the king? 'Isolt
Of the White Hands' they call'd her: the sweet
 name
Allured him first, and then the maid herself,
Who served him well with those white hands of hers,
And loved him well, until himself had thought 400
He loved her also, wedded easily,
But left her all as easily, and return'd.
The black-blue Irish hair and Irish eyes
Had drawn him home — what marvel ? then he laid
His brows upon the drifted leaf and dream'd. 405

He seem'd to pace the strand of Brittany
Between Isolt of Britain and his bride,
And show'd them both the ruby-chain, and both
Began to struggle for it, till his queen
Graspt it so hard that all her hand was red. 410
Then cried the Breton, 'Look, her hand is red !
These be no rubies, this is frozen blood,
And melts within her hand — her hand is hot
With ill desires, but this I gave thee, look,

Is all as cool and white as any flower.'   415
Follow'd a rush of eagle's wings, and then
A whimpering of the spirit of the child,
Because the twain had spoil'd her carcanet.

He dream'd; but Arthur with a hundred spears
Rode far, till o'er the illimitable reed,   420
And many a glancing plash and °sallowy isle,
The wide-wing'd sunset of the misty marsh
Glared on a huge °machicolated tower
That stood with open doors, whereout was roll'd
A roar of riot, as from men secure   425
Amid their marshes, ruffians at their ease
Among their harlot-brides, an evil song.
'Lo there,' said one of Arthur's youth, for there,
High on a grim dead tree before the tower,
A goodly brother of the Table Round   430
Swung by the neck: and on the boughs a shield
Showing a shower of blood in a field °noir,
And therebeside a horn, inflamed the knights
At that dishonor done the gilded spur,
Till each would clash the shield and blow the horn.   435
But Arthur waved them back.   Alone he rode.
Then at the dry harsh roar of the great horn,
°That sent the face of all the marsh aloft
An ever upward-rushing storm and cloud
Of shriek and plume, the Red Knight heard, and all,

Even to tipmost lance and topmost helm,   441
In blood-red armor sallying, howl'd to the King:

  'The teeth of Hell flay bare and gnash thee flat!—
Lo! art thou not that eunuch-hearted king
Who fain had clipt free manhood from the world—445
The woman-worshipper? Yea, God's curse, and I!
Slain was the brother of my paramour
By a knight of thine, and I that heard her whine
And snivel, being eunuch-hearted too,
Sware by the °scorpion-worm that twists in hell   450
And stings itself to everlasting death,
To hang whatever knight of thine I fought
And tumbled. Art thou king?—Look to thy life!'

  He ended: Arthur knew the voice; the face
Wellnigh was helmet-hidden, and the name   455
Went wandering somewhere darkling in his mind.
And Arthur deign'd not use of word or sword,
But let the drunkard, as he stretch'd from horse
To strike him, overbalancing his bulk,
Down from the causeway heavily to the swamp   460
Fall, as the crest of some slow-arching wave,
Heard in dead night along that table-shore,
Drops flat, and after the great waters break
Whitening for half a league, and thin themselves,
Far over sands marbled with moon and cloud,   465

From less and less to nothing; thus he fell
Head-heavy; then the knights, who watch'd him, roar'd
And shouted and leapt down upon the fallen,
There trampled out his face from being known,   470
And sank his head in mire, and slimed themselves;
Nor heard the King for their own cries, but sprang
Thro' open doors, and swording right and left
Men, women, on their sodden faces, hurl'd
The tables over and the wines, and slew
Till all the rafters rang with woman-yells,   475
And all the pavement stream'd with massacre:
Then, echoing yell with yell, they fired the tower,
Which half that autumn night, like the live North,
Red-pulsing up thro' °Alioth and Alcor,
Made all above it, and a hundred meres   480
About it, as the water °Moab saw
Come round by the east, and out beyond them flush'd
The long low dune and lazy-plunging sea.

So all the ways were safe from shore to shore,
But in the heart of Arthur °pain was lord.   485

Then, out of Tristram waking, the red dream
Fled with a shout, and that low lodge return'd,
Mid-forest, and the wind among the boughs.
He whistled his good war-horse left to graze
Among the forest greens, vaulted upon him,   490

And rode beneath an ever-showering leaf,
Till °one lone woman, weeping near a cross,
Stay'd him. 'Why weep ye?' 'Lord,' she said, 'my man
Hath left me or is dead;' whereon he thought —
'What, if she hate me now? I would not this.   495
What, if she love me still? I would not that.
I know not what I would' — but said to her,
'Yet weep not thou, lest, if thy mate return,
He find thy favor changed and love thee not' —
Then pressing day by day thro' Lyonnesse   500
Last in a °roky hollow, belling, heard
The hounds of Mark, and felt the goodly hounds
°Yelp at his heart, but, turning, past and gain'd
Tintagil, half in sea and high on land,
A crown of towers.

     Down in a casement sat,   505
A low sea-sunset glorying round her hair
And glossy-throated grace, Isolt the queen.
And when she heard the feet of Tristram grind
The °spiring stone that scaled about her tower,
Flush'd, started, met him at the doors, and there   510
Belted his body with her white embrace,
Crying aloud: 'Not Mark — not Mark, my soul!
The footstep flutter'd me at first: not he!
Catlike thro' his own castle steals my Mark,

But warrior-wise thou stridest thro' his halls   515
Who hates thee, as I him — even to the death.
My soul, I felt my hatred for my Mark
Quicken within me, and knew that thou wert nigh.'
To whom Sir Tristram smiling, ' I am here :
Let be thy Mark, seeing he is not thine.'   520

     And drawing somewhat backward she replied:
' Can he be wrong'd who is not even his own,
But save for dread of thee had beaten me,
Scratch'd, bitten, blinded, marr'd me somehow — Mark ?
What rights are his that dare not strike for them ? 525
Nor lift a hand — not, tho' he found me thus !
But harken ! have ye met him ? hence he went
To-day for three days' hunting — as he said —
And so returns belike within an hour.
Mark's way, my soul ! — but eat not thou with Mark,
Because he hates thee even more than fears,   530
Nor drink ; and when thou passest any wood
Close vizor, les! an arrow from the bush
Should leave me all alone with Mark and hell.
My God, the measure of my hate for Mark   535
Is as the measure of my love for thee !'

     So, pluck'd one way by hate and one by love,
Drain'd of her force, again she sat, and spake
To Tristram, as he knelt before her, saying:

' O hunter, and O blower of the horn,   540
Harper, and thou hast been a rover too,
For, ere I mated with my shambling king,
Ye twain had fallen out about the bride
Of one — his name is out of me — the prize,
If   prize   she   were — what   marvel ? — she   could
    see —   545
Thine, friend; and ever since my craven seeks
To wreck thee villainously : but, O Sir Knight,
What dame or damsel have ye kneel'd to last ? '

And Tristram, ' Last to my °Queen Paramount,
Here now to my queen paramount of love   550
And loveliness — ay, lovelier than when first
Her light feet fell on our rough Lyonnesse,
Sailing from Ireland.'

                    Softly laugh'd Isolt:
' Flatter me not, for hath not our great Queen
My dole of beauty °trebled ? ' and he said :   555
' Her beauty is her beauty, and thine thine,
And thine is more to me — soft, gracious, kind —
Save when thy Mark is kindled on thy lips
Most gracious ; but she, haughty, even to him,
Lancelot ; for I have seen him wan enow   560
To make one doubt if ever the great Queen
Have yielded him her love.'

                                    To whom Isolt:
'Ah, then, false hunter and false harper, thou
Who brakest thro' the scruple of my bond,
Calling me thy white hind, and saying to me   565
That Guinevere had sinn'd against the highest,
And I — misyoked with such a want of man —
That I could hardly sin against the lowest.'

    He answer'd: 'O my soul, be comforted!
If this be sweet, to sin in leading-strings,   570
If here be comfort, and if ours be sin,
Crown'd warrant °had we for the crowning sin
That made us happy; but how ye greet me — fear
And fault and doubt — no word of that fond tale —
Thy deep heart-yearnings, thy sweet memories   575
Of Tristram in that year he was away.'

    And, saddening on the sudden, spake Isolt:
'I had forgotten all in my strong joy
To see thee — yearnings? — ay! for, hour by hour,
Here in the never-ended afternoon,   580
O, sweeter than all memories of thee,
Deeper than any yearnings after thee
Seem'd those far-rolling, westward-smiling seas,
Watch'd from this tower.   Isolt of Britain dash'd
Before Isolt of Brittany on the strand,   585
Would that have chill'd her bride-kiss? Wedded her?

Fought in her father's battles ? wounded there ?
The King was all fulfill'd with gratefulness,
And she, my namesake of the hands, that heal'd
Thy hurt and heart with unguent and caress —   590
Well — can I wish her any huger wrong
Than having known thee ? her too hast thou left
To pine and waste in those sweet memories.
O, were I not my Mark's, °by whom all men
Are noble, I should hate thee more than love.'   595

And Tristram, fondling her light hands, replied :
' Grace, queen, for being loved : she loved me well.
Did I love her ? the name at least I loved.
Isolt ? — I fought his battles, for Isolt !
The night was dark ; the true star set. Isolt !   600
The name was ruler of the dark — Isolt ?
Care not for her ! patient, and prayerful, meek,
Pale-blooded, she will °yield herself to God.'

And Isolt answer'd : ' Yea, and why not I ?
Mine is the larger need, who am not meek,   605
Pale-blooded, prayerful. Let me tell thee now.
Here one black, mute midsummer night I sat,
Lonely, but musing on thee, wondering where,
Murmuring a light song I had heard thee sing,
And once or twice I spake thy name aloud.   610
Then flash'd a °levin-brand ; and near me stood,

In fuming sulphur blue and green, a fiend —
Mark's way to steal behind one in the dark —
For there was Mark: " He has wedded her," he said,
Not said, but hiss'd it; then this crown of towers   615
So shook to such a roar of all the sky,
That here in utter dark I swoon'd away.
And woke again in utter dark, and cried,
" I will flee hence and give myself to God " —
And thou wert lying in thy new °leman's arms.'   620

Then Tristram, ever dallying with her hand,
' May God be with thee, sweet, when old and gray,
And past desire !' a saying that anger'd her.
' " May God be with thee, sweet, when thou art old,
And sweet no more to me ! "   I need Him now.   625
For when had Lancelot utter'd aught so gross
Even to the swineherd's °malkin in the mast ?
The greater man the greater courtesy.
Far other was the Tristram, Arthur's knight !
But thou, thro' ever harrying thy wild beasts —   630
Save that to touch a harp, tilt with a lance
Becomes thee well — art grown wild beast thyself.
How darest thou, if lover, push me even
In fancy from thy side, and set me far
In the gray distance, half a life away,   635
Her to be loved no more ?   Unsay it, unswear !
Flatter me rather, seeing me so weak,

Broken with Mark and hate and solitude,
Thy marriage and mine own, that I should suck
Lies like sweet wines: lie to me; I believe.   640
Will ye not lie? not swear, as there ye kneel,
And solemnly as when ye sware to him,
The man of men, our King — My God, the power
Was once in vows when men believed the King!
They lied not then who sware, and thro' their vows
The King prevailing made his realm: — I say,   646
Swear to me thou wilt love me even when old,
Gray-hair'd, and past desire, and in despair.'

Then Tristram, pacing moodily up and down:
'Vows! did you keep the vow you made to Mark   650
More than I mine? Lied, say ye? Nay, but learnt,
The vow that binds too strictly snaps itself —
My knighthood taught me this — ay, being snapt —
We run more counter to the soul thereof
Than had we never sworn. I swear no more.   655
I swore to the great King, and am foresworn.
For once — even to the height — I honor'd him.
" Man, is he man at all? " methought, when first
I rode from our rough Lyonnesse, and beheld
That victor of the Pagan throned in hall —   660
His hair, a sun that ray'd from off a brow
Like hill-snow high in heaven, the steel-blue eyes,
The golden beard that clothed his lips with light —

т

Moreover, that weird legend of his birth,
With Merlin's mystic babble about his end   665
Amazed me; then, his foot was on a stool
Shaped as a dragon; he seem'd to me no man,
But °Michael trampling Satan; so I sware,
Being amazed : but this went by — The vows!
O, ay — the wholesome madness of an hour —   670
They served their use, their time; for every knight
Believed himself a greater than himself,
And every follower eyed him as a God;
Till he, being lifted up beyond himself,
Did mightier deeds than elsewise he had done,   675
And so the realm was made : but then their vows —
First mainly thro' that sullying of our Queen —
Began to gall the knighthood, asking whence
Had Arthur right to bind them to himself ?
Dropt down from heaven ? wash'd up from out the
    deep ?   680
They fail'd to trace him thro' the flesh and blood
Of our old kings : whence then ? a doubtful lord
To bind them by inviolable vows,
Which flesh and blood perforce would violate :
For feel this arm of mine — the tide within   685
Red with free chase and heather-scented air,
Pulsing full man ; can Arthur make me pure
As any maiden child? lock up my tongue
From uttering freely what I freely hear ?

Bind me to one? The wide world laughs at it. 690
And worldling of the world am I, and know
The °ptarmigan that whitens ere his hour
Woos his own end; we are not angels here
Nor shall be: vows — I am a woodman of the woods,
And hear the °garnet-headed yaffingale 695
Mock them: my soul, we love but while we may;
And therefore is my love so large for thee,
Seeing it is not bounded save by love.'

Here ending, he moved toward her, and she said:
'Good: an I turn'd away my love for thee 700
To some one thrice as courteous as thyself —
For courtesy wins woman all as well
As valor may, but he that closes both
Is perfect, he is Lancelot — taller indeed,
Rosier and comelier, thou — but say I loved 705
This knightliest of all knights, and cast thee back
Thine own small saw, "We love but while we may,"
Well then, what answer?'

He that while she spake,
Mindful of what he brought to adorn her with,
The jewels, had let one finger lightly touch 710
The warm white apple of her throat, replied,
°'Press this a little closer, sweet, until —
Come, I am hunger'd and half-anger'd — meat,

Wine, wine — and I will love thee to the death,
And out beyond into the dream to come.'   715

So then, when both were brought to full accord,
She rose, and set before him all he will'd ;
And after these had comforted the blood
With meats and wines, and satiated their hearts —
Now talking of their woodland paradise,   720
The deer, the dews, the fern, the founts, the lawns ;
Now mocking at the much ungainliness,
And craven shifts, and long crane legs of Mark —
Then Tristram laughing caught the harp and sang :

'Ay, ay, O, ay — the winds that bend the brier ! 725
A star in heaven, a star within the mere !
Ay, ay, O, ay — a star was my desire,
And one was far apart and one was near :
Ay, ay, O, ay — the winds that blow the grass !
And one was water and one star was fire,   730
And one will ever shine and one will pass.
Ay, ay, O, ay — the winds that move the mere !'

Then in the light's last glimmer Tristram show'd
And swung the ruby carcanet.   She cried,
'The collar of some Order, which our King   735
Hath newly founded, all for thee, my soul,
For thee, to yield thee grace beyond thy peers.'

'Not so, my queen,' he said, 'but the red fruit
Grown on a magic oak-tree in mid-heaven,
And won by Tristram as a tourney-prize,   740
And hither brought by Tristram for his last
Love-offering and peace-offering unto thee.'

He spoke, he turn'd, then, flinging round her neck,
Claspt, and cried, 'Thine Order, O my queen!'
But, while he bow'd to kiss the jewell'd throat,   745
Out of the dark, just as the lips had touch'd,
Behind him rose a shadow and a shriek —
'Mark's way,' said Mark, and clove him thro' the brain.

That night came Arthur home, and while he climb'd,
All in a death-dumb autumn-dripping gloom,   750
The stairway to the hall, and look'd and saw
The great Queen's bower was dark, — about his feet
A voice clung sobbing till he question'd it,
'What art thou?' and the voice about his feet
Sent up an answer, sobbing, 'I am thy fool,   755
And I shall never make thee smile again.'

GUINEVERE

Queen Guinevere had fled the court, and sat
There in the holy house at °Almesbury
Weeping, none with her save a little maid,
A °novice: one low light betwixt them burn'd
Blurr'd by the creeping mist, for all abroad,   5
Beneath a moon unseen albeit at full,
The white mist, like a °face-cloth to the face,
Clung to the dead earth, and the land was still.

For hither had she fled, her cause of flight
Sir Modred; he that like a subtle beast   10
Lay couchant with his eyes upon the throne,
Ready to spring, waiting a chance: for this
He chill'd the popular praises of the King
With silent smiles of slow disparagement;
And °tamper'd with the Lords of the White Horse,   15
Heathen, the °brood by Hengist left; and sought
To make disruption in the Table Round
Of Arthur, and to splinter it into feuds
Serving his traitorous end; and all his aims
Were sharpen'd by strong hate for Lancelot.   20

For thus it chanced one morn when all the court,
Green-suited, but with plumes that °mock'd the may,
Had been — their wont — a-maying and return'd,
That Modred still in green, all ear and eye,
Climb'd to the high top of the garden-wall   25
To spy some secret scandal if he might,
And saw the Queen who sat betwixt her best
Enid and ° lissome Vivien, of her court
The wiliest and the worst; and more than this
He saw not, for Sir Lancelot passing by   30
Spied where he crouch'd, and as the gardener's hand
Picks from the °colewort a green caterpillar,
So from the high wall and the flowering grove
Of grasses Lancelot pluck'd him by the heel,
And cast him as a worm upon the way;   35
But when he knew the prince tho' marr'd with dust,
He, reverencing king's blood in a bad man,
Made such excuses as he might, and these
Full knightly without scorn : for in those days
No knight of Arthur's noblest dealt in scorn;   40
But, if a man were halt, or hunch'd, in him
By those whom God had made full-limb'd and tall,
Scorn was allow'd as part of his defect,
And he was answer'd softly by the King
And all his Table.   So Sir Lancelot holp   45
To raise the prince, who rising twice or thrice
Full sharply smote his knees, and smiled, and went :

But, ever after, the small violence done
Rankled in him and ruffled all his heart,
As the sharp wind that ruffles all day long   50
A little bitter pool about a stone
On the bare coast.

              But when Sir Lancelot told
This matter to the Queen, at first she laugh'd
Lightly, to think of Modred's dusty fall,
Then shudder'd, as the village wife who cries,   55
'I shudder, °some one steps across my grave;'
Then laugh'd again, but faintlier, for indeed
She half-foresaw that he, the subtle beast,
Would track her guilt until he found, and hers
Would be for evermore a name of scorn.   60
Henceforward rarely could she front in hall,
Or elsewhere, Modred's narrow foxy face,
Heart-hiding smile, and gray persistent eye.
Henceforward too, the °Powers that tend the soul,
To help it from the °death that cannot die,   65
And save it even in extremes, began
To vex and plague her.   Many a time for hours,
Beside the placid breathings of the King,
In the dead night, grim faces came and went
Before her, or a vague spiritual fear —   70
Like to some doubtful noise of creaking doors,
Heard by the watcher in a haunted house,

That keeps the °rust of murder on the walls —
Held her awake: or if she slept she dream'd
°An awful dream; for then she seem'd to stand   75
On some vast plain before a setting sun,
And from the sun there swiftly made at her
A ghastly something, and its shadow flew
Before it till it touch'd her, and she turn'd —
When lo! her own, that broadening from her feet, 80
And blackening, swallow'd all the land, and in it
Far cities burnt, and with a cry she woke.
And all this trouble did not pass but grew,
Till even the clear face of the guileless King,
And trustful courtesies of household life,   85
Became her bane; and at last she said,
'O Lancelot, get thee hence to thine own land,
For if thou tarry we shall meet again,
And if we meet again some evil chance
Will make the smouldering scandal break and blaze 90
Before the people and our lord the King.'
And Lancelot ever promised, but remain'd,
And still they met and met. Again she said,
'O Lancelot, if thou love me get thee hence.'
And then they were agreed upon a night —   95
When the good King should not be there — to meet
And part for ever. Vivien, lurking, heard.
She told Sir Modred. Passion-pale they met
And greeted. Hands in hands, and eye to eye,

Low on the border of her couch they sat   100
Stammering and staring.   It was their last hour,
A madness of farewells.   And Modred brought
His creatures to the basement of the tower
For testimony; and crying with full voice,
'Traitor, come out, ye are trapt at last,' aroused   105
Lancelot, who rushing outward lionlike
Leapt on him, and hurl'd him headlong, and he fell
Stunn'd, and his creatures took and bare him off,
And all was still.   Then she, 'The end is come,
And I am shamed for ever;' and he said: 110
'Mine be the shame; mine was the sin: but rise,
And fly to my strong castle over-seas:
There will I hide thee till my life shall end,
There hold thee with my life against the world.'
She answer'd: 'Lancelot, wilt thou hold me so?   115
Nay, friend, for we have taken our farewells.
Would God that thou couldst hide me from myself!
Mine is the shame, for I was wife, and thou
Unwedded; yet rise now, and let us fly,
For I will draw me into °sanctuary,   120
And bide my doom.'   °So Lancelot got her horse,
Set her thereon, and mounted on his own,
And then they rode to the divided way,
There kiss'd, and parted weeping: for he past,
Love-loyal to the least wish of the Queen,   125
Back to his land; but she to Almesbury

Fled all night long by glimmering waste and weald,
And heard the spirits of the waste and weald
Moan as she fled, or thought she heard them moan:
And in herself she moan'd 'Too late, too late!'   130
Till in the cold wind that foreruns the morn,
A blot in heaven, the raven, flying high,
Croak'd, and she thought, 'He spies a field of death;
For now the heathen of the Northern Sea,
Lured by the crimes and frailties of the court,   135
Begin to slay the folk and spoil the land.'

And when she came to Almesbury she spake
There to the nuns, and said, 'Mine enemies
Pursue me, but, O peaceful Sisterhood,
Receive and yield me sanctuary, nor ask   140
Her name to whom ye yield it till her time
To tell you;' and her beauty, grace, and power
Wrought as a charm upon them, and they spared
To ask it.

So the stately Queen abode
For many a week, unknown among the nuns,   145
Nor with them mix'd, nor told her name, nor sought,
Wrapt in her grief, for °housel or for shrift,
But communed only with the little maid,
Who pleased her with a babbling heedlessness
Which often lured her from herself; but now,   150

This night, a rumor wildly blown about
Came that Sir Modred had usurp'd the realm
And leagued him with the heathen, while the King
°Was waging war on Lancelot: then she thought,
'With what a hate the people and the King   155
Must hate me,' and bow'd down upon her hands
Silent, until the little maid, who brook'd
No silence, brake it, uttering ' Late ! so late !
What hour, I wonder now ? ' and when she drew
No answer, by and by began to hum   160
An air the nuns had taught her : ' Late, so late !'
Which when she heard, the Queen look'd up, and said,
'O maiden, if indeed ye list to sing,
Sing, and unbind my heart that I may weep.'
Whereat full willingly sang the little maid.   165

°' Late, late, so late ! and dark the night and chill !
Late, late, so late ! but we can enter still.
Too late, too late ! ye cannot enter now.

'No light had we : for that we do repent,
And learning this, the bridegroom will relent.   170
Too late, too late ! ye cannot enter now.

'No light : so late ! and dark and chill the night !
O, let us in, that we may find the light !
Too late, too late ! ye cannot enter now.

'Have we not heard the bridegroom is so sweet? 175
O, let us in, tho' late, to kiss his feet!
No, no, too late! ye cannot enter now.'

So sang the novice, while full passionately,
Her head upon her hands, remembering
Her thought when first she came, wept the sad Queen,
Then said the little novice prattling to her: 181

'O pray you, noble lady, weep no more;
But let my words — the words of one so small,
Who knowing nothing knows but to obey,
And if I do not there is penance given — 185
Comfort your sorrows; for they do not flow
From evil done: right sure am I of that,
Who see your tender grace and stateliness.
But weigh your sorrows with our lord the King's,
And weighing find them less; for gone is he 190
To wage grim war against Sir Lancelot there,
Round that strong castle where he holds the Queen;
And °Modred whom he left in charge of all,
The traitor — Ah, sweet lady, the King's grief
For his own self, and his own Queen, and realm, 195
Must needs be thrice as great as any of ours!
For me, I thank the saints, I am not great;
For if there ever come a grief to me
I cry my cry in silence, and have done:

None knows it, and my tears have brought me good. 200
But even were the griefs of little ones
As great as those of great ones, yet this grief
Is added to the griefs the great must bear,
That, howsoever much they may desire
Silence, they cannot weep behind a cloud;   205
As even here they talk at Almesbury
About the good King and his wicked Queen,
And were I such a King with such a Queen,
Well might I wish to veil her wickedness,
But were I such a King it could not be.'   210

Then to her own sad heart mutter'd the Queen,
'Will the child kill me with her innocent talk?'
But openly she answer'd, 'Must not I,
If this false traitor have displaced his lord,
Grieve with the common grief of all the realm?'   215

'Yea,' said the maid, 'this is all woman's grief,
That *she* is woman, whose disloyal life
Hath wrought confusion in the Table Round
Which good King Arthur founded, years ago,
With signs and miracles and wonders, there   220
At Camelot, ere the coming of the Queen.'

Then thought the Queen within herself again,
'Will the child kill me with her foolish prate?'
But openly she spake and said to her,

'O little maid, shut in by nunnery walls,   225
What canst thou know of Kings and Tables Round,
Or what of signs and wonders, but the signs
And simple miracles of thy nunnery?'

    To whom the little novice garrulously:
'Yea, but I know: the land was full of signs   230
And wonders ere the coming of the Queen.
So said my father, and himself was knight
Of the great Table — at the founding of it,
And rode thereto from Lyonnesse; and he said
That as he rode, an hour or maybe twain   235
After the sunset, down the coast, he heard
Strange music, and he paused, and turning — there,
All down the lonely coast of Lyonnesse,
Each with a beacon-star upon his head,
And with a wild sea-light about his feet,   240
He saw them — headland after headland flame
Far on into the rich heart of the west:
And in the light the white °mermaiden swam,
And strong man-breasted things stood from the sea,
And sent a deep sea-voice thro' all the land,   245
To which the °little elves of chasm and cleft
Made answer, sounding like a distant horn.
So said my father — yea, and furthermore,
Next morning, while he past the dim-lit woods,
Himself beheld three spirits mad with joy   250

Come dashing down on a tall wayside flower,
That shook beneath them as the thistle shakes
When three gray linnets wrangle for the seed:
And still at evenings on before his horse
The flickering fairy-circle wheel'd and broke   255
Flying, and link'd again, and wheel'd and broke
Flying, for all the land was full of life.
And when at last he came to Camelot,
A wreath of airy dancers hand-in-hand
Swung round the lighted lantern of the hall;   260
And in the hall itself was such a feast
As never man had dream'd; for every knight
Had whatsoever meat he long'd for served
By hands unseen; and even as he said
Down in the cellars merry bloated things   265
Shoulder'd the spigot, straddling on the butts
While the wine ran: so glad were spirits and men
°Before the coming of the sinful Queen.'

Then spake the Queen and somewhat bitterly,
'Were they so glad? ill prophets were they all,   270
Spirits and men: could none of them foresee,
Not even thy wise father with his signs
And wonders, what has fallen upon the realm?'

To whom the novice garrulously again:
'Yea, one, a bard; of whom my father said,   275

Full many a noble war-song had he sung,
Even in the presence of an enemy's fleet,
Between the steep cliff and the coming wave;
And many a mystic lay of life and death
Had chanted on the smoky mountain-tops, 280
When round him bent the spirits of the hills
With all their dewy hair blown back like flame.
So said my father — and °that night the bard
Sang Arthur's glorious wars, and sang the King
As wellnigh more than man, and rail'd at those 285
Who call'd him the false son of Gorloïs:
For there was no man knew from whence he
    came;
But after tempest, when the long wave broke
All down the thundering shores of °Bude and
    Bos,
There came a day as still as heaven, and then 290
They found a naked child upon the sands
Of dark Tintagil by the Cornish sea,
And that was Arthur; and they foster'd him
Till he by °miracle was approven King:
And that his grave should be a mystery 295
From all men, like his birth; and could he find
A woman in her womanhood as great
As he was in his manhood, then, he sang,
The twain together well might change the world.
But even in the middle of his song 300

U

He falter'd, and his hand fell from the harp,
And pale he turn'd and reel'd, and would have
    fallen,
But that they stay'd him up; nor would he tell
His vision; but what doubt that he foresaw
°This evil work of Lancelot and the Queen?'   305

      Then thought the Queen, 'Lo! they have set her on,
Our simple-seeming abbess and her nuns,
To play upon me,' and bow'd her head nor spake.
Whereat the novice crying, with clasp'd hands,
Shame on her own garrulity garrulously,   310
Said the good nuns would check her gadding
    tongue
Full often, 'and, sweet lady, if I seem
To vex an ear too sad to listen to me,
Unmannerly, with prattling and the tales
Which my good father told me, check me too   315
Nor let me shame my father's memory, one
Of noblest manners, tho' himself would say
Sir Lancelot had the noblest; and he died,
Kill'd in a tilt, come next, five summers back,
And left me; but of others who remain,   320
And of the two first-famed for courtesy —
And pray you check me if I ask amiss —
But pray you, which had noblest, while you moved
Among them, Lancelot or our lord the King?'

Then the pale Queen look'd up and answer'd her : 325
'Sir Lancelot, as became a noble knight,
Was gracious to all ladies, and the same
In open battle or the tilting-field
Forbore his own advantage, and the King
In open battle or the tilting-field   330
Forbore his own advantage, and these two
Were the most nobly-manner'd men of all;
For manners are not idle, but the fruit
Of loyal nature and of noble mind.'

'Yea,' said the maid, 'be manners such fair fruit?
Then Lancelot's needs must be a thousand-fold   336
Less noble, being, as all rumor runs,
The most disloyal friend in all the world.'

To which a mournful answer made the Queen :
'O, closed about by narrowing nunnery-walls,   340
What knowest thou of the world and all its lights
And shadows, all the wealth and all the woe ?
If ever Lancelot, that most noble knight,
Were for one hour less noble than himself,
Pray for him that he scape the °doom of fire,   345
And weep for her who drew him to his doom.'

'Yea,' said the little novice, 'I pray for both;
But I should all as soon believe that his,

Sir Lancelot's, were as noble as the King's,
As I could think, sweet lady, yours would be   350
Such as they are, were you the sinful Queen.'

    So she, like many another babbler, hurt
Whom she would soothe, and harm'd where she would
        heal;
For here a sudden flush of wrathful heat
Fired all the pale face of the Queen, who cried: 355
' Such as thou art be never maiden more
For ever! thou their tool, set on to plague
And play upon and harry me, petty spy
And traitress!'   When that storm of anger brake
From Guinevere, aghast the maiden rose,   360
White as her veil, and stood before the Queen
As tremulously as foam upon the beach
Stands in a wind, ready to break and fly,
And when the Queen had added, ' Get thee hence!'
Fled frighted.   Then that other left alone   365
Sigh'd, and began to gather heart again,
Saying in herself : ' The simple, °fearful child
Meant nothing, but my own too-fearful guilt,
Simpler than any child, betrays itself.
But help me, Heaven, for surely I °repent!   370
For what is true repentance but in thought—
Nor even inmost thought to think again
The sins that made the past so pleasant to us ?

And I have sworn never to see him more,
To see him more.'

                    And even in saying this,   375
Her memory from old habit of the mind
Went slipping back upon the golden days
In which she saw him first, when °Lancelot came,
Reputed the best knight and goodliest man,
Ambassador, to yield her to his lord   380
Arthur, and led her forth, and far ahead
Of his and her retinue moving, they,
Rapt in sweet talk or lively, all on love
And sport and tilts and pleasure, — for the time
Was may-time, and as yet no sin was dream'd —   385
Rode under groves that look'd a paradise
Of blossom, °over sheets of hyacinth
That seem'd the heavens upbreaking thro' the
    earth,
And on from hill to hill, and every day
Beheld at noon in some delicious dale   390
The silk pavilions of King Arthur raised
For brief repast or afternoon repose
By couriers gone before; and on again,
Till yet once more ere set of sun they saw
The Dragon of the great Pendragonship,   395
That crown'd the state pavilion of the King,
Blaze by the rushing brook or silent well.

But when the Queen immersed in such a trance,
And moving thro' the past unconsciously,
Came to that point where first she saw the King   400
Ride toward her from the city, sigh'd to find
Her journey done, glanced at him, thought him cold,
High, self-contain'd, and passionless, not like him,
'Not like my Lancelot' — °while she brooded thus
And grew half-guilty in her thoughts again,   40~
There rode an armed warrior to the doors.
A murmuring whisper thro' the nunnery ran,
Then on a sudden a cry, 'The King!'   She sat
Stiff-stricken, listening; but when armed feet
Thro' the long gallery from the outer doors   41~
Rang coming, prone from off her seat she fell,
And grovell'd with her face against the floor.
There with her milk-white arms and shadowy hair
She made her face a darkness from the King,
And in the darkness heard his armed feet   415
Pause by her; then came silence, then a voice,
Monotonous and hollow like a ghost's
Denouncing judgment, but, tho' changed, the King's:

'Liest thou here so low, the child of one
I honor'd, happy, °dead before thy shame?   420
°Well is it that no child is born of thee.
The children born of thee are sword and fire,
Red ruin, and the breaking up of laws.

The °craft of kindred and the godless hosts
Of heathen swarming o'er the Northern Sea; 425
Whom I, while yet Sir Lancelot, my right arm
The mightiest of my knights, abode with me,
Have everywhere about this land of Christ
In twelve great battles ruining overthrown.
And knowest thou now from whence I come — from
    him,
                                                    430
From waging bitter war with him; and he,
That did not shun to smite me in worse way,
Had yet that grace of courtesy in him left,
He spared to lift his hand against the King
Who made him knight: but many a knight was slain;
And many more and all his kith and kin 436
Clave to him, and abode in his own land.
And many more when Modred raised revolt,
Forgetful of their troth and fealty, clave
To Modred, and a remnant stays with me. 440
And of this remnant will I leave a part,
True men who love me still, for whom I live,
To guard thee in the wild hour coming on,
Lest but a hair of this low head be harm'd.
Fear not: thou shalt be guarded till my death. 445
Howbeit I know, if ancient prophecies
Have err'd not, that I march to meet my doom.
Thou hast not made my life so sweet to me,
That I the King should greatly care to live;

For thou hast spoilt the purpose of my life.   450
Bear with me for the last time while I show,
Even for thy sake, the sin which thou hast sinn'd.
For when the Roman left us, and their law
Relax'd its hold upon us, and the ways
Were fill'd with rapine, here and there a deed   455
Of prowess done redress'd a random wrong.
But I was first of all the kings who drew
The °knighthood-errant of this realm and all
The realms together under me, their Head,
In that fair Order of my Table Round,   460
A glorious company, the flower of men,
To serve as model for the mighty world,
And be the fair beginning of a time.
I made them lay their hands in mine and swear
To reverence the King, as if he were   465
Their conscience, and their conscience as their King,
To break the heathen and uphold the Christ,
To ride abroad redressing human wrongs,
To speak no slander, no, nor listen to it,
To honor his own word as if his God's,   470
To lead sweet lives in purest chastity,
To love one maiden only, cleave to her,
And worship her by years of noble deeds,
Until they won her; for indeed I knew
Of no more subtle master under heaven   475
Than is the maiden passion for a maid,

Not only to keep down the base in man,
But teach high thought, and amiable words
And courtliness, and the desire of fame,
And love of truth, and all that makes a man.   480
And all this throve before I wedded thee,
Believing, " Lo, mine helpmate, one to feel
My purpose and rejoicing in my joy ! "
Then came thy shameful sin with Lancelot ;
Then came the sin of Tristram and Isolt ;   485
Then others, following these my mightiest knights,
And drawing foul ensample from fair names,
Sinn'd also, till the loathsome opposite
Of all my heart had destined did obtain,
And all thro' thee ! so that this life of mine   490
I guard as God's high gift from scathe and wrong,
Not greatly care to lose ; but rather think
How sad it were for Arthur, should he live,
To sit once more within his lonely hall,
And miss the wonted number of my knights,   495
And miss to hear high talk of noble deeds
As in the golden days before thy sin.
For which of us who might be left could speak
Of the pure heart, nor °seem to glance at thee ?
And in thy bowers of Camelot or of Usk   500
Thy shadows still would glide from room to room,
And I should evermore be vext with thee
In hanging robe or vacant ornament,

Or ghostly footfall echoing on the stair.
For think not, tho' thou wouldst not love thy
      lord,
Thy lord has wholly lost his love for thee.   505
I am not made of so °slight elements.
Yet must I leave thee, woman, to thy shame.
°I hold that man the worst of public foes
Who either for his own or children's sake,   510
To save his blood from scandal, lets the wife
Whom he knows false abide and rule the house:
For being thro' his cowardice allow'd
Her station, taken everywhere for pure,
She like a new disease, unknown to men,   515
Creeps, no precaution used, among the crowd,
Makes wicked lightnings of her eyes, and saps
The fealty of our friends, and stirs the pulse
With devil's leaps, and poisons half the young.
Worst of the worst were that man he that reigns!   520
Better the King's waste hearth and aching heart
Than thou reseated in thy place of light,
The mockery of my people and their bane!'

    He paused, and in the pause she crept an inch
Nearer, and laid her hands about his feet.   525
Far off a solitary trumpet blew.
Then waiting by the doors the war-horse neigh'd
As at a friend's voice, and he spake again:

· Yet think not that I came to urge thy crimes;
I did not come to curse thee, Guinevere, 530
I, whose vast pity almost makes me die
To see thee, laying there thy golden head,
My pride in happier summers, at my feet.
The wrath which forced my thoughts on that fierce law,
The °doom of treason and the flaming death,— 535
When first I learnt thee hidden here,—is past.
The pang—which, while I weigh'd thy heart with °one
Too wholly true to dream untruth in thee,
Made my tears burn—is also past—in part.
And all is past, the sin is sinn'd, and I, 540
Lo, I forgive thee, as Eternal God
Forgives! do thou for thine own soul the rest.
But how to take last leave of all I loved?
O golden hair, with which I used to play
Not knowing! O imperial-moulded form, 545
And beauty such as never woman wore,
Until it came a kingdom's curse with thee—
I cannot touch thy lips, °they are not mine,
But Lancelot's; nay, they never were the King's.
I cannot take thy hand; that too is flesh, 550
And in the flesh thou hast sinn'd; and mine own flesh,
Here looking down on thine polluted, cries,
"I loathe thee:" yet not less, O Guinevere,
For I was ever virgin save for thee,
My love thro' flesh hath wrought into my life 555

So far that my doom is, I love thee still.
Let no man dream but that I love thee still.
Perchance, and so thou purify thy soul,
And so thou lean on our fair father Christ,
Hereafter in that world where all are pure   560
We two may meet before high God, and thou
Wilt spring to me, and claim me thine, and know
I am thine husband — not a small soul,
Nor Lancelot, nor another.   Leave me that,
I charge thee, my last hope.   Now must I hence.   565
Thro' the thick night I hear the trumpet blow:
They summon me their King to lead mine hosts
Far down to that great battle in the west,
Where I must strike against the man they call
My sister's son — no kin of mine, who leagues   570
With Lords of the White Horse, heathen, and knights,
Traitors — and strike him dead, and meet myself
Death, or I know not what mysterious doom.
And thou remaining here wilt learn the event;
But hither shall I never come again,   575
Never lie by thy side, see thee no more —
Farewell !'

        And while she grovell'd at his feet
She felt the King's breath wander o'er her neck,
And in the darkness o'er her fallen head
Perceived the waving of his hands that blest.   580

Then, listening till those armed steps were gone,
Rose the pale Queen, and in her anguish found
The casement : 'peradventure,' so she thought,
'If I might see his face, and not be seen,'
And lo, he sat on horseback at the door !   585
And near him the sad nuns with each a light
Stood, and he gave them charge about the Queen,
To guard and foster her for evermore.
And while he spake to these his helm was lower'd,
To which for crest the golden dragon clung   590
Of Britain ; so she did not see the face,
Which then was as an angel's, but she saw,
Wet with the mists and smitten by the lights,
The Dragon of the great Pendragonship
Blaze, making all the night a steam of fire.   595
And even then he turn'd ; and more and more
The moony vapor rolling round the King,
Who seem'd the phantom of a giant in it,
Enwound him fold by fold, and made him gray
And grayer, till himself became as mist   600
Before her, moving ghostlike to his doom.

Then she stretch'd out her arms and cried aloud,
'O Arthur !' there her voice brake suddenly,
Then — as a stream that spouting from a cliff
Fails in mid air, but gathering at the base   605
Re-makes itself, and flashes down the vale —
Went on in passionate utterance :

                                           'Gone — my lord!
Gone thro' my sin to slay and to be slain!
And he forgave me, and I could not speak.
Farewell? I should have answer'd his farewell.   610
His mercy choked me.   Gone, my lord the King,
My own true lord! how dare I call him mine?
The shadow of another cleaves to me,
And makes me one pollution: he, the King,
Call'd me polluted: shall I kill myself?   615
What help in that?   I cannot kill my sin,
If soul be soul; nor can I kill my shame;
No, nor by living can I live it down.
The days will grow to weeks, the weeks to months,
The months will add themselves and make the years, 620
The years will roll into the centuries,
And mine will ever be a name of scorn.
I must not dwell on that defeat of fame.
Let the world be; that is but of the world —
What else? what hope? I think there was a hope;
Except he mock'd me when he spake of hope,   626
His hope he call'd it; but he never mocks,
For mockery is the fume of little hearts.
And blessed be the King, who hath forgiven
My wickedness to him, and left me hope   630
That in mine own heart I can live down sin
And be his mate hereafter in the heavens
Before high God!   Ah great and gentle lord,

Who wast, as is the conscience of a saint
Among his warring senses, to thy knights — 635
To whom my false voluptuous pride, that took
Full easily all impressions from below,
Would not look up, or half-despised the height
To which I would not or I could not climb —
I thought I could not breathe in that fine air, 640
That pure severity of perfect light —
I yearn'd for warmth and color which I found
In Lancelot — now I see thee what thou art,
Thou art the highest and most human too,
Not Lancelot, nor another. Is there none 645
Will tell the King I love him tho' so late?
Now — ere he goes to the great battle? none:
Myself must tell him in that purer life,
But now it were too daring. Ah my God,
What might I not have made of thy fair world, 650
Had I but loved thy highest creature here?
It was my duty to have loved the highest;
It surely was my profit had I known;
It would have been my pleasure had I seen.
We needs must love the highest when we see it, 655
Nor Lancelot, nor another.'

Here her hand
Grasp'd made her vail her eyes: she look'd and saw
The novice, weeping, suppliant, and said to her,

' Yea, little maid, for am *I* not forgiven ?'
Then glancing up beheld the holy nuns   660
All round her, weeping ; and her heart was loosed
Within her, and she wept with these and said:

' Ye know me then, that wicked one, who broke
The vast design and purpose of the King.
O, shut me round with narrowing nunnery-walls,   665
Meek maidens, from the voices crying, " Shame ! "
I must not scorn myself ; he loves me still.
Let no one dream but that he loves me still.
So let me, if you do not shudder at me,
Nor shun to call me sister, dwell with you ;   670
Wear black and white, and be a nun like you,
Fast with your fasts, not feasting with your feasts ;
Grieve with your griefs, not grieving at your joys,
But not rejoicing ; mingle with your rites ;
Pray and be pray'd for ; lie before your shrines ;   675
Do each low office of your holy house ;
Walk your dim cloister and distribute °dole
To poor sick people, richer in His eyes
Who ransom'd us, and °haler too than I ;
And treat their loathsome hurts and heal mine
          own ;   680
And so wear out in alms-deed and in prayer
The sombre close of that voluptuous day
Which wrought the ruin of my lord the King.'

She said: they took her to themselves; and she
Still hoping, fearing 'is it yet too late?'   685
Dwelt with them, till in time their abbess died.
Then she, for her good deeds and her pure life,
And for the power of ministration in her,
And likewise for the high rank she had borne,
Was chosen abbess, there, an abbess, lived   690
For three brief years, and there, an abbess, past
To where beyond these voices there is peace.

THE PASSING OF ARTHUR

THAT story which the bold °Sir Bedivere,
First made and latest left of all the knights,
Told, when the man was no more than a voice
In the white <u>winter of his age</u>, to those
With whom he dwelt, new faces, other minds.   5

For on their march to °westward, Bedivere,
Who slowly paced among the slumbering host,
Heard in his tent the moanings of the King:

°'I found Him in the shining of the stars,
I mark'd Him in the flowering of His fields,   10
But in His ways with men I find Him not.
I waged His wars, and now I pass and <u>die.</u>
O me! for why is all around us here
As if some lesser god had made the world,
But had not force to shape it as he would,
Till the High God behold it from beyond,   15
And enter it, and make it beautiful?
Or else as if the world were wholly fair,
But that these eyes of men are dense and dim,
And have not power to see it as it is: 20

Perchance, because we see not to the close ; —
For I, being simple, thought to work His will,
And have but stricken with the sword in vain ;
And all whereon I lean'd in wife and friend
Is traitor to my peace, °and all my realm　　　25
Reels back into the beast, and is no more.
My God, thou hast forgotten me in my death :
Nay — God my Christ — I pass but shall not die.'

Then, ere that last weird battle in the west,
There came on Arthur sleeping, Gawain kill'd　　30
In Lancelot's war, the ghost of Gawain blown
Along a wandering wind, and past his ear
Went shrilling : 'Hollow, hollow all delight !
Hail, King ! to-morrow thou shalt pass away.
Farewell ! there is an isle of rest for thee.　　35
And I am blown along a wandering wind,
And hollow, hollow, hollow all delight !'
And fainter onward, like wild birds that change
Their season in the night and wail their way
From cloud to cloud, down the long wind the dream　40
Shrill'd ; but in going mingled with dim cries
Far in the moonlit haze among the hills,
As of some lonely city sack'd by night,
When all is lost, and wife and child with wail
Pass to new lords ; and Arthur woke and call'd :　　45
'Who spake ? A dream. O light upon the wind,

Thine, Gawain, was the voice — are these dim cries
Thine ? or doth all that haunts the waste and wild
Mourn, knowing it will go along with me ? '

This heard the bold Sir Bedivere and spake: 50
'O me, my King, let pass whatever will,
Elves, and the harmless glamour of the field ;
But in their stead thy name and glory cling
To all high places like a golden cloud
For ever : but as yet thou shalt not pass.   55
Light was Gawain in life, and light in death
Is Gawain, for the ghost is as the man ;
And care not thou for dreams from him, but rise —
I hear the steps of Modred in the west,
And with him many of thy people, and knights   60
Once thine, whom thou hast loved, but grosser grown
Than heathen, spitting at their vows and thee.
Right well in heart they know thee for the King.
Arise, go forth and conquer as of old.'

Then spake King Arthur to Sir Bedivere: 65
' Far other is this battle in the west
Whereto we move than when we strove in youth,
And brake the petty kings, and fought with Rome,
Or thrust the heathen from the Roman wall,
And shook him thro' the north.   Ill doom is mine   70
To war against my people and my knights.

The king who fights his people fights himself.
And they my knights, who loved me once, the stroke
That strikes them dead is as my death to me.
Yet let us hence, and find or feel a way   75
Thro' this blind haze which, ever since I saw
One lying in the dust at Almesbury,
°Hath folded in the passes of the world.'

   Then rose the King and moved his host by night,
And ever push'd Sir Modred, league by league,   80
Back to the sunset bound of Lyonnesse —
A land of old upheaven from the abyss
By fire, to sink into the abyss again;
Where fragments of forgotten peoples dwelt,
And the long mountains ended in a coast   85
Of ever-shifting sand, and far away
The phantom circle of a moaning sea.
There the pursuer could pursue no more,
And he that fled no further fly the King;
And there, that day when the great light of heaven 90
°Burn'd at his lowest in the rolling year,
On the waste sand by the waste sea they closed.
Nor ever yet had Arthur fought a fight
Like this last, dim, weird battle of the west.
A death-white mist slept over sand and sea,   95
Whereof the chill, to him who breathed it, drew
Down with his blood, till all his heart was cold

With formless fear; and even on Arthur fell
Confusion, since he saw not whom he fought.
For friend and foe were shadows in the mist,   100
And friend slew friend not knowing whom he slew;
And some had visions out of golden youth,
And some beheld the faces of old ghosts
Look in upon the battle; and in the mist
Was many a noble deed, many a base,   105
And chance and craft and strength in single fights,
And ever and anon with host to host
Shocks, and the splintering spear, the hard mail hewn,
Shield-breakings, and the clash of brands, the crash
Of battle-axes on shatter'd helms, and shrieks   110
After the Christ, of those who falling down
Look'd up for heaven, and only saw the mist;
And shouts of heathen and the traitor knights,
Oaths, insult, filth, and monstrous blasphemies,
Sweat, writhings, anguish, laboring of the lungs   115
In that close mist, and cryings for the light,
Moans of the dying, and °voices of the dead.

     Last, as by some one deathbed after wail
Of suffering, silence follows, or thro' death
Or death-like swoon, thus over all that shore,   120
Save for some whisper of the seething seas,
A dead hush fell; but when the dolorous day
Grew drearier toward twilight falling, came

A bitter wind, clear from the north, and blew
The mist aside, and with that wind the tide   125
Rose, and the pale King glanced across the field
Of battle: but no man was moving there;
Nor any cry of Christian heard thereon,
Nor yet of heathen; only the wan wave
Brake in among dead faces, to and fro   130
Swaying the helpless hands, and up and down
Tumbling the hollow helmets of the fallen,
And shiver'd brands that once had fought with Rome,
And rolling far along the gloomy shores
The voice of days of old and days to be.   135

Then spake King Arthur to Sir Bedivere,
And whiter than the mist that all day long
Had held the field of battle was the King:

'Hearest thou this great voice that shakes the world
And wastes the narrow realm whereon we move,   140
And beats upon the faces of the dead,
My dead, as tho' they had not died for me? —
O Bedivere, for on my heart hath fallen
Confusion, till I know not what I am,
Nor whence I am, nor whether I be king;   145
Behold, I seem but king among the dead.'

Then spake the bold Sir Bedivere: 'My King;
King everywhere! and so the dead have kings,

There also will I worship thee as king.
Yet still thy life is whole, and still I live   150
Who love thee; but who hates thee, he that brought
The heathen back among us, yonder stands,
Modred, unharm'd, the traitor of thine house.

    Then spake the King: 'My house has been my doom.
But call not thou this traitor of my house   155
Who hath but dwelt beneath one roof with me.
My house are rather they who swore my vows,
Yea, even while they brake them, own'd me king.
And well for thee, saying in my dark hour,
When all the °purport of my throne hath fail'd,   160
That quick or dead thou holdest me for king.
King am I, whatsoever be their cry;
And one last act of kinghood shalt thou see
Yet, ere I pass.'   And uttering this the King
Made at the man: then Modred smote his liege   165
Hard on that helm which many a heathen sword
Had beaten thin; while Arthur at one blow,
Striking the last stroke with Excalibur,
Slew him, and, all but slain himself, he fell.

    So all day long the noise of battle roll'd   170
Among the mountains by the winter sea;
Until King Arthur's Table, man by man,
Had fallen in Lyonnesse about their lord,

King Arthur.   Then, because his wound was deep,
The bold Sir Bedivere uplifted him,   175
And bore him to a chapel nigh the field,
A broken chancel with a broken cross,
That stood on a dark strait of barren land:
On one side lay the Ocean, and on one
Lay a °great water, and the moon was full.   180

Then spake King Arthur to Sir Bedivere:
'The sequel of to-day °unsolders all
The goodliest fellowship of famous knights
Whereof this world holds record.   Such a sleep
They sleep — the men I loved.   I think that we   185
Shall never more, at any future time,
Delight our souls with talk of knightly deeds,
Walking about the gardens and the halls
Of Camelot, as in the days that were.
I perish by this people which I made, —   190
Tho' Merlin sware that I should come again
To rule once more; but, let what will be be,
I am so deeply smitten thro' the helm
That without help I cannot last till morn.
Thou therefore take my brand Excalibur,   195
Which was my pride: for thou rememberest how
In those old days, one summer noon, an arm
Rose up from out the bosom of the lake,
Clothed in white samite, mystic, wonderful,

Holding the sword — and how I row'd across   200
And took it, and have worn it, like a king;
And, wheresoever I am sung or told
In aftertime, this also shall be known.
But now delay not: take Excalibur,
And °fling him far into the middle mere;   205
Watch what thou seest, and lightly bring me word.'

   To him replied the bold Sir Bedivere:
'It is not meet, Sir King, to leave thee thus,
Aidless, alone, and smitten thro' the helm —
A little thing may harm a wounded man;   210
Yet I thy <u>hest</u> will all perform at full,
Watch what I see, and lightly bring thee word.'

   So saying, from the ruin'd shrine he stept,
And in the moon athwart the place of tombs,
Where lay the mighty bones of ancient men,   215
Old knights, and over them the sea-wind sang
Shrill, chill, with flakes of foam.   He, stepping down
By zigzag paths and juts of pointed rock,
Came on the shining levels of the lake.

   There drew he forth the brand Excalibur,   220
And o'er him, drawing it, the winter moon,
Brightening the skirts of a long cloud, ran forth
And sparkled keen with frost against the hilt;

For all the haft twinkled with diamond sparks,
Myriads of topaz-lights, and jacinth-work   225
Of subtlest jewellery.   He gazed so long
That both his eyes were dazzled as he stood,
This way and that dividing the swift mind,
In act to throw: but at last it seem'd
Better to leave Excalibur conceal'd   230
There in the many-knotted °water-flags,
That whistled stiff and dry about the marge.
So strode he back slow to the wounded King.

Then spake King Arthur to Sir Bedivere:
'Hast thou perform'd my mission which I gave?   235
What is it thou hast seen? or what hast heard?'

And answer made the bold Sir Bedivere:
'I heard the ripple °washing in the reeds,
And the wild water °lapping on the crag.'

To whom replied King Arthur, faint and pale: 240
'Thou hast betray'd thy nature and thy name,
Not rendering true answer, as beseem'd
Thy fealty, nor like a noble knight;
For surer sign had follow'd, either hand,
Or voice, or else a motion of the mere.   245
This is a shameful thing for men to lie.
Yet now, I charge thee, quickly go again,

As thou art °lief and dear, and do the thing
I bade thee, watch, and lightly bring me word.'

   Then went Sir Bedivere the second time   250
Across the ridge, and paced beside the mere,
Counting the dewy pebbles, fixt in thought;
But when he saw the wonder of the hilt,
How curiously and strangely chased, he smote
His palms together, and he cried aloud: 255

   'And if indeed I cast the brand away,
Surely a precious thing, one worthy note,
Should thus be lost for ever from the earth,
Which might have pleased the eyes of many men.
What good should follow this, if this were done?   260
What harm, undone?   Deep harm to disobey,
Seeing obedience is the bond of rule.
Were it well to obey then, if a king demand
An act unprofitable, against himself?
The King is sick, and knows not what he does.   265
What record or what relic of my lord
Should be to aftertime, but empty breath
And rumors of a doubt?   But were this kept,
Stored in some treasure-house of mighty kings,
Some one might show it at a joust of arms,   270
Saying: "King Arthur's sword, Excalibur,
Wrought by the lonely Maiden of the Lake.

Nine years she wrought it, sitting in the deeps
Upon the hidden bases of the hills.''
So might some old man speak in the aftertime   275
To all the people, winning reverence.
But now much honor and much fame were lost.'

So spake he, °clouded with his own conceit,
And hid Excalibur the second time,
And so strode back slow to the wounded King.   280

Then spoke King Arthur, breathing heavily:
'What is it thou hast seen? or what hast heard?'

And answer made the bold Sir Bedivere:
'I heard the water lapping on the crag,
And the long ripple washing in the reeds.'   285

To whom replied King Arthur, much in wrath:
'Ah miserable, and unkind, untrue,
Unknightly, traitor-hearted!   Woe is me!
Authority forgets a dying king,
Laid °widow'd of the power in his eye   290
That bow'd the will.   I see thee what thou art,
For thou, the latest-left of all my knights,
In whom should meet the °offices of all,
Thou wouldst betray me for the precious hilt;
Either from lust of gold, or like a girl   295

Valuing the giddy pleasure of the eyes.
Yet, for a man may fail in duty twice,
And the third time may prosper, get thee hence:
But, if thou spare to fling Excalibur,
I will arise and slay thee with my hands.'   300

    Then quickly rose Sir Bedivere, and ran,
And, leaping down the ridges lightly, plunged
Among the bulrush beds, and clutch'd the sword,
And strongly wheel'd and threw it. The great
    brand
Made lightnings in the splendor of the moon,   305
And flashing round and round, and whirl'd in an
    arch,
Shot like a streamer of the °northern morn,
Seen where the moving isles of winter shock
By night, with noises of the Northern Sea.
So flash'd and fell the brand Excalibur;   310
But ere he dipt the surface, rose an arm
Clothed in white samite, mystic, wonderful,
And caught him by the hilt, and brandish'd him
Three times, and drew him under in the mere.
And lightly went the other to the King.   315

    Then spoke King Arthur, drawing thicker breath:
'Now see I by thine eyes that this is done.
Speak out: what is it thou hast heard, or seen?'

And answer made the bold Sir Bedivere:
'Sir King, I closed mine eyelids, lest the gems   320
Should blind my purpose, for I never saw,
Nor shall see, here or elsewhere, till I die,
Nor tho' I live three lives of mortal men,
So great a °miracle as yonder hilt.
Then with both hands I flung him, wheeling him;   325
But when I look'd again, behold an arm,
Clothed in white samite, mystic, wonderful,
That caught him by the hilt, and brandish'd him
Three times, and drew him under in the mere.'

And answer made King Arthur, breathing hard: 330
'My end draws nigh; 'tis time that I were gone.
Make broad thy shoulders to receive my weight,
And bear me to the margin; yet I fear
My wound hath taken cold, and I shall die.'

So saying, from the pavement he half rose,   335
Slowly, with pain, reclining on his arm,
And looking wistfully with wide blue eyes
As in a picture.   Him Sir Bedivere
Remorsefully regarded thro' his tears,
And would have spoken, but he found not words;   340
Then took with care, and kneeling on one knee,
O'er both his shoulders drew the languid hands,
And rising bore him thro' the place of tombs.

But, as he walk'd, King Arthur panted hard,
Like one that feels a °nightmare on his bed   345
When all the house is mute.   So sigh'd the King,
Muttering and murmuring at his ear, 'Quick, quick!
I fear it is too late, and I shall die.'
But the other swiftly strode from ridge to ridge,
°Clothed with his breath, and looking, as he walk'd,   350
Larger than human on the frozen hills.
He heard the deep behind him, and a cry
Before.   His own thought drove him like a goad.
°Dry clash'd his harness in the icy caves
And barren chasms, and all to left and right   355
The bare black cliff clang'd round him, as he based
His feet on juts of slippery crag that rang
Sharp-smitten with the dint of armed heels —
And on a sudden, lo, the level lake,
And the long glories of the winter moon!   360

Then saw they how there hove a dusky barge,
Dark as a funeral scarf from stem to stern,
Beneath them; and descending they were ware
That all the decks were dense with stately forms,
Black-stoled, black-hooded, like a dream — by these   365
Three queens with crowns of gold: and from them rose
°A cry that shiver'd to the tingling stars,
And, as it were one voice, an agony
Of lamentation, like a wind that shrills

All night in a waste land, where no one comes,   370
Or hath come, since the making of the world.

   Then murmur'd Arthur, 'Place me in the barge.'
So to the barge they came. There those three queens
Put forth their hands, and took the King, and wept.
But she that rose the tallest of them all   375
And fairest laid his head upon her lap,
And loosed the shatter'd casque, and chafed his
    hands,
And call'd him by his name, complaining loud,
And dropping bitter tears against a brow
Striped with dark blood: for all his face was white 380
And colorless, and like the wither'd moon
Smote by the fresh beam of the springing east;
And all his °greaves and cuisses dash'd with drops
Of onset; and the light and lustrous curls —
That made his forehead like a rising sun   385
High from the dais-throne — were parch'd with
    dust,
Or, clotted into points and hanging loose,
Mixt with the knightly growth that fringed his lips.
So like a shatter'd column lay the King;
Not like that Arthur who, with lance in rest,   390
From spur to plume a star of tournament,
Shot thro' the lists at Camelot, and charged
Before the eyes of ladies and of kings.

Then loudly cried the bold Sir Bedivere:
'Ah! my Lord Arthur, whither shall I go?   395
Where shall I hide my forehead and my eyes?
For now I see the true old times are dead,
When every morning brought a °noble chance,
And every chance brought out a noble knight.
Such times have been not since the light that led   400
The °holy Elders with the gift of myrrh.
But now the whole Round Table is dissolved
Which was an °image of the mighty world,
And I, the last, go forth companionless,
And the days darken round me, and the years,   405
Among new men, strange faces, other minds.'

And slowly answer'd Arthur from the barge:
'The old order changeth, yielding place to new,
And God fulfils himself in many ways,
°Lest one good custom should corrupt the world.   410
Comfort thyself: what comfort is in me?
I have lived my life, and that which I have done
May He within himself make pure! but thou,
If thou shouldst never see my face again,   414
Pray for my soul.   More things are wrought by prayer
Than this world dreams of.   Wherefore, let thy voice
Rise like a fountain for me night and day.
For what are men better than sheep or goats
That nourish a blind life within the brain,

If, knowing God, they lift not hands of prayer   420
Both for themselves and those who call them friend?
For so the whole round earth is every way
Bound by gold chains about the feet of God.
But now farewell.   I am going a long way
With °these thou seest — if indeed I go —   425
For all my mind is clouded with a doubt —
To the island-valley of °Avilion;
Where falls not hail, or rain, or any snow,
Nor ever wind blows loudly; but it lies
Deep-meadow'd, happy, fair with °orchard lawns   430
And bowery hollows crown'd with summer sea,
Where I will heal me of my grievous wound.'

So said he, and the barge with oar and sail
Moved from the brink, like some full-breasted swan
That, °fluting a wild carol ere her death,   435
Ruffles her pure cold plume, and takes the flood
With swarthy webs.   Long stood Sir Bedivere
Revolving many memories, till the hull
Look'd one black dot against the verge of dawn,
And on the mere the wailing died away.   440

But when that moan had past for evermore,
The stillness of the dead world's winter dawn
Amazed him, and he groan'd, ° ' The King is gone.'
And therewithal came on him the weird rhyme,
' From the great deep to the great deep he goes.'   445

Whereat he slowly turn'd and slowly clomb
The last hard footstep of that iron crag,
Thence mark'd the black hull moving yet, and cried:
' He passes to be king among the dead,
And after healing of his grievous wound   450
He comes again; but — if he come no more —
O me, be yon dark queens in yon black boat,
Who shriek'd and wail'd, the three whereat we gazed
On that high day, when, clothed with living light,
They stood before his throne in silence, friends   455
Of Arthur, who should help him at his need?'

Then from the dawn it seem'd there came, but faint
As from beyond the limit of the world,
Like the last echo born of a great cry,
Sounds, as if some fair city were one voice   460
Around a king returning from his wars.

Thereat once more he moved about, and clomb
Even to the highest he could climb, and saw,
Straining his eyes beneath an arch of hand,
Or thought he saw, the speck that bare the King,   465
Down that long water opening on the deep
Somewhere far off, pass on and on, and go
From less to less and vanish into light.
And the new sun rose bringing the new year.

NOTES

THE COMING OF ARTHUR

1. Leodogran, the King of Cameliard. See Malory's *Morte Darthur*, Book 1, chapter xvi. Leodogran was one of the petty kings referred to in line 5. **Cameliard** is apparently, according to Wright, the district called Carmelide in the English metrical romance of Merlin. Its location is uncertain.

8. heathen host. Littledale, in his essays on *Idylls of the King*, says, " In the opening lines Tennyson describes very closely the state of affairs which existed in Britain at the time of the landing of Hengist and Horsa, — that great event with which English history begins."

13. first Aurelius. He was a descendant of the last Roman general who claimed the purple as Emperor in Britain. See Green's *Making of England*, pp. 28, 37. He usurped the kingdom from Vortigern and gained some advantages from Hengist, but was overthrown in a final battle. After his death by poison, his brother, Uther, ruled for a time and defeated the Saxons in a number of battles, but at last was poisoned also. Geoffrey of Monmouth says : " For there was near the court a spring of very clear water, which the king used to drink of. This the detestable conspirators made use of to destroy him, by so poisoning the water which sprang up that the next time the king drank of it he was seized with sudden death, as were also a hundred other persons after him."

17. puissance. The form of this idyll is more archaic than that of any other except the last. This may be observed often in the choice of words. Puissance is a word which was common both in the Old French and Middle English. It came into both languages from the Latin.

17. Table Round. Wace, a French Chronicler of the twelfth century, first mentions the Round Table. It was instituted, he says, in the years of peace which intervened between Arthur's conquests and his successful campaign against Lucius of Rome. "All the barons and knights of the civilized world, together with their ladies, flocked to Arthur's court. For the noble barons, each of whom held himself better than any other, and was unwilling to take a place lower than any other, Arthur made the Round Table, of which the Bretons tell so many stories. At this table his vassals sat in equal dignity. They sat in perfect equality, and they were served in perfect equality. Not one of them could boast of sitting higher than his peers. All were seated with the same honor; no one was distinguished."

26. the wolf would steal, etc. Littledale says, " The description of the wolves stealing and suckling human babes is not only based on myths like the Roman legend, but on the well-authenticated fact in natural history that these animals do sometimes suckle human children that they have carried off. There is, however, no known case of children thus reared arriving at maturity. Quite possibly Tennyson is referring to the lycanthropi of the

Greeks and Romans, the loups-garous of the French, and the were-wolves of the Teutons and English.''

34. Groan'd for the Roman legions. Tennyson here referred to the *Groans of the Britons* of Gildas, who says that the Britons wrote to the Roman Senate after the Roman legions had been withdrawn, that '' the barbarians drive us into the sea ; the sea throws us back on the barbarians ; thus two modes of death await us, we are either slain or drowned.'' He further says that, ''The Roman legion had no sooner returned home in joy and triumph, than their former foes, like hungry and ravening wolves, rushing with greedy jaws upon the fold, which is left without a shepherd, attacked the Britons.''

36. Urien. In the first edition, Tennyson followed Malory and called this king Rience, but later changed it. He was the husband of Arthur's sister, Morgan le Fay, and was a king of North Wales. He it was who wanted Arthur's beard to complete a mantle which he was making from the beards of the kings whom he had slain. Malory, I, xxiv.

39. amazed, in the sense of confused or perplexed.

47. Guinevere. The character of Guinevere appears in many mediæval romances in the French, English and Celtic languages, and is everywhere characterized by beauty, strength and queenly dignity, as well as by the guilty love which has linked her name with that of Lancelot. Tennyson has followed, in the main, the conception of Malory, but has added a charm of gracious womanliness and the benediction of a final repentance and forgiveness from the kingly husband, whom she had so deeply wronged. Two noteworthy modern poems, besides the *Idylls*, dealing with the character of Guinevere are, *The Defence of Guinevere* by William Morris, and *The Marriage of Guinevere*, by Richard Hovey.

50. The golden symbol. The dragon was the symbol of leadership, hence was used as the emblem of royal power and authority. In Pendragon, the first syllable was the Welsh word, *pen*, meaning head. Pendragon is attached to the names of both Uther and Arthur in these poems to denote supreme and dread majesty. Cf. *Lancelot and Elaine*, lines 430–440, and 526.

58. drave the heathen. Notice the archaic form of the verb. The invading hordes from northern Europe had not yet adopted Christianity, hence are called heathen or pagans. Observe the thoroughness with which Arthur performed his task.

72–73. Gorloïs . . . Anton. These allusions are explained in the passage beginning with line 177. Malory calls Gorloïs the Duke of Tintagil in Cornwall. Anton is the Sir Ector of Malory.

75. Travail. Observe the intensity of feeling indicated by the figurative language of this line, and by the strong expressions in the rest of the passage.

92–93. dark land . . . dead world. In what sense does Arthur use these expressions?

94. he speaks, etc. The poet often speaks of himself, and sometimes of Malory, as "he who tells the tale." This mode of referring to the narrator is common in old French romances.

99. the morning star. Arthur's new-born love for Guinevere, coupled with his eager hope of winning her, quickens all his faculties, mental and physical, alike.

103. long-lanced battle. Battle may mean not only the actual conflict of armed forces, but the forces themselves. Robertson says, " The cavalry, by way of distinction, was called the battle, and on it alone depended the fate of every action." In Shakespeare's *Henry V* occurs this passage : —

> " Fire answers fire, and through their paly flames
> Each battle sees the other's umber'd face."

Malory, I, xv, says of this conflict : " All these knights rode on afore with spears on their thighs, and spurred their horses mightily as the horses might run. And the eleven kings with part of their knights rushed with their horses as fast as they might with their spears, and there they did on both parties marvellous deeds of arms."

110. kings. This list of kings is taken from Malory's account of this battle, I, x–xv.

116. As dreadful as, etc. The full force of this simile should be observed.

120. Ho! they yield. In the original story, it is Merlin, not Arthur, who stops the battle. Riding up on a great black horse, he said to Arthur : " Thou hast never done. Hast thou not done enough ? Of threescore thousand this day hast thou left on live fifteen thousand, and it is time to say Ho ! . . . And therefore withdraw you unto your lodgings, and rest you as soon as you may, and reward your good knights with gold and silver, for they have well deserved it ; there may no riches be too dear for them, for so many men as ye have there were never men did more of prowess than they have done to-day, for ye have matched this day with the best fighters of the world." **Ho, a word**

used to command a stop in some action, was probably a shortened form of hold, and is written *whoa* when it is used to stop a horse.

121. painted battle. Observe the strength and vividness of this simile. A similar expression may be found in Coleridge's *Ancient Mariner*.

124. laughed upon his warrior. Picture carefully the setting of this remarkable and dramatic scene between Arthur and Lancelot, and decide what high qualities of character are brought out in each.

127. liege. The word means, — free from obligation to service except as within the relations of lord and vassal. A liege lord is a sovereign lord or feudal superior.

129. I know thee for my king. It was this battle that finally settled Arthur's right to the throne, and with it began the splendid career of conquest and statesmanship which Tennyson has pictured so beautifully in these poems. It is true that there is little historic foundation upon which to rest the story of Arthur's brilliant career. But it has become so crystallized in romance and poesy that his name may be written in the list of the world's great mythical heroes.

132. Man's word is God in man. Littledale has paraphrased this pregnant sentence in this way, " A man's promise is a divine thing, therefore it must be regarded as especially sacred."

133. I trust thee to the death. How well Arthur kept this compact, and how ill Lancelot, should be observed throughout the tales that follow.

134. foughten field. In the first edition of this poem this line read,

"Then Arthur from the field of battle sent."

What improvement, if any, is found in the present reading?
Foughten field is found several times in Tennyson.

136. to King Leodogran. These three knights were among the first to attach themselves to Arthur, and they remained faithful to him to the end, though they appear only as minor characters in the Idylls. Bedivere it is who, alone of all the Round Table, is left to assist Arthur after he has received his mortal wound. The passage, which follows, relating to Arthur's suit for the hand of Guinevere is practically all Tennyson's conception. In Malory, Arthur sends Merlin to Leodogran, who willingly gives Guinevere and sends the great Round Table as a present.

150. Merlin is the central figure in a cycle of mediæval romances and lays. His name is first given as Ambrosius Merlinus, but is afterwards shortened to Merlin. He was noted as a worker of magic and became closely connected with the Arthurian legends as the protector of Arthur, and later as his adviser, friend, and powerful helper. His magic is never at fault and never conquered until he meets Vivien, as portrayed in the sad and tragic Idyll of that name.

155. and wrote. Malory, I, xv, says: "And there he told how Arthur and the two kings had sped at the great battle, and how it ended, and told the names of every king and knight of worship that was there. And so Bleise wrote the battle, word by word, as Merlin told him, how it began, and by whom, and in likewise how it was ended, and who had the worse. All the battles that were done in Arthur's days, Merlin did his master Bleise do write."

160. O friend. Leodogran tells his chamberlain that if

Arthur had helped him in battle in the same way he had helped him with his answers to his questions, that is not at all, his kingdom would by this time have been destroyed.

166. the cuckoo. It is a fact in natural history that the cuckoo is wont to lay its eggs in the nests of other birds, who thus are compelled to assume the care of the young intruders. Sometimes the indignation of the foster-parents is shown by chasing the intruder out of the nest and away from the neighborhood.

186. Tintagil castle. This castle was located on a picturesque promontory off the Cornish coast. It figures not only in the romance of Gorloïs and Igraine, but also in that of Tristram and Iseult. See Malory, VIII, xiii. For a good description of this interesting place, see Maynadier's *The Arthur of the English Poets*, pp. 184–185.

187. Ygerne. In Malory the name appears as Igraine.

189. Bellicent, called elsewhere Morgan le Fay, was the daughter of Gorloïs and Igraine, and hence was the half-sister of Arthur.

194. bright dishonor, that is, the guilty splendor of King Uther's love.

197. Then Uther. In this connection read also the account in *Guinevere*, ll. 282–299.

207. wrack. The common form of wreck in various Elizabethan writers.

228. Brought Arthur forth. See Malory, I, iii–iv, for the story of the miraculous sword by which Arthur proved his right to the succession. Littledale suggests that Tennyson constantly eliminates supernatural and magical incidents from the narrative in order to diminish as much as possible the incongruity arising from the commingling of grotesque medieval sorcery with solemn Christian mysteries.

244. The kingdom of Orkney was in the north of Scotland.

247. A doubtful throne. Leodogran likens a doubtful throne to an iceberg, which has drifted into summer seas and which will soon topple over. These six lines stand in the place of four in the first edition.

> "A doubtful throne is ice on summer seas —
> Ye come from Arthur's court; think ye this king —
> So few his knights, however brave they be —
> Hath body enow to beat his foemen down?"

Compare the present passage with the original and decide whether it has been improved by the expansion.

266. But when he spake. Many regard the *Idylls* as a great allegory which pictures the struggles of the soul, in its higher life, with the evils and temptations of the flesh. If this view is accepted, the beautiful description of the coronation scene may be considered as symbolical of the soul starting out upon its earthly career with the intensity of its consecration, its youthful vigor and its divine purity indicated by the heraldic colors, flame-color, green and blue. Through the stained glass windows above his head the benediction of " the crucified " falls upon him. Near by with helpful sympathy, stand the "three fair queens," — the Christian Graces, Faith, Hope and Love, who shall finally receive him, when the course of his life is run, in the funeral barge and conduct him to the fair shore of " Avilion." The compelling force of such a soul is shown by the " momentary likeness of the king," which " flashes from eye to eye through all their order."

279–282. And there I saw. In this symbolism, **Merlin** typifies the power of intellect, whose vast, unmeasured stores of wisdom, accumulated through the ages, lend themselves as loyal vassals to his service. The **Lady of the Lake** seems to symbolize religion. **Who knows a subtler magic** than that of Merlin, because the spiritual powers are higher and more powerful than the intellectual. She is clothed in garments of crystalline purity and gives to Arthur the sword of the spirit with which the conquests of righteousness are to be made. The absolute tranquillity of the divine life is shown in the calm depths of her dwelling place, and she walks upon the waters undisturbed by the storms that sweep the seas around her. This description of the Lady of the Lake should be compared with that in *Gareth and Lynette*, beginning with line 210.

284. white samite. Samite comes from a Greek word meaning six-threaded, and was applied originally to a heavy silk material, each thread of which was supposed to be made of six fibers twisted together. Later it came to mean a heavy silk material which had a satin-like gloss.

285. huge, cross-hilted sword. In Malory, I, xxiii, is given this account of the gift of the sword, Excalibur, to Arthur. " And, as they rode, Arthur said, I have no sword. No force, said Merlin, hereby is a sword that shall be yours and I may. So they rode until they came to a lake, the which was a fair water and broad, and the midst of the lake Arthur was aware of an arm clothed in white samite, that held a fair sword in hand. Lo, said Merlin, yonder is the sword I spoke of. What damsel is that, said Arthur? That is the Lady of the Lake, said Merlin. . . . Anon withal came the damsel unto Arthur and saluted him and he her again. Damsel, said Arthur, what sword is that, that yonder the arm holdeth above the water? I would it were mine for I have no sword." After which the damsel tells him he may have the sword if he will promise her a gift whenever she shall ask for it. He promises and goes out in a shallop, and takes it.

290. A voice as of the waters. See line 380. Cf. " I heard a voice from heaven as the voice of many waters," Rev. xiv, 2.

294. Excalibur. The name is said to mean cut steel. For a fuller description of this wonderful sword, see *The Passing of Arthur*.

298. elfin Urim. Urim is a Hebrew plural meaning lights or flames, and were supposed to be jewels which were worn by the high priest. **Elfin**, gifted with fairy charms.

299. blade so bright. Malory has this sentence, " Then he drew his sword, Excalibur, but it was so bright in his enemies' eyes, that it gave light like thirty torches."

312. swallows and **swifts** are groups of the same family. In some parts of England the swift is known as the black swallow.

329. this king is fair. Bellicent questions the relationship because she and all the family of Gorloïs were dark, as was Uther, but Arthur was light, with golden hair. In the *Last Tournament*, lines 661–663 we read,

> "His hair, a sun that ray'd from off a brow
>   Like hill-snow high in heaven, the steel-blue eyes,
>   The golden beard that clothed his lips with light."

362. Fairy changeling. According to popular superstition, the elves which fairies sometimes left in the place of beautiful children, whom they had stolen, could be distinguished by their shrunken and shrivelled little forms.

379. a ninth one. There is a Welsh tradition that the waves are the sheep of a mermaid, and that every ninth one, being larger than the rest, is a ram.

401. riddling triplets. The old bardic rhymes were often in triplets. They were riddling because their meaning was hidden. The meaning may be something as follows : — Shadow, sunshine, and the rainbow of hope. Arthur will know more when he grows older, and the wits of old men, like Bleys, may wander so that they know not what they speak. Truth may mean one thing to one man and another thing to another, but, however it may be clothed, it will prevail. Life is a mystery and no one knows why the blossom blows. Life begins in the darkness of mystery and into the mystery of darkness it goes.

410. From the great deep to the great deep he goes. Cf. *Passing of Arthur*, line 445. There is a belief still current among the peasants of Brittany that Arthur will awaken out of his sleep and come again. Malory, XXII, vii, says : " Yet some men say in many parts of England that Arthur is not dead, but had by the will of our Lord Jesu in another place. And men say that he shall come again, and he shall win the holy cross. I will not say it shall be so, but rather I will say, here in this world he changed his life. But many say that there is written upon his tomb this verse :

" 'Hic jacet Arthurus Rex quondam Rexque futurus.' "

443. And Leodogran awoke. How is this vision interpreted, and in what way did it influence Leodogran ?

447. Sir Lancelot. Malory does not introduce Lancelot until the sixth book, while Tennyson brings him in at the beginning of the action of the poem. This is probably to intensify the strength of the ties that bound them, and to make Lancelot's duplicity all the more heinous. Yet it would seem as if Arthur placed temptation in the way of both, when he sent Lancelot to bring Guinevere to the Court, through a long journey and at the most beautiful season of the year. Perhaps it was necessary to do this in order to afford some excuse for two, whose characters were so noble and blameless by nature, to break their binding vows and become faithless to him to whom they owed so much of love and service.

452. Dubric was a high church dignitary, being the primate of Britain and the Papal legate, as well as Archbishop of Caerleon-upon-Usk.

454. altar-shrines. Malory states that the king was wedded at Camelot, in the church of St. Stephen's, with great solemnity.

456. The fair beginners, etc. To whom does this refer, and in what sense is it used?

476. Great lords from Rome. Rome had once held possession of Britain and had now sent to collect the customary tribute. This incident of the poem has no historic foundation.

481. Blow trumpet. Stopford Brooke says, with reference to this song: "It embodies the thought of the poem. grips the whole meaning of it together. And its sound is the sound of martial triumph, of victorious weapons in battle, and of knights in arms. We hear in the carefully varied chorus, in the very rattle and shattering of vowels

z

in the words, the beating of axe on helm and shaft on shield. Rugged, clanging, clashing lines, — it is a splendid effort of art."

511. Roman wall. The Romans built a wall across Britain, not far from the present boundary line between England and Scotland, to protect the southern portion from the barbarians who occupied the country to the north. Even this wall they were unable to protect and defend in the later years of their occupation.

517. twelve great battles. According to Nennius, a chronicler of the ninth century, Arthur overcame the barbarians in twelve great battles, of which the names are given. In the battle of Castellum Guinnion, Arthur carried on his shoulders the image of the Holy Virgin Mary, and the pagans were put to flight that day, and there was a great slaughter of them. At the battle of Mount Badon there fell by Arthur's own hand in one day nine hundred and sixty of the heathen.

GARETH AND LYNETTE

This Idyll was published in 1872, and a note says, "With this poem the author concludes the *Idylls of the King. Gareth* follows the *Coming of Arthur.*"

The first four hundred and thirty lines are original with Tennyson, unless a slight suggestion was found in the story of Peredur in the Mabinogion. After that the story follows the account of Malory in the main. This account may be found in the sixth book of *Le Morte Darthur*, and should be read in connection with the Idyll.

The scene of the poem is conceived as being laid in the

springtime, and it is characterized by the freshness and vigor of youth, and the sweetness and beauty of the joyous springtide. Everywhere is the activity of a new and vigorous life. Arthur is seen on the judgment seat tempering his justice with a mercy which was a stranger to the age. His state is in the process of building, and all his Round Table, rejoicing in the present fulfilment, are looking forward with a larger hope to a greater and more glorious future. Arthur appears here as a great constructive statesman rather than as a warrior as in the preceding Idyll. He is building his state on the broad foundations of justice and mercy, and is adopting as his watchwords — help for the helpless and rescue for the oppressed.

The shadow of evil has not yet fallen upon the court. The men are brave with the grace of self-denial, and the women are beautiful with the graciousness of virtue and purity.

Gareth is a high-born youth, who is eager for high achievement and confident in his own power to attain the greatest honor. Regardless of all discouragements, he presses cheerfully on until he accomplishes his quest and wins the highest meed of praise. It may be said that, in Gareth, Tennyson has given us his most perfect hero, not even excepting Galahad, for Galahad has no touch of earth, while Gareth is altogether of earth and of the highest type of true manhood.

The poem itself, in its wealth of imagery, its beauty of expression, and its high ideals, is altogether the most delightful of the *Idylls*. It is worthy of study as the joyous beginning of a tale which is destined to end in the gloom of disappointment and death.

2. Gareth. The sons of Lot and Bellicent were Gawain, Agravaine, Gaheris, Modred and Gareth, but only Gawain, Modred, and Gareth figure in the Idylls. Malory says that Gareth " was the goodliest young man and the fairest that ever they all saw, and he was large and long and broad in the shoulders and well-visaged, and the fairest and largest-handed that ever man saw."

2. showerful. Is this a regular word, or one coined for the occasion? Comment on its appropriateness.

3. spate. The river in flood. The word is of Celtic origin. Notice the alliteration in these lines. In what way does it add to the effectiveness of the passage?

4. Lost footing. What figure?

18. yield. In the sense of reward, repay. Cf. *Hamlet*, IV, 5, 41 ; *Antony and Cleopatra*, IV, 2, 33.

20. dis-caged. Tennyson often uses these compounds with *dis-*, *e.g.* dis-linked, dis-helmed, dis-princed, dis-edged.

21. ever-highering. Higher is very rarely used as a verb. It would almost seem as if Gareth, in his youthful enthusiasm, had invented the word.

40. the goose and the golden eggs. See Tennyson's humorous poem, entitled *The Goose*.

46. Book of Hours. An illuminated prayer-book.

47. haunting. The verb haunt is sometimes used intransitively in the sense of visiting often.

> "I have charged thee not to haunt about my doors."
> — *Othello*, I, 1.

51. leash. A line used to hold hounds or coursing dogs. Among sportsmen it also means a brace and a half, that is, three.

56. clomb is an old form for climbed, but is now obsolete except in poetry.

73. Lot. According to Malory, Lot, who was a brave and powerful king, was slain by King Pellinore, who was later slain by Gawain in revenge for his father's death.

84. red berries charm the bird. A proverbial saying, meaning that they allure the bird in the same way that jousts and wars allure Gareth.

85. jousts. A military contest or spectacle in which two adversaries attacked each other, usually with blunted lances, though sometimes with sharp weapons as in war.

87. often. Here used as an adjective.

90. burns. From an old Anglo-Saxon word, meaning a brook. It is used almost exclusively in Scotland and North England.

93. comfortable. Notice the active sense in which the adjective is used. So in *All's Well*, I, 1 : " Be comfortable to my mother."

104. But. Only.

105. good lack. An exclamation implying wonder or surprise. It seems to have been a variation of good Lord.

114. Shame. This allegory of Fame and Shame may be compared with Goldsmith's allegory of Guilt and Shame in *The Vicar of Wakefield*, Chap. XV.

122. frequent. The adjective and the verb have the same form, but are accented differently. Does the scansion of this line indicate which this word is? Its special use here should be observed.

130. Not an hour, etc. Gareth says, " I will not stay an hour if ye will but yield me permission to go." Is this merely boyish eagerness and petulance, or is it the impatience of a manly spirit fretting to begin its life's work?

133. Not proven? Gareth questions his mother's statement that Arthur has not been proven king, and asks if he who has destroyed the last remnants of the Roman power and crushed the power of the pagans, who sought to overrun the land, has not given sufficient proof of his right to the throne.

139. one. Used in the sense of the same, hence unchanged.

140. She answered. She quotes his words, " Will ye walk through fire? Then will I give you something that will test your determination."

147. quick . . . quick. Notice the play upon words.

150. Serve. She thinks that the mere prospect of performing menial tasks for the wage of bed and board alone will be so repugnant to the proud spirit of the prince that he will prefer to stay at home rather than go to the Court of the king under such conditions. But she fails to appreciate his dauntless spirit.

151. kitchen-knaves. Knave, like the German *knabe*, meant originally only a boy, or a servant. Here it is used in its earlier sense and not in its later meaning of a dishonest, rascally fellow.

152. bar. Originally a bar was a barrier or something which was an obstacle to progress. Here it is the counter over which refreshments are served in an inn.

154. a twelvemonth and a day. Not an unusual expression for a year. The extra day was added to make sure of a full measure.

157. villain kitchen-vassalage. Villain is from the

Latin *villa*, meaning a village, hence a villager or low-born person. It was used in feudalism to indicate the lowest class of serfs. It soon came to mean a man of ignoble character as well as birth. It is interesting to trace the development of the present meaning from the original, in such words, and the student should not fail to do so.

185. Camelot. In the edition of Tennyson's works edited by his son, Vol. III, appears this passage : " The earliest fragment of an epic that I can find among my father's MSS. in my possession was probably written about 1833, and is a sketch in prose. I give it as it stands. ' On the latest limit of the West in the land of Lyonnesse, where, save the rocky isles of Scilly, all is now wild sea, rose the sacred Mount of Camelot. It rose from the deeps with gardens and bowers and palaces, and, at the top of the mount, was King Arthur's hall, and the holy Minster with the Cross of Gold. Here dwelt the King in glory apart, while the Saxons, whom he had overthrown in twelve battles, ravaged the land, and ever came nearer and nearer.

" ' The Mount was the most beautiful in the world, sometimes green and fresh in the beam of the morning, sometimes all one splendor, folded in the golden mists of the West. But all underneath it was hollow, and the mountain trembled, when the seas rushed bellowing through the porphyry caves : and there ran a prophecy that the mountain and the sea on some wild morning would topple into the abyss and be no more.' " The Camelot of the *Idylls* is, of course, purely imaginary, but there has been much speculation as to its possible location. Some authorities make it some twenty miles southeast of Glastonbury in Somerset, on the steep hill called Cadbury Castle, others would locate it near Winchester, and still others in Wales.

186. Far off, etc. This mystical description of Camelot is one of the finest passages in the *Idylls*. In ease and grace of diction ; the choice of words, which clearly express the exact shade of meaning ; in vivid and delicately colored imagery ; in its rare and beautiful symbolism and the smooth flow of musical cadences the passage is hardly excelled in the whole range of English poetry. Cf. the lyrics in the *Princess*.

207. To plunge old Merlin, etc. Gareth may here refer to the old belief that it was possible to destroy the sorceries of a magician by plunging him into the waters of certain seas. The Red Sea was believed to be specially efficacious.

212. The Lady of the Lake. The description which follows seems clearly intended to be allegorical, and may be interpreted as follows: The Lady of the Lake represents the true religion. Although, in person, she takes but little part in the action of the poem, she stands as the sponsor and protector of the king. She gives him his sword to show that his authority and power are derived from and based on divine justice. She is present at his wedding, and thus gives sanction to the institution of marriage. And when his life approaches its visible ending, she receives back the sword, and thus confers upon him the blessing of immortality.

Her dress ripples away like water to show that the forms of religion are ever changing.

Her arms, **like the cross**, support the cornice, thus showing that the substance of religion is unchanging, and that
it is a strong foundation and support of all civilization.

The **drops of water** symbolize the life-giving and refresh-
ing influences of religion.

The **sword** is the emblem of divine justice.

A **censer** symbolizes the purifying and sweetening influences of religion.

Worn with wind and storm. The world antiquity of
religion.

The sacred fish. The fish was the emblem of Christ, and
is found cut in the tombs in the catacombs and other
burial places of the early Christians. The initial letters
of Jesus Christ, Son of God, Savior, in the Greek, form the
Greek word which means fish.

Arthur's wars carved around. The warfare of right
against wrong, of the ideal against the evils of the world,
all centers about religion.

New things and old. Ancient conflicts are always repeating themselves in new forms. We are confused unless
we remember that the differences in time are as nothing,
for the deep principles of the strife are the same.

The **three queens** are Faith, Hope, and Charity.

223. inveterately. From two Latin words which mean
substantially for the ages. Veteran comes from the same
root. Here it means deep-rooted.

229. dragon-boughts are the coiled and knotted tails of
dragons.

236. an ancient man. Merlin.

248. Seer. This word is used in the sense of one who sees
visions and thus may foretell the future.

248. playing on him. The old man spoke half in earnest and half mockingly.

249. seen the good ship. There is a curious mirage, which is sometimes seen at the seashore, where ships are reflected upside down in the sky. This phenomenon is most frequently witnessed in Calabria, in Italy, where the natives say it is the work of the fairy Morgana, the Morgan le Fay of the Arthurian legends.

252. And here is truth. A mocking reference to the untruth told by Gareth.

256. sacred mountain cleft. Merlin's speech is mystical and symbolical. The building of the city may represent the growth of civilization, especially in its higher spiritual and æsthetic phases. The fairy king and fairy queens, who have come from the sacred mountain-cleft, that is, Mount Parnassus, are the arts, mythologies and religions, which have come from the east to wield their potent influences upon the upbuilding of spiritual life. It is built to music because to be complete it must be harmonious in all its parts, and harmony is the soul of music. (In this connection the student should read Browning's *Abt Vogler.*)

261. King. Merlin contends that the King, that is, the soul, is the living reality, and that all else is fading and transitory. It is, therefore, a shame not to be governed by the high ideals of the soul, and yet they are so high that they are not possible of mortal attainment.

273. never built at all. Civilization never ceases to develop, yet it never attains that perfection, beyond which there can be no farther growth.

275. reverence thine own beard. The white beard should
be a symbol of truth. Gareth is confused and puzzled,
and concludes that Merlin is making fun of him.

293. Let love be blamed, etc. Notice the confusion in
his grammar in this line.

298. did their days in stone. Wrought the history of
their reigns in the solid stones of the city.

299. Merlin's hand. Many great works were ascribed
to the art and magic of Merlin, of which the greatest were
the building of Arthur's palace at Camelot. Other works
were Stonehenge, the palace of Uther Pendragon, and four
magic fountains. Reference is made to these fountains
in different mediæval romances. One of these fountains is
referred to by Ariosto in *Orlando Furioso:* —

> "This spring was one of those four fountains rare,
>   Of those in France produced by Merlin's sleight,
>   Encompassed round about by marble fair,
>   Shining and polished, and than milk more white.
>   There in the stone choice figures chiselled were,
>   By that magician's godlike labor dight."

302. spire to heaven. To show its divine aspirations.

306. And out of bower. The student should observe
the wholesome life of the city while it is following the
example and leadership of the king, and see how it deterio-
rates and grows evil as it gradually separates itself from
his high ideals under the influence of the queen and her
guilty love for Lancelot. The *Idylls* may be called the
epic of a sin.

314. doom. Judgment or justice. Originally it was
used in a neutral sense, but now it implies an adverse

decision or condemnation. Gareth was frightened lest his imposture should be discovered and punished.

319. Sir Gawain. Why should he fear to meet Sir Gawain or Sir Modred?

333. Whether would ye? Another of the archaic expressions in which this Idyll abounds. It means, Which will ye choose?

343. Thine enemy. What light does this passage throw upon the character of the king?

351. standeth seized. A legal term, formerly used, meaning, has obtained possession.

359. Sir Kay. The foster-brother of Arthur, and the cynic of the Court.

362. gyve and gag. In former times scolding women were bound to a ducking-stool and a sort of iron muzzle or mask fastened to their faces. This is probably what Sir Kay refers to.

367. Aurelius Emrys. Emrys is the Celtic form of Ambrosius, referred to in the *Coming of Arthur*, line 13.

369. rough humor. The use of **humor** in this connection is interesting, and should be looked up.

376. Mark. Tennyson makes Mark the embodiment of hypocrisy and thus the antitype of Arthur.

380. charlock was a common name for wild mustard, whose abundant blossoms were of a pale but brilliant yellow.

383. Delivering. Reporting.

386. cousin. Used in the sense of kinsman. According to Malory Tristram was the son of Mark's sister. Tristram is the hero of a romantic cycle hardly less interesting and comprehensive than that of Arthur. See

Arnold's *Tristram and Iseult*, and Swinburne's *Tristram of Lyonnesse*, also Wagner's *Tristram and Isolde*. Mark's idea was that, because he was of higher rank than Tristram, he was entitled all the more to this high honor of knighthood.

411. reave. Deprive. This verb is still found in bereave, and in the participle reft.

422. lap him up in cloth of lead. Referring to the custom of wrapping a dead body in a sheet of lead.

423. craven. Mean-spirited.

430. evermore. Continuously.

431. Last, Gareth. From this point Tennyson follows the narrative of Malory.

442. thine. Thy master.

444. Wan=sallow. Pale and sickly, as a plant which feels its root attacked by some parasite.

445. Lo ye now! This passage should be compared with Malory's version of the same episode, VII, i.

447. God wot. Wot is the first and third personal form of the old verb witan, " to know," which is not now in use, except in the single set form " to wit."

447. brewis. An old English form of broth. It comes from or is associated with the verb brew.

448. an. An archaic form of *and*, meaning if.

451. Lancelot. The attitudes of Lancelot and Kay towards Gareth are characteristic of the two men. Kay is narrow-minded, cynical, and wholly uncharitable, while Lancelot is broadly tolerant and trustful, the flower of chivalry, and, so far, at least, the embodiment of every virtue. The student should watch for any signs of deterioration in the character of Lancelot as the action progresses, and try to discover the cause.

452. sleuth-hound. Sleuth means the track of a beast or a man, and a sleuth-hound is one that follows such a trail by scent. It is commonly applied to a bloodhound.

454. fluent. Flowing, not often used in such connection.

461. will poison, etc. The reference may be to the death of King Aurelius, one of Arthur's predecessors, who died of poison.

465. Sir Fair-hands. Malory, VII, i, makes Kay say: ". . . for I dare undertake he is villain born, and never will make man, for and he had come of gentlemen, he would have asked you of horse and armour, but such as he is, so he asketh. And since he has no name, I shall give him a name that shall be Beaumains, that is Fair-hands, and into the kitchen I shall bring him."

476. broach. Originally any sharp-pointed thing, hence a spit upon which meat was roasted before the fire.

489. tarns. An early English and Scotch word, meaning a small mountain lake or pool, especially one which has no visible feeders.

490. Caer-Eryri. Littledale says that this is a Welch word which means literally Snowdon Field. Snowdon is a mountain in Wales, and is the highest in either Wales or England. It is noted for its grandeur and the extensive view which may be had from its summit.

491. A naked babe. This is still another form of the legend of Arthur's birth.

492. Isle Avilion. The Isle of the Apples was the paradise of the Celts. It has been located at Glastonbury, but in Tennyson its location is very vague. See *The Passing of Arthur*, lines 428–432.

496. roundelay. Any song in which a line or refrain is

frequently repeated. The songs of birds are frequently spoken of in poetry as roundelays.

498. prodigious is usually applied to something immensely or unbelievably large, but here means strange or wonderful.

501. gap-mouthed. Notice how aptly the unusual expression conveys the desired meaning.

504. like a sudden wind, etc. The student should make a careful study of Tennyson's similes with a special view to their appropriateness and sources. To what extent do they show that he was a careful student and observer of nature?

508. by two yards, etc. Malory, VII, ii, says, "And when there were any masteries done thereat would he be, and there might none cast bar nor stone to him by two yards."

519. in-crescent and de-crescent. Would there be any difference in the meaning of these words if they were written without hyphens? Increase and decrease came from the same original words.

524, ragged oval. The lists in which tournaments were ridden were oval in shape. Ragged means uneven or with ragged edges.

528. Peter's knee. A figurative expression meaning to the gates of heaven, as Peter was known as the guardian or gate-keeper of heaven.

529. news. This word was originally a plural, and thus might be used with the plural adjective. Notice the incoherency of his speech. What does it indicate with regard to his state of mind?

532. staggered. Cf. line 29 of this Idyll.

536. the King's calm eye. In Malory there is no hint that the king knew Gareth's identity. Gareth asks two boons of the king, that he shall grant him this adventure, and that he may receive knighthood at the hands of Lancelot. The king grants both, and Lancelot knights Gareth after a passage at arms in which neither gains the advantage and in which Gareth announces himself to Lancelot.

561. Have I not earned, etc. A jesting allusion to his kitchen service.

566. lusty. Meaning originally pleasant, merry, and hence full of life, vigorous.

568. quest is used here as a term of Chivalry and means a going out in search of knightly adventure. On Arthur's lips it means an adventure undertaken for the sake of righting some wrong.

571. the lions on thy shield. Cf. *Lancelot and Elaine*, line 658, " Sir Lancelot's azure lions crowned in gold."

575. May-blossom. In England this name is given to the Lily of the Valley, which flower is probably meant here because of its waxen whiteness. It also is given to the Haw, which blossoms in May and is also white.

577. Tip-tilted. A rare word, possibly one of Tennyson's own coining. Notice here as elsewhere the grace and accuracy with which the poet adapts his words to the meaning which he desires to express. He was always an artist in his choice and use of words.

579. for. Used as a conjunction only to introduce an independent clause or sentence, giving a reason for or justification for something previously said. It means in such connection, *since*.

582. The lord of half a league. Every noble is practically confined to his tower by the bandits.

584. lonest. Lone, abbreviated from alone, is not subject to comparison either in form or sense. Is anything gained by the use of this forced superlative?

586. that best blood. The wine of the sacrament which is symbolical of the blood of Christ.

592. Lynette. In Malory's account, the maiden refuses to give the name of the one for whom she desires to secure succor and Arthur refuses to send one of his knights, upon which Gareth rushes in and demands the quest for himself. In what way, if any, is Tennyson's version an improvement?

592. noble. In the sense of high-born.

593. Lyonors. In Malory, this lady is named Liones.

596. Castle Perilous. " The old romances contain many such names as Castle Perilous. Thus in *Morte Darthur*, we find the Forest Perilous, the Chapel Perilous, the Perilous Lake, the Siege Perilous, and this Castle Perilous, near the Isle of Avilion." — LITTLEDALE.

603. purport. This word is not a synonym for purpose, although it is used here in much the same sense. Observe the different derivations of the two words.

607. holy life. To wed a holy life means to become a nun, that is " a bride of Christ." In this connection read *St. Agnes' Eve.*

610. this Order. See the passage in *Guinevere* beginning with line 457.

614. old knight-errantry. The old knights, who roamed the country without restraint of law or high purpose before the foundation of the Round Table.

2 A

616. from the moment. As the impulse of the moment may impel them.

618. fantasy. The older form of fancy. Here a whim or caprice.

619. Morning Star, etc. The three substantives in this line are in apposition with Day in the preceding. This conceit of the men is in the form of an allegory of human life in which they represent, respectively, youth, middle life, old age, and death.

626. scape, not 'scape. This is an independent form in use during the Elizabethan age.

636. topple. Observe the three different ways in which this word may be used. Shakespeare in *Macbeth* has this line, "Though castles topple on their warders' heads." In the *Death of Wellington*, Tennyson speaks of "The toppling crags of duty." The third use is found in this passage.

638. Brought down, etc. What rhetorical figure?

639. worthy to be a knight. What qualities in Gareth called forth this exclamation from the king?

642. slew the may-white. Her forehead flushed with anger.

651. gave upon a range. Opened upon or commanded a view.

657. But one was counter. The other was opposite to the hearth.

658. highest-crested, etc. The knight in full armor, with loftiest crest, could ride through.

669. a fuel-smothered fire. A replenished fire looks half dead until the fresh fuel catches and suddenly bursts into full flame, so Gareth cast off his outer robe of service and appeared in the full brilliancy of a new and glittering armor.

671. Dull-coated things. Cf. Tennyson's *The Two Voices :* —

> "To-day I saw the dragon-fly
> Come from the wells where he did lie
> An inner impulse rent the vail
> Of his old husk: from head to tail
> Came out clear plates of sapphire mail.
> He dried his wings: like gauze they grew;
> Thro' crofts and pastures wet with dew
> A living flash of light he flew."

675. donned. Put on. Don is a contraction of do on, just as doff is contracted from do off.

677. storm-strengthened. It was customary to take the wood for spears and bows from trees that stood alone by themselves in some exposed place where they had had no protection from the storms, because the fibre of such trees was tougher and more durable than that of trees which grew in the midst of a forest.

678. trenchant. Keen-edged, sharp.

684. lanes of shouting. Cf. " lane of access," line 646; and " silent faces," line 717.

686. but as the cur. The following note on this passage was made by Mr. Tennyson's son : " When we lived in Kent we had two large dogs, one a large white one, an uneducated ruffian always chained to an apple tree, the other a larger black one, and much more of a gentleman. One day while I was passing with this last too near the tree, the white one seized hold of him and tore his ear.

Then followed a duel. I separated them with some difficulty, and then took my dark friend on a walk of some six miles. All the way out and half the way back he growled and swore to himself about every five minutes."

693. the King hath past his time. The king is in his dotage.

695. For an your fire, etc. Notice the play upon the literal and figurative meanings of the word *fire*.

700. Crazed. To whom does he refer by this question?

703. peacocked. The peacock is the symbol of vanity and the verb derived from it means puffed up with pride in one's appearance.

706. so. Used in a conditional sense and equivalent to provided.

715. ye are overfine. See line 466. In what sense does Sir Kay use the word fine?

729. agaric. A kind of fungus growth which is sometimes found on trees in some parts of Europe. **holt** is an old Saxon word meaning a wood. It is not in use except occasionally in poetry.

730. carrion comes from a Latin word *caro* which means flesh, but has come to mean a dead and putrifying body. Our adjective carnal comes from the same root.

732. shrilling. Shrill used as a verb is equivalent to the Scottish skirl, and means to utter a keen, high-pitched sound.

> " Then gan the bagpipes and the hornes to shrill
>   And shriek aloud."
>
> —SPENSER, *Faerie Queene*, VI, viii, 46.

733. Avoid. Used in the sense of avaunt, and implies contempt and abhorrence.

738. ungentle. "And right as Beaumains overtook the damsel, right so came Sir Kay, and said, Beaumains, what, know ye not me? Then he turned his horse and knew it was Sir Kay, that had done him all the despite as ye have heard before. Yea, said Beaumains, I know you for an ungentle knight of the court, and therefore beware of me." — *Morte Darthur*, VII, iv.

742. sod and shingle. Showing the violence of the conflict. The word shingle comes from an Anglo-Saxon word meaning to sing, and is applied to coarse gravel because of the grating noise made by a horse's hoofs in passing through it.

751. loon. From an Anglo-Saxon word meaning a clown-ish fellow. It is a different word from loon meaning a kind of bird.

766. beknaved. Called knave.

771. Spit. She sarcastically calls his sword a spit, with reference to his kitchen service.

779. eagle-owl. "The comparison between the pool gleaming red in the twilight, and the eye of an eagle-owl, burning round and bright in the darkness, may have the fault of being too uncommon to really illustrate the description, but it is a simile that an ornithologist can appreciate. Indeed, a book might be written on the bird-lore of Tennyson, as has been well done by Mr. Harting in the case of Shakespeare." — LITTLEDALE.

781. Serving man. "So thus as they rode in the woods, there came a man flying all that ever he might. Whither wilt thou? said Beaumains. O lord, he said, help me, for hereby in a slade are six thieves that have taken my lord and bound him, so I am afeard lest they will slay him

Bring me thither, said Beaumains. And so they rode together until they came thereas was the knight bound, and then he rode unto them and struck one unto the death, and then another, and at the third stroke he slew the third thief: and then the other three fled. And he rode after them, and he overtook them, and then those three thieves turned again and assailed Beaumains hard, but at last he slew them, and returned and unbound the knight."— *Morte Darthur*, VII, v.

791. haling. The older form of hauling.

796. oilily bubbled. Notice how the sound suggests the meaning.

799. caitiff. An epithet of a false knight.

800. wreaked themselves. Avenged themselves. This verb formerly took for its object either the offender or the offence. It is now not often used except in such expressions as to wreak vengeance on one.

804. wan. Originally this word meant dark, gloomy, when applied to the weather or to water, as here. Later it came to mean colorless, sickly of hue. Cf. *The Passing of Arthur*, line 29.

806. grimly. Now obsolete. It is used occasionally to describe ghosts.

807. Good now. Littledale says, "Good is probably used as a form of address, 'my good sir, now,' as in *Hamlet*."

815. a light laugh, etc. Lynette laughs in derision at the knight's reference to Arthur's Table. Tennyson frequently uses this play on words. The student should observe Lynette's attitude towards Gareth, and especially the signs of change as she begins to show an increasing interest and a more tolerant spirit.

820. rout. A crowd of people in disorder.

828. cate. A delicacy.

829. a peacock in his pride. "At table, peacocks were never introduced, except on the most important and magnificent occasions : and he who carved them was considered honored in the highest degree. The feathers from the tail of the peacock were formed by ladies of quality into a crown, for the purpose of decorating their favorite troubadours or minstrels. The eyes were considered to represent the attention of the whole world fixed upon them. And in those days of chivalry, so constantly was the peacock the object of the solemn vows of the knights, that its image was hung up in the place, where they exercised themselves in the management of their horses and weapons : and before it, when roasted and dressed in its plumage, and placed with great pomp and ceremony, as the top dish, at the most splendid feasts, all the guests, male and female, took a solemn vow : the knights vowing bravery, and the ladies engaging to be loving and faithful." Littledale further says, " Tennyson does not introduce this dainty dish without a purpose : Lynette is to be reminded by the peacock in his pride that ladies should be loving and kind to their champions — a lesson she stands rather in need of."

839. frontless. Without shame or modesty.

844. to stick swine. This expression is from Malory. " Fie, fie, said she, Sir Knight, ye are uncourteous to set a kitchen page before me, him beseemeth better to stick a swine than to sit before a damsel of high parentage."

862. avail. Profit.

871. Lion and stoat. It has often happened that wild

animals under influence of terror have taken refuge together in some safe place, and the weaker ones have forgotten their fears. The comparison between the lion and
the stoat is an interesting one. The lion is high-born, and
the stoat, or the weasel, is an outcast.

873. ruth. Sorrow for the misery of another.

882. Among the ashes. Is the story of Cinderella, as
referred to here, an anachronism?

887. Took at a leap. Notice the personification. Is the
use of this figure effective?

889. Lent-lily. The daffodil is so called because it blooms
at Lent. It is also sometimes called the Lent-rose.

896. Sir Morning Star. This passage is probably allegorical, though it may be read as a purely romantic adventure. Mr. Tennyson said in referring to certain reviews of
the *Idylls*, which laid special stress upon their allegorical
significance, " They have taken my hobby and ridden it
too hard, and have explained some things too allegorically,
although there is an allegorical or perhaps rather a para-
bolic drift in the poem. . . . There is no single fact or incident in the *Idylls*, however seemingly mystical, which
cannot be explained without any mystery or allegory
whatever." — Tennyson's *Works*, Vol. III. (Edited by
Hallam, Lord Tennyson.) Mr. Elsdale has stated the
allegory as follows: " The serpent river is the stream of
time. Its three long loops the three ages of life, — youth,
middle age, old age. The guardians of the crossings are the
personified forms of the temptations suited to these different ages." The student should interpret this whole
episode as an allegory.

908. Avanturine. Avanturine, sometimes called the

panther-stone, is a kind of gray-green or brown quartz with sparkles in it. The first reading was —

> "Like stars within the stone Avanturine."

." This simile was taken from a fine piece of the stone Avanturine, kept in an étui-case belonging to my mother. ' Look at it,' my father said, ' see the stars in it, worlds within worlds.' " — Tennyson's *Works*, Vol. III, p. 465.

934. lightly. In the sense of quickly. Malory, VII. xii, has the expression, " lightly they avoided their horses."

939. central bridge. What figure of speech?

970. she sang. " Lynette has now seen that Gareth is a gentleman and no knave, and admiration of his valor awakens a different feeling in her heart. Her songs conceal rather than reveal this dawning love : maiden modesty will not permit her to abate one jot of her mis-sayings and revilings.

" Her first song indicates the sudden light that has dawned upon her : her morning dream has once proved true — that her love would smile upon her that day.

" She urges Gareth to take her counsel, but ends with seeming scorn : ' Care not for shame : thou art not knight but knave.' However, she answers him reasonably when he remonstrates with her.

" After the Sun is overthrown, her love has smiled upon her twice : her dream that she would find a victorious champion that day — a knight who would achieve her quest and become her love — has twice been proved true. Her revilings take a more mocking, but less bitter tone. What does he know of flowers save as garnitures of dishes : or of birds, save when turning on a spit ! But there is no trace of scorn of Gareth in her proud reply to Sir Evening Star. . . . Thrice hath her dream come true — or rather, three omens have proved her dream true — her dream of a victorious and loving champion." — LITTLEDALE.

1001. Noonday Sun. In Malory, the second knight was a green knight. The symbolism does not appear in the original story.

1002. flower. The dandelion.

1008. brother. He thinks Gareth is his brother because he carries the shield of the Morning Star.

1048. rosemaries and bay. It was customary to garnish meats, when they formed the chief dish at the table, with these aromatic herbs.

1052. mavis. The song thrush. **merle.** The common blackbird. These birds are all song birds. Does this fact add a sting to her raillery?

1067. harden'd skins. This wrapping represents the unyielding nature of the habits which have been forming through a lifetime. They clothe a person in an armor of evil, if he has been a sinful man, which nothing can penetrate, and he becomes wholly insusceptible to all good influences. Can the same be said of good habits?

1107. Well done. Lynette now definitely abandons her reviling, and shows her interest, not only in the issue of the conflict, but in the welfare of her knight.

1117. Southwesterns. The southwest gales.

1118. buoy is the object of could bring under understood.

1130. trefoil. The three-leaved clover. Three conflicts have been won.

1141. Hast mazed my wit. She finds herself at a loss

to understand the situation. Arthur had apparently scorned her in giving her his kitchen-knave as a champion. The knave has proved himself brave and knightly, yet is no knight. She shows herself a lady of true instincts by acknowledging her error, and Gareth proves his magnanimity by meeting her in the same spirit.

1156. Lets down his other leg. The heron, when resting, stands on one leg, but when he gets ready to fly, he puts down the other leg so he may spring from the ground with sufficient force to enable him to begin his flight.

1163. comb. A Welsh word meaning a hollow between two hills. It is used only in southwestern England and Wales and a part of Ireland.

> "From those heights
> We dropped at pleasure into sylvan combs."
> — WORDSWORTH, *Excursion*, iii.

1172. vexillary. Standard-bearer in the Roman legion. Such an inscription was carved on a cliff that overhangs the river Gelt in Cumberland, near Brampton. Remains of the inscription may still be seen. They were well known to Tennyson.

1174. Phosphorus, etc. The Latin names for Morning Star, Noonday, Evening, Night, and Death.

1179. cave. The soul chased by these five personations of time is flying to the cave where he may be safe under the protection of religion.

1184. error. Wandering from the path.

1273. Ramp, etc. The lions on Lancelot's shield.

1277. from my hold on these. He gains **virtue,** — **fire,** — from his hold on the lions on Lancelot's shield.

1281. Arthur's Harp. A star which lies near the pole-star and Arcutrus, the three forming a triangle likened unto a harp. It is referred to in the *Last Tournament*, line 331.

1313. Thus — and not else. The passage means, — If Lancelot fights for his shield he will probably win it, as he is the stronger man, but I shall not yield it in any other way.

1314. urged all the devisings. Told all the devices.

1318. fineness. In the sense of finesse, stratagem.

1336. Came lights and lights. Lights appeared here and there in succession.

1347. With white breast-bone. With breastbone and bare ribs painted white on his armor.

1348. And crown'd with fleshless laughter. Crowned with a grinning skull.

1367. blink the terror. Shrink from looking at it.

1378. This episode, as well as all the allegorical part of the three battles which preceded, is Tennyson's. In Malory, the last champion is the hardest to conquer and he is overcome only after a long and desperate battle. It might be questioned whether it would have been possible for Gareth to cleave the helm asunder and still leave the head within unharmed. The allegory may mean that death, which seems the most formidable, is easily conquered and yields to a fresh new life. Or it may mean, as Little-dale suggests, that Gareth had found his most terrible opponent give place to love.

1392. he that told the tale. The first, — Malcry; the second, — Tennyson.

THE MARRIAGE OF GERAINT

The Geraint Idylls are based on the romance of Geraint, the Son of Erbin, in the Mabinogion, and none of the incidents are to be found in Malory. The Mabinogion is a general title given by Lady Charlotte Guest to twelve tales which she translated from the Welsh, and which were found in a fourteenth century MSS., called *The Red Book of Hergest*. This book is now published in cheap form in *Every Man's Library*, and should be read by all students who are interested in the old tales connected with the Arthurian cycle.

These two Idylls were originally one, but were separated in the second edition of Tennyson's works. The original Idyll, known as *Enid*, was much longer than the others; but, by the division, the attention was better concentrated upon the two chief incidents.

The first 144 lines of the first Idyll really belong to the second, but by introducing them in the beginning, the interest is aroused by the plunge into the middle of the story.

29. A horror. The shadow of the one sin which was to overturn all the work of the great king and destroy the Round Table is already beginning to fall, and all the sufferings of this tale may be traced to it.

39. common sewer of all his realm. This line is repeated in *Geraint and Enid*, line 894. Observe how much stronger and more vivid the figurative expression is than any plain statement.

40. fair permission. Fair is used in the sense of gracious or free.

49. worship. This word is now commonly used to denote adoration or homage paid to God or some deity. It was formerly used to mean fervent admiration directed towards any one.

50. Forgetful, etc. This striking repetition of the single word in five lines adds much to the beauty as well as to the strength and vividness of the passage. It is used with striking effect in a number of passages in *Taliesin*, one of the romances of the Mabinogion.

60. molten is the old past participial form of the verb to melt. Observe the strength of the word. His manhood is not only gone, but is broken up and fused beyond hope of rehabilitation. **Uxoriousness** is an excessive and foolish fondness for one's wife.

68. taint. Cf. line 31.

70. each by either. The first edition had "each by other." In what way has the line been affected by the change?

77. As slopes, etc. Tennyson himself says, " I made this simile from a stream, and it is different, tho' like Theocritus, *Idyll*, XXII, 48 ff." When some one objected that he had taken this simile from Theocritus, he answered : " It is quite different. Geraint's muscles are not compared to the rounded stones, but to the stream pouring vehemently over them."— Tennyson's *Works*, Vol. III, p. 469. The passage from Theocritus referred to is

"Broad were his shoulders, vast his orbed chest,
  And nigh the shoulder on each brawny arm
  Stood out the muscles, huge as rolling stones
  Caught by some rain-swollen river and shapen smooth
  By its wild eddyings."

The student should make a critical comparison of the two passages.

116. For all my pains, etc. In spite of all his precautions, his separation from Arthur's court, his enforced isolation from all warlike activities and the defences which his jealous love had erected, still she had become tainted and had fallen in love with some knight in Arthur's court. Geraint's treatment of the innocent Enid should be compared with the high magnanimity which the great Arthur showed towards the guilty Guinevere.

124. hurled. The first edition has "snatched." Contrast the two words.

126. palfrey. An ordinary riding horse as distinguished from a war horse.

128. spurs are yet to win. Referring to the slights which had been put upon him because of his inactivity.

136. cedarn. Cf. oaken.

138. sprigs of summer. It is even now the custom to put away clothes for the summer with sprigs of lavender or other sweet-smelling herbs placed between them.

145. For Arthur, etc. The monarchs of England and France were accustomed to hold courts on the great anniversaries of Easter, Whitsuntide, and Christmas.

145. Whitsuntide comprises the week following Whitsunday, which is the seventh Sunday after Easter. It takes its name from the white garments worn by the candidates for baptism.

146. Caerleon upon Usk. The traditional seat of Arthur's government. It was located in Monmouthshire, three miles northeast of Newport.

148. forester of Dean. The forest of Dean was an exten-

sive tract in Gloucestershire beyond the Severn. In the
original story, the forester said to Arthur, " In the Forest
I saw a stag, the like of which beheld I never yet." " What
is there about him ? " asked Arthur, " that thou never yet
didst see his like ? " " He is of pure white, Lord, and he
does not herd with any other animal through stateliness
and pride, so royal is his bearing."

158. dreaming, etc. This passage does not appear in
the original. Tennyson introduces it here in order to
show the gradual growth of the evil and its reflection in
the increasing contentions of the court.

185. Cavall. Arthur's dog, Cavall, is one of the noted
dogs of history or tradition. The tradition is current
that one day, when Arthur was hunting a wild boar with his
dog, Cavall left a footprint upon a flat stone. Thereupon
Arthur built a carn and placed the stone with the footprint
on top of it. It is said that one may carry away the stone
to ever so great a distance, but the next day it is back in
place again.

209. instinctive. Observe the peculiar use.

213. Wroth to be wroth. Angry because he had permitted himself to become angry at such a vile creature.

217. this vermin to their earths. This use of vermin as
both a collective and a plural is unusual even at the time
of which Tennyson is writing. The word means from its
origin a worm, but has been applied to any noxious insect
or animal. It was commonly applied to such animals as
rats, mice, otters, weasels, and polecats. Perhaps Geraint
had this last-named unsavory animal in mind. **Earths** is
the conventional word for hole, used as a term of the
chase.

220. for pledge. Some article of value being left as security for payment.

230. a beggar from the hedge. Cf. line 724. Also read in this connection Tennyson's early poem, *King Cophetua and the Beggar Maid.*

231. bridals. Bridal was originally used only as a noun. It was a contraction of bride-ale, hence meant the nuptial feast.

235. vile. Of small price, hence mean, contemptible.

255. hostel. Hospital and hotel are other forms of the same word. It means a house of entertainment.

260. The sparrow-hawk preys on sparrows and other small birds. Because of this fact it was considered a type of meanness and cowardice.

262. the dusty sloping beam. A beam of light from the setting sun.

273. Spleen. Anger. The spleen has been supposed to be the seat of various emotions.

274. Pips. Littledale suggests that Geraint was not posted in diseases of chickens, as pips is a disease which attacks the tongue and cannot in any way be said to eat up " your sparrow-hawk."

276. rustic cackle. What simile is intended here? Note Geraint's contempt.

282. arms. Explain the repetition of *arms.*

306. passion. The word meant originally suffering. Here it is used in the sense of eagerness.

319. wilding. This word may be either a noun or an adjective. Is it more effective here than the simple word *wild* would have been?

322. monstrous ivy-stems. In England the ivy grows

2.B

luxuriantly and fully answers the description given here.
It is not uncommon in poetry to compare the roots of trees
or masses of vines to snakes.

330. lander. One who lands. An unusual word, but
not coined by Tennyson as some have suggested.

336. liquid note beloved by men. The nightingale is
famous for its beautiful song. It winters in Africa and
arrives in England the first or second week in April, where
its coming is eagerly awaited by bird lovers.

339. coppice. Copse, a wood or thicket composed of
small trees or bushes. Chaucer spoke of the colors of
young trees in the springtime.

> "Some very red, and some a glad light green."

344. Here, by God's grace. The triteness of Geraint's
introduction to Enid by a song is lost in the classic beauty
of the passage and its wealth of simile and allusion.

345. the song. Stopford Brooke in his *Tennyson*, page
289, says, " And Enid sings that song of fortitude in
poverty, of the mastery of the soul in good or evil fortune,
which is so finely written that it speaks the very soul of
enduring manhood and womanhood all over the world.
There is as much strength as there is beauty in the whole
scene ; and the two comparisons of the effect on Geraint of
Enid's voice are one of the noblest instances we can give of
that sweet keen delicacy in Tennyson which, in contrast
with his bluff power, is so pleasant a surprise."

363. dim brocade. Brocade is a silken fabric variegated
with gold and silver, or with raised flowers, foliage, or other
ornaments. Dim means faded.

364. vermeil-white. Vermeil means a bright red or

vermilion. The whole expression means white tinged with red.

368. God's rood. Rood at first meant a rod, but came to mean a crucifix. The word appears in the name of the royal palace in Edinburgh, Holyrood.

386. A costrel. A small vessel of wood, leather, or earthenware. In the Mabinogion the story runs as follows: " And, behold ! the maiden came back, and a youth with her, bearing on his back a costrel full of good purchased mead, and a quarter of young bullock. And in the hands of the maiden was a quantity of white bread, and she had some manchet bread in her vail, and she came into the chamber. 'I could not obtain better than this,' said she, ' nor with better should I have been trusted.' ' It is good enough,' said Geraint. And they caused the meat to be boiled ; and when their food was ready they sat down."

389. manchet bread. A small roll or loaf of bread made from the finest and whitest wheat flour. The word is now obsolete.

412. under-shapen. A word of rare use, meaning undersized or dwarfish.

419. They take. Cf. line 276.

440. Limours. He appears in *Geraint and Enid* in the passage beginning with line 277.

443. wild land. That part of Geraint's territory which had not yet been brought to order by Arthur.

451. Affirming. The account in the Mabinogion is essentially different : " I had a nephew, son of my brother, and I took his possessions to myself ; and when he came to his strength, he demanded of me his property, but

I withheld it from him. So he made war upon me, and wrested from me all I possessed." Tennyson makes the young man wholly a wanton aggressor.

481. Except the lady he loves best, etc. This condition was often imposed upon a knight in mediæval times before he would be admitted to a tourney or sometimes even to a castle.

513. prove her heart. Find out her feelings.

535. To quicken to the sun. To show signs of color and hence of life.

537. jousts. A knightly tilt in which two adversaries attacked each other with blunted lances.

539. twain. An obsolete masculine form of *two*.

543. Chair of Idris. Idris was one of the three primitive bards of Wales and was the reputed inventor of the harp. The Chair of Idris, Cader-Idris, next to Snowdon, is the highest mountain in Wales. Cf. Arthur's Seat, near Edinburgh.

545. errant knights. Wandering knights.

547. Flow'd in. Special significance of this word?

565. distant walls. It has been suggested that this " clapping of phantom hands " was the echo of the applause from the field returned by the walls of the town, but this is not probable. Those in attendance were overawed by the tyranny of the Sparrow-Hawk and they would not dare applaud his defeat. It is more likely that the friends of Yniol, who would hardly dare to attend the tournament, were watching at a distance and the phantom applause was theirs.

579. Edyrn, son of Nudd. He appears again in *Geraint and Enid*, in the passage beginning with line 780.

593–596. In the first edition this passage reads: —

> "And, being young, he changed himself and grew
> To hate the sin, that seem'd so like his own,
> Of Modred, Arthur's nephew, and fell at last
> In the great battle fighting for the King."

The great battle was the last one, described in *The Passing of Arthur*, in which practically all the knights of the Round Table who still remained faithful were killed.

597. third day. See line 222.

598. low splendor. Does this refer to the rising or setting of the sun?

631. All branch'd, etc. With branches and flowers gold-embroidered on it.

641. sold and sold. Sold one after another.

654. And dreamt herself, etc. This beautiful and pathetic dream does not appear in the Mabinogion. In the *Idylls*, Tennyson has given us three beautiful, sweet, and pure women, Lynette, Enid, and Elaine. He has also given us three of a different type, Guinevere, Vivien, and Etarre. The student should study and individualize these characters. The humility, patience, and sweetness of Enid, together with her generous and unchanging love, make her one of the noteworthy female characters of all poetry.

661. a turkis. One of the old spellings of turquoise. Its color is blue, while that of the garnet is red.

672. mixen. An obsolete word meaning a dunghill.

712. noble maintenance. The maintaining of a fitting state for a noble family.

724. a ragged robin. A red wild flower which is common

in English hedgerows. Probably her mother is thinking of a ragged beggar maiden by the wayside.

730. those of old. In the book of Esther, we read that, after the banishment of Vashti from the royal presence, the King Ahasuerus appointed officers in all the provinces of his kingdom to gather together all the fair young women, and bring them into the presence of the king that he might select the fairest to become his queen. Enid's mother thinks that even though search were made throughout Arthur's realm, a maid fairer than Enid could not be found.

743. Whom Gwydion, etc. The tale is from the Mabinogion. Math says to Gwydion: "Well, we will seek, I and thou, by charms and illusion, to form a wife for him out of flowers . . . so they took the blossoms of the oak, and the blossoms of the broom, and the blossoms of the meadow-sweet, and produced from them a maiden, the fairest and most graceful that man ever saw. And they baptized her, and gave her the name of Blodenwedd."

744. bride of Cassivelaun. "Milton tells us that it was the desire of British pearls that led the Roman Cæsar to invade Britain, but the laureate follows the more poetic Welsh tradition, that it was for the love of a fair British maiden named Flur, who was beloved also by the British chieftain Cassivelaunus. Flur had been carried away by a Gaulish prince, an ally of Cæsar, to whom he had presented the lady. Cassivelaunus led an army of sixty-one thousand men in pursuit, and after slaying six thousand of Cæsar's followers recaptured his beloved."

762. That she ride with me in her faded silk. The

Mabinogion has, " Let not the damsel array herself,"
said Geraint, " except in her vest and her veil, until she
come to the Court of Arthur, to be clad by Guinever in
such garments as she may choose." So the maiden did
not array herself.

764. Like flaws. Sudden gusts of wind which lay or lodge
grain. Corn is used for any kind of grain.

771. Never man rejoiced. Is not this an evidence of
supreme disregard for Enid's feelings?

814. A prophet certain of my prophecy. See *Geraint and
Enid*, line 247.

818. gaudy-day. Some merry, festal day.

829. white sails flying on the yellow sea. Swinburne
says : " On the first bright day I ever spent on the
eastern coast of England I saw the truth of this touch. . . .
There on the dull, yellow, formless floor of dense, dis-
colored sea, so thick with clotted sand that the water
looked massive and solid as the shore, the white sails flashed
whiter against it and along it as they fled, and I knew once
more the truth of what I had never doubted — that the
eye and hand of Tennyson may always be trusted at once
and alike to see and to express the truth."

GERAINT AND ENID

This Idyll takes up the narrative, where it was broken
off, at line 144, in the preceding Idyll, and goes straight
forward to the end, following the original story in the
Mabinogion, but with a number of variations, which
generally add to the dramatic interest. The student

should not fail to read the original and compare Tennyson's work with it.

1. O purblind, etc. Why does the poet begin with this invocation? In what special way is it appropriate at this point in the action of the poem? **Purblind** means here dim-sighted.

3. forge. Observe the peculiar force of this word in this connection.

7. where we see, etc. Cf. *I Corinthians* xiii. 12.

20. Effeminate, etc. Cf. *The Marriage of Geraint*, line 107.

30. marches. March means a bound or border, hence a frontier. It was most commonly applied to the border lands between England and Scotland, and England and Wales.

49. great plover. The whistle of this bird is so like that of a man that it often deceives wanderers on the heaths. Dyer in his *English Folk-lore* says that there is a curious notion about some species of plovers that their bodies are inhabited by the souls of those Jews who took part in the crucifixion of Christ.

52. If there be such in me, etc. Referring to "that unnoticed failing" in line 47.

76. Did I wish, etc. In the Mabinogion Geraint's reply is, "Thou hadst only to hold thy peace as I bade thee. I wish but for silence not for warning." In the first edition the line read, "Did I wish your silence or your warning?" In later editions, the line was changed to read as at present. What was the reason for the change?

86. cubit. Originally the word meant a bend or an elbow.

It finally came to be a unit of linear measure based on the length of the forearm.

94. three dead wolves. Cf. *The Coming of Arthur*, line 873.

101. ruth. Cf. *Gareth and Lynette*, line 873.

116. Caerleon. Cf. *The Marriage of Geraint*, line 146.

119. shallow shade. Edge of the wood. Notice the contrast with " deep " and " gloom " following.

120. stubborn-shafted. Having an unyielding shaft or trunk. What is gained by the alliteration in this and the preceding expression?

123. shook her pulses. Made her pulses beat more rapidly.

125. set on. Attack.

151. not obey. The position of the negative is unusual, though it is sometimes so placed in Shakespeare.

155. Short fits. Observe how the structure of this sentence suggests the agonized breathlessness of the action.

157. erred. Failed to strike the point aimed at.

159. corselet. That part of the armor which protected the breast.

164. windy walls. Observe the similar use of this expression in the *Palace of Art*, line 72. The student should not fail to observe how carefully Tennyson chooses his adjectives, and how often he makes an alliterative phrase with them. In what sense may the cliff walls be said to be " windy " ?

171. That listens. Observe the special beauty and fitness of this simile. It was suggested to the poet by a scene near Festiniog, in Wales.

189. disedge. Cf. *Gareth and Lynette*, line 20.

198. meadow gemlike, etc. A grassy plain set in the

brown wilderness like a gem. Meadow probably comes
from a word meaning to mow.

202. victual. This singular form has now gone out of use.

218. guerdon. Reward or recompense.

245. errant. Wandering.

247. false doom. Cf. *The Marriage of Geraint*, line 814.

250. humorous ruth. Pity mixed with amusement.

258. Listless annulet. Rings of grasses or rushes made
without purpose.

267. supporters of a shield. That is, in a coat of arms.
Supporters is a term used in heraldry.

277. Limours. Cf. *The Marriage of Geraint*, line 440.
In the Mabinogion this earl was a stranger to Enid.
Tennyson has intensified the revolting features of this
episode in order to emphasize the jealousy of Geraint and
to make the contrast still greater between his unreasoning
anger and the gentle patience of Enid.

291. took the word, etc. In telling his licentious tales, he
used words of double meaning.   Observe the revoltingly
discourteous treatment of Enid.

300. My free leave. This permission granted to Limours
and the insult contained in the sentence has been called
the crowning injury which Geraint heaped upon Enid.
It also illustrates the depths of infamous misjudgment into
which jealousy, the meanest of all evil passions, will lead a
man.   To what extent is the sin of Guinevere responsible
for the sufferings of Enid?

306. pilot star. The North star, by which pilots were
wont to guide their ships over the ocean.

324. lovers' quarrels. Milton says, " Lovers' quarrels
oft in pleasing concord end."

325. bicker. Wrangle, quarrel.

329. loves you no more. Is not this statement of Limours true?

341. there is the keep. Limours means to say that he does not contemplate the death of Geraint, but that he will imprison him in the keep, or in the central stronghold of a castle.

364. a broken egg-shell. Meaning a wholly worthless object.

382. rout of random followers. Rout means here a tumultuous rabble, and **random** means gathered at haphazard.

410. Suddenly honest. A touch of humor which is not often found in the *Idylls*.

431. As careful robins, etc. "This line was made one day while my father was digging, as was his wont, in the kitchen garden at Farringford, when he was much amused by the many watchful robins around him." — Tennyson's *Works*, edited by Hallam, Lord Tennyson, Vol. III, p. 473.

449. bicker. Here means to move quickly. Cf. *The Brook:* —

> "I come from haunts of coot and hern,
>   I make a sudden sally,
>   And sparkle out among the fern,
>   To bicker down a valley."

461. dry shriek. An expression taken from the Latin poets. It means that he has ridden so fast in the dust and heat that his throat is parched and dry.

470. crystal dykes. Ditches filled with clear water.

475. cressy islets. Masses of cress matted together in the water.

477. boon. Used here in the sense of convivial. It is from the French word *bon*, meaning good.

485. Not a hoof left. When a knight conquered another in battle, the horse and armor of the defeated knight became the property of the victor, by the laws of Chivalry.

490. shall we fast or dine? Shall we go hungry or shall we take his armor and pay for our dinner with it?

499. sickens nigh to death. It is possible that Tennyson had Enoch Arden in mind when he wrote these lines.

523. Cf. *The Last Tournament*, line 492.

525. perilous. Because he might risk his own life by showing pity for a victim of the fierce Earl Doorm.

532 smoke. With clouds of dust raised by his headlong flight.

550. idiot tears. Tears which, in either case, were foolishly shed.

565. litter-bier. A litter is a portable bed or couch. Bier comes from a word meaning to bear. In the Mabinogion the incident is related, " . . . and to see if he yet would live, he had him carried with him in the hollow of his shield and upon a bier . . . and when they arrived there, Geraint was placed upon a litter couch in front of the table that was in the hall." Cf. the familiar saying of the Spartan mother.

572. settle. A long wooden bench with a high back.

300. spears, for spearmen. What figure?

631. the old serpent. *Revelation* xii. 9.

632. As the worm, etc. Tennyson says, "I used to watch worms drawing in withered leaves on the lawn at Farringford."

635. gracious here means both physical loveliness and great spiritual purity and beauty.

679. Weed. From the Anglo-Saxon, meaning a garment. Cf. widows' weeds.

687. shoaling sea, etc. Whoever has noticed the tints of the water as it shoals towards the beach from the deep sea will appreciate the beauty of the simile, and also the genius of the poet in choosing rare and beautiful similes.

727. shore. An obsolete past participle of shear.

762. And never yet. Stopford Brooke says of the passage which follows, " . . . we do not wonder that Tennyson was so moved with his own creation as to write about her (Enid) some of the loveliest lines he ever wrote about womanhood."

763. four rivers. "And a river went out of Eden to water the garden; and from thence it was parted, and became into four heads." — *Genesis* ii. 10.

768. happy mist. "But there went up a mist from the ground, and watered the whole face of the earth." — *Genesis* ii. 6.

791. By overthrowing, etc. Explain the paradox.

820. hollow land. Volcanic region.

830. With one main purpose. See line 838 fol.

841. that ever answered Heaven. Reflected back the blue of heaven.

892. delegated hands. He had trusted to others to report the condition of the country, and to exercise his authority, without giving it his personal attention. .

902. vicious quitch. Quitch-grass is a weed grass somewhat resembling wheat and difficult to eradicate. In this country, it is called witch-grass.

928. Bala lake. The largest lake in Wales and so situated that the southwest wind blows along its whole length and swells the waters of the Dee, which flows from it. Professor Masson says, " The holy Dee is sacred with Druidic and Arthurian legends."

935. the White Horse. Littledale says : " There is a huge figure of a horse, 374 feet long, cut in the turf on a chalky hillside near Wantage in Berkshire. It was made to commemorate Alfred's victory over the Danes in the reign of Ethelred. The white horse was an emblem of Hengist. It represented the horse of Odin, the war-god of northern mythology." Thomas Hughes has written a book on *The Scouring of the White Horse.*

957. the spiteful whisper. See *The Marriage of Geraint,* lines 56–60.

969. fighting for the blameless king. Lady Charlotte Guest in a note says : —

" The name of Geraint, the son of Erbin, is familiar to all lovers of ancient Welsh literature, through the beautiful elegy composed on him by his fellow-warrior, the venerable bard Llywarch Hen. He was a prince of Devon, and fell fighting valiantly against the Saxons, under Arthur's banner, in the battle of Llongborth."

> "Before Geraint, the terror of the foe,
>   I saw steeds fatigued with the toil of battle,
>   And after the shout was given, how dreadful was the onset.
>
> Before Geraint, the scourge of the enemy,
>   I saw steeds white with foam,
>   And after the shout of battle a fearful torrent.

At Llongborth I saw the raging of slaughter,
And an excessive carnage
And warriors blood-stained from the assault of Geraint

At Llongborth was Geraint slain,
A valiant warrior from the woodlands of Devon.
Slaughtering his foes as he fell."

LANCELOT AND ELAINE

The two Idylls, *Balin and Balan* and *Merlin and Vivien*, which intervene between the Geraint Idylls and this, are omitted here. In them the progress of evil at the court is clearly shown. The moral deterioration of the Round Table has been very rapid since the time of Geraint. Scandal is no longer whispered, but is the current gossip of all. Evil, in the person of Vivien, has taken up her permanent abode at the Court, and his knights no longer pursue with single hearts and fixed purpose the high ideals of the king.

For the first time Lancelot is brought into the foreground. Hitherto he has dominated the poem like some gigantic mountain peak, which, though hidden by enveloping clouds, still thrills the air and earth with a sense of its hidden majesty. He was the friend chosen by the king to escort Guinevere to the court for her high marriage. Thinking he was the king, when first she saw him, she fell in love with him and him she wedded in her heart when her outward troth was plighted before the altar to the immaculate king. Again we catch a glimpse of him, wholly noble and human, in *Gareth and Lynette*, and

once more in the garden scene in *Balin and Balan*. Now
we see him in all his strength and all his weakness. Plainly
the poet pictures his splendid qualities of mind and heart,
sullied, as they are, by the dark stains of his unholy
passion.

Guinevere appears as the selfish, passionate shadow of
her former self. How great the change since first she rode
forth amid the blossoms of that May so many years ago
to take her place as the consort of the blameless king!
With his ideals she has no sympathy, for his person no
affection, and for his daily life no vestige of interest. Her
whole being is swallowed up by her love for Lancelot, and
she takes no pains to conceal it from any one except the
king. Clearly she appears as the cause of the moral ruin
of the noblest knight of them all, and the infection of her
wilful sin is spreading throughout the entire court, and
effectually thwarting the most exalted purpose of the
Round Table, that for which it was founded, the quest of
the Holy Grail. For it was only as these knights grew in
spiritual grace and purity of thought and life that they
could become fitted for the exalted mission. The vows
which made each one the champion of the right against
the wrong, the weak against the strong, were only a preparation for the consummate deed which was to crown the
whole Round Table with the glory of transcendent achievement.

As sin first came into the world through the medium of
the most beautiful and closed the gates of Paradise, so
now the choicest flower in this royal garden became the
source and prime cause of its devastation.

Contrasted strongly with Guinevere is Elaine, the high

type of womanly purity and perfectness. Littledale says: "Tennyson's power of drawing the characters of simple and lovable women is here seen to perfection. It is easy enough to represent a woman in whom the elements of good and evil are mingled, or in whom the latter predominate, — such a character is in no danger of being too neutral-tinted or monotonous ; but it is a far harder task to depict women like Enid and Elaine, fair and lovable beings, with all the charm of purity and goodness, but moving steadfastly within the orbit of homely simple duties, and lacking the effect of deviation, the contrast of light and shade, that we see in the lives of less clear-natured women. In delineating these gracious creatures Tennyson stands unrivalled ; and in his rare sympathy with such types of womanly purity we may perceive the almost feminine delicacy of his mind."

The outline of the story of Elaine, the poet has taken from the *Morte Darthur*, XVIII, chapters viii to xxi.

1. Elaine the fair. Observe that the poet plunges into the middle of the story as he does in *The Marriage of Geraint*.

2. the lily maid of Astolat. Malory calls her Elaine le Blank, that is, *blanche*, meaning white. Astolat is Guilford in Surrey.

4. the sacred shield of Lancelot. Sacred, because she held him the greatest and purest of all knights, and he had left his shield blazoned with the records of his deeds in her care.

7. soilure. From an old French word meaning filth. It was customary for knights to keep their shields in silken cases when not in use. These cases were often fabricated and ornately decorated by their lady-loves.

2 c

10. tinct, — or tint, the modern spelling. **Wit** means fancy.

22. Caerlyle. A border town in northern England on the Eden river. Caer, appearing in this and the following name, means a wall or fortification, hence these places were undoubtedly fortified towns or strongholds.

23. Camelot is a legendary spot, where Arthur is said to have held his court.

27. lived in fantasy. Gave herself up to romantic day-dreams.

35. Lyonesse. A mythical region near Cornwall, which appears only in the Arthurian romances. It is said to be now submerged more than forty fathoms deep under the water between the Land's End and the Scilly Islands. It calls to mind the fabled Atlantis.

36. tarn. A small mountain lake without visible outlet.

39. two brothers. The story of the two brothers who fought is alluded to in *The Last Tournament*, line 47.

53. shingly scaur. A bare and broken place on the side of the hill with small stones scattered over it.

59. Divinely. Providentially.

67. still. Continually.

75. this world's hugest. London.

94. lets. From a different root from the word which means to permit. It is now obsolete, but had the meaning of hinder, prevent.

95. Glanced first, etc. This episode marks the first entrance of suspicion into the heart of the king, but his nature is so frank and his own character so stainless that he dismisses it. For the first time, Lancelot has stained his life with a lie, one of the basest sins of which a knight could be guilty. The advancing and corrupting power of the great sin is shown.

97. To blame, etc. Cf. Malory, XVIII, viii. "And so by the way the king lodged in a town called Astolat, that is now in English called Guilford, and there the king lay in the castle. So when the king was departed, the queen called Sir Lancelot unto her, and said, Sir Lancelot ye are greatly to blame, thus to hold you behind my lord: what trow ye, what will your enemies and mine say and deem? not else but see how Sir Lancelot holdeth him ever behind the king, and so doth the queen, for that they would be together: and thus will they say, said the queen to Sir Lancelot, have ye no doubt thereof."

102. vext at having lied in vain. A false shame that is excited, not by the sin, but by the fact that the sin was in vain.

106. myriad cricket. In *Enoch Arden* occurs "The myriad shriek of wheeling ocean-fowl."

110. allowed. Accepted and approved.

121. faultless. Notice the use of the word by each one of the two. Is there any difference in the use? Guinevere shows her own unworthiness when she utters her scornful words about the king.

130. vows impossible. Cf. *Gareth*, line 266.

133. For who loves me, etc. Cf. *Guinevere*, line 633, and the passage following.

138. vermin voices. The alliteration serves to bring out more strongly the bitterness of these words.

144. Compare Lancelot's character with that of the king as delineated here.

146. A moral child, etc. Arthur's guileless simplicity

and utter truthfulness could not be appreciated by the deceitful mind of the queen and caused her to despise him. To what extent is her word true where she says, " Else he had not lost me! "

157. They prove to him his work. They show that his ideals are beginning to mould and shape their lives.

176. Elaine. The student should read Malory, XVIII, ix, and then compare Tennyson's treatment of this character to see how much more beautiful and full of sweet humanity is the conception of the poet than that of the old romancer.

181. Livest between the lips. This is a literal translation of a line from the *Eneid*, 201.

201. but Lavaine, etc. This is one of the lighter touches which relieve the gloom of this tragic and pathetic Idyll.

246. Had marred his face. This description of Lancelot is noteworthy. The struggle of a great and noble nature against a sin that was utterly abhorrent and yet too sweet to be conquered was so elemental as to mark his features and at times drive him into the solitudes of the wilderness, like the man with the unclean spirit, in *Luke* vii. 29. Perhaps Tennyson had in mind Sir Ector's eulogy on Lancelot after his death, — Malory, XXI, xiii : " Ah, Lancelot, he said, thou were head of all Christian knights and now I dare say, said Sir Ector, thou Sir Lancelot, there thou liest, that thou were never matched of earthly knight's hand ; and thou were the courtliest knight that ever bare shield ; and thou were truest friend to thy lover that ever bestrode a horse ; and thou were the truest lover of a sinful man that ever loved woman ; and thou were the kindest man that strake with sword ; and thou were the goodliest person ever came among press of knights; and thou was the meekest man and the gentlest that ever ate in hall among ladies; and thou were the sternest knight to thy mortal foe that ever put spear in rest."

269. glanced at Guinevere. Spoke of Guinevere.

279. Badon hill. The last of the twelve battles which Arthur was said to have fought against the heathen. Nennius, in his *Chronicles*, says, Arthur killed nine hundred and forty in this battle with his own hand alone, no one but the Lord affording him assistance.

280. rapt. From a Latin word meaning carried away.

287. the violent Glem. These are the battles as listed by Nennius: " The first battle in which he was engaged, was at the mouth of the river Glem. The second, third, fourth, and fifth, were on another river, by the Britons called Duglas, in the region Linius. The sixth on the river Bassus. The seventh in the wood Celidon, which the Britons call Cat Coit Celidon. The eighth was near Gernion Castle, where Arthur bore the image of the Virgin Mary, mother of God, on his shoulders, and through the power of our Lord Jesus Christ, and the holy Mary, put the Saxons to flight, and pursued them the whole day with great slaughter. The ninth was at the city of Legion, which is called Caer Leon. The tenth was on the banks of the river Trat Treuroit. The eleventh was on the mountain Breguoin, which we call Cat Bregion. The twelfth was a most severe contest, when Arthur penetrated to the hill of Badon."

314. The fire of God. Cf. *The Coming of Arthur*, line 127.

325. to make him cheer. To make him glad with a friendly reception.

338. rathe. An obsolete word of which rather, the comparative, is still in use. It means early.

354. rapt. She stood exalted in ecstasy as she gazed upon his face.

401. A hermit, etc. This fine passage describing the hermit's cave is all the poet's own. Malory has no reference to the cave.

406. The green light, etc. This fancy of the green from the meadows reflecting itself in the whiteness of the inner roofs is compared by Littledale to a passage from Shelley's *Dream of the Unknown* : —

> "Floating water-lilies, broad and bright,
>   Which lit the oak which overhung the hedge
>   With moonlight beams of their own watery light."

409. noise of falling showers. Whoever has heard the rustling of the leaves of these trees at night will realize the force of the simile.

422. Pendragon. Means supreme head and was applied only to Uther and Arthur.

429. Lay like a rainbow, etc. Because of the brilliant colors worn by the ladies seated there.

440. with all ease. With perfect harmony.

442. nameless king. See lines 45–46.

446. crescent. Increasing, growing.

453. held the lists. Awaited the attack.

459. bode. Past participle of bide, meaning delayed.

480. as a wild wave. In a letter from Tennyson to his wife occurs this passage, " Next day (July 24, 1858) very fine, but in the night towards morning storm arose and our topmast was broken off. I stood next morning a long time by the cabin door and watched the green sea looking like a mountainous country, far-off waves with foam at the top looking like snowy mountains bounding the scene; one great wave, green-shining, past with all its crests smoking high up beside the vessel. As I stood there came a sudden hurricane and roared drearily in the funnel for twenty seconds and past away." Quoted in Tennyson's *Works*, Vol. III, p. 484.

535. Gawain was the brother of Gareth and was one of the most prominent knights at Court, but not for his good qualities. In Tennyson he is fickle, light-minded, unstable and altogether a mischief-maker and scandal-monger. In the quest of the Holy Grail, he is told by a holy hermit, "When ye were first made knight ye should have taken you to knightly deeds and virtuous living, and ye have done the contrary, for ye have lived mischievously for many years." It was the irony of fate that he should have been chosen for this quest as he was the enemy of Lancelot and the Queen.

548. restless heart. Notice the beauty of the expression. Tennyson uses a similar expression in *Maud*, I, xiv, 2.

> "Maud's own little oak room
> (Which Maud, like a precious stone
> Set in the heart of the carven gloom,
> Lights with herself. . . ."

556. Sir Modred was the traitor of the Round Table, always plotting the overthrow of Arthur and the downfall of his great ideals.

567. tarriance. A word of rare use meaning delay.

583. Our true Arthur. Notice how ingeniously she mixes up her own words with those of Lancelot.

592. So fine a fear. The king is gently sarcastic in this saying.

608. Traitor. What was the cause of this paroxysm of anger on the part of the queen?

707. our courtesy. Every knight had taken the most solemn oath to do the king's will. Gawain had been sent to perform a mission, and now lightly boasts that his false courtesy absolves him from his oath to do the king's will.

728. Marred her friend's aim. Spoiled the effect of her friend's malice.

807. battle-writhen. Twisted or distorted by stress of battle.

871. His honor rooted in dishonor, etc. A fine example of Tennyson's epigrammatic power.

883. What the rough sickness meant. She could understand his impatience born of suffering, but his moodiness she could not fathom and grieved over it.

898. burthen. The refrain of a song.

905. victim's flowers. It was the custom when human sacrifices were offered, in heathen religions, to wreathe the victim with flowers.

923. that I live to hear is yours. It is due to you that I am alive to-day to hear you.

924. Then suddenly. Stopford Brooke says of this passage: " She rises to the very verge of innocent maidenliness in passionate love, but she does not go over the verge. And to be on the verge and not pass beyond it is the very peak of innocent girlhood when seized by overmastering love.

It was as difficult to represent Elaine as to represent Juliet; and Tennyson has succeeded well where Shakespeare succeeded beautifully. It is great praise, but it is well deserved." This comparison should be discussed by the class.

939. quit. Requite, repay.

953. half my realm beyond the seas. Malory, XX, xvii, says, "But to say the sooth Sir Lancelot and his nephews were lords of all France and of the lands that longed unto France, he and his kindred rejoiced in all through Sir Lancelot's noble prowess."

969. That were against me. Sir Lancelot was known as the perfect example of knightly courtesy.

977. tact. An intuitive sense.

997. she made a little song. Tennyson touched the high-water mark of his poetic genius in his impassioned lyrics. For perfection of form and musical cadence there are few if any lyrics which surpass those in *The Princess*, with which every student of Tennyson ought to be familiar. This song is one of simple beauty and deep pathos, the death song of a sweet-souled and pure-minded maiden, innocent of the evils of society, yet the victim directly of the sin which is surely corrupting the court of Arthur and destroying his work.

1015. the Phantom of the house. Referring to the banshee, which was supposed to attend every great family in Ireland. It was a species of fairy, who, in the shape of a little hideous old woman, has been known to appear, and heard to sing in a mournful, supernatural voice under the windows of great houses to warn the family that some of them were soon to die.

1048. muse. Wonder.

1092. ghostly man. One who has to do with the soul or spirit, hence a priest.

1093. shrive me clean. Give absolution after confession.

1134. to that stream. The Thames, which flows by London where Arthur is now holding court (line 76). If Astolat was near Guilford, it was only about twenty-five miles from London, and not far from the river which is swept by the ocean tides some miles above London.

1140. And on the black decks. In this connection *The Lady of Shalott* should be read.

1170. oriel. A deeply recessed window. It comes from a Latin word which means gilded or richly decorated.

1178. tawnier. The neck of the cygnet is of a yellowish tinge, while the neck of the swan is pure white. The exaggerated comparison falls little short of flattery.

1198. Lancelot of the Lake. He was so called because in the old romances he was brought up in the castle of Vivien, the Lady of the Lake.

1209. For her. Compare the jealousy of Guinevere with the trustfulness of Elaine in the passage beginning with line 1079.

1217. her pearls. See line 601.

1233. slowly past the barge. Notice the dramatic power of this passage. While the queen is working herself up to the climax of her bitter jealousy, the barge with the silent form of her supposed rival is slowly floating before the window from which she casts the diamonds.

1143. the face. Perhaps reference is made to the Great Stone Face of Hawthorne.

1256–1257. Sir Percivale . . . Sir Galahad. The two

purest and holiest knights of the Round Table, and therefore the ones most fit to bear the body of the lily maid.

1264. Most noble lord. In Malory, XVIII, xx, we read: " And this was the intent of the letter: Most noble knight, Sir Lancelot, now hath death made us two at debate for your love; I was your lover that men called the fair maiden at Astolat; therefore unto all ladies I make my moan; yet pray for my soul, and bury me at the least and offer ye my mass-penny. This is my last request. And a clean maiden I died. I take God to witness. Pray for my soul, Sir Lancelot, as thou art peerless. — This was all the substance in the letter."

1299. Sea was her wrath. Her wrath was like the sea, over which the storm has passed, but which has not yet returned to peace and tranquillity.

1316. to thy worship. To thy honor.

1319. that shrine. Westminster Abbey, the most famous church in England, was built by Edward the Confessor on the site of an earlier church.

1346. affiance. Trust, confidence.

1375. Unbound as yet. Arthur had not noticed the love of Lancelot and Guinevere which was so patent to all others.

1408. Alas for Arthur's greatest knight. The inherent nobility of Lancelot's character is shown in passages such as this. Many times he is represented as struggling against the evil which had overcome him, sometimes with such determination that he absented himself from the haunts of men and wandered in the wilderness as one demented. Such an episode in his life is detailed in the Holy Grail.

1418. Not knowing he should die a holy man. See Malory, XXI, ix, x.

THE HOLY GRAIL

This Idyll was first published in 1869 and is based on Malory, XIII–XVII, though the poet's invention and imagination have so expanded and enriched the original narrative that his indebtedness to the legends of the past seems slight. He says, himself: "The Holy Grail is one of the most imaginative of my poems. I have expressed there my strong feeling as to the Reality of the Unseen. The end where the king speaks of his work and of his visions is intended to be the summing up of all in the highest note by the highest of men."

The quest of the Holy Grail was to have been the crowning achievement of the Round Table, and toward it, as a final goal, Arthur had consciously directed all his own activities and those of his court. In order to attain this quest it was necessary that his knights should rise from the lower to the higher levels of life, that they should press persistently upward until they had reached that state of moral and social perfection which was the highest ideal of knighthood. In the realization of this purpose, he had been increasingly thwarted by the growing power of evil, finding its birth first in the heart of the queen and spreading like an infectious disease throughout the court and the remoter circles beyond. Thus the offence of one, and that the most beloved, was destined to bring to nought all his efforts to achieve the triumph of his great ideals as well as to bring confusion and final destruction to the Round Table.

When each knight had perfected his character through self-denial and the persistent pursuit of righteousness, his life was to be crowned by the final quest, but it was necessary that all, and not one or two alone, should pass successfully through the period of preparation, and thus stand together in one great social and moral order which should be powerful to win the world to the higher ideals. Now the time is not ripe, for few have attained the necessary high plane of living, and failure in this means failure in all; for if the supreme task is impossible, despair must follow the failure of the quest and utter moral collapse will be the result.

" This Idyll marks the turn of the tide in Arthur's fortunes; the succeeding poems display the ebbing of his influence and authority until that last scene when all seems lost, and he departs for a time from a world unripe for regeneration."

2. Sir Percivale. The hero of many mediæval legends which center around the search for the Grail. These legends have appeared in the literature of nearly all European nations, but probably originated among the Welsh in the romance of Peredur, a name which means " searcher for the basin." The character is the same as that which forms the hero of Wagner's great music drama, Parsifal.

4. silent life of prayer. In the days of Chivalry, when a knight had finished his career of warfare and adventure, he was supposed to crown his earthly life by retiring to a monastery and spending his last days in prayer and meditation.

5. cowl. The hood which was attached to the monastic robe.

13. world-old yew tree. The yew tree was an evergreen with dark, thick foliage. It was slow-growing and long-lived.

15. smoke. The pollen of the yew was so abundant that it was blown from the trees by the wind in clouds so thick that they looked like smoke.

21. the pale. The usual term for the limits of the monastery grounds.

30. Nay, said the knight. From this point on, the Idyll takes the form of a dialogue with the monk as questioner and Percival the narrator of the story. This Idyll touches upon the supernatural much more strongly than any other and involves a wider range of the imagination. It is much more effective to call upon one who has passed through all the scenes to narrate his experiences than for the poet to depict them in his own person.

31. the Holy Grail. There is a vast body of romances, some pagan and many Christian, relating to the Holy Grail. It was supposed to be the cup which Christ had used at the Last Supper and in which Joseph of Arimathea had collected His blood after the crucifixion. It remained in the possession of Joseph until his death, which is supposed to have occurred in Britain. The cup was gifted with miraculous powers, such as providing food for the hungry and saving lives in the presence of danger. Joseph was supposed to have built a sanctuary for the Grail at Glastonbury, where it remained for many years, but finally departed because of the corruption of the times.

38. We are green. That is, we are gifted with the true life from the heavenly standpoint, though from earthly standards we may appear dead and moldering.

41. refectory. A hall or apartment in a monastery or convent where meals were eaten.

48. Aromat. Used for Arimathea.

49. the day of darkness. The temple was on Mount Moriah and the wandering of the dead after the crucifixion is told in *St. Matthew* xxvii. 50–53.

52. Glastonbury, where, etc. The winter thorn is a variety of thorn which puts forth leaves and blossoms at Christmas time. It is said to have originated at Glastonbury abbey, where the original thorn had sprung from the staff of Joseph, which had supported his steps during his wanderings from the Holy Land to Britain.

61. Arviragus. One of the sons of Cymbeline, who figured in Shakespeare's play of that name. He was supposed to have reigned as king of Britain from 44 to 72 A.D.

63. Wattles. Reeds. The old legend says that the first church was built of wattles.

70. Than sister. Percivale's sister is the third of Tennyson's pure and meek women. The mystic, shadowy character of this sweet, unearthly maid accords well with that of her spiritual mate, Sir Galahad.

107. Sweet brother, etc. Notice the peculiar musical rhythm, which pulsates with deep and tender emotion, and which is in perfect harmony with the strange, weird incident which it depicts.

118. Rose-red, etc. It was vibrating with a life which was at once intense and beneficent. Compare its appearance to Galahad, line 473, and to Lancelot, line 839.

135. Galahad is the personification of that perfect purity which has never yielded to temptation. He has preserved his innocence because he has had his mind so intent on the quest of the Grail that he has been impervious to human ambition as well as to human sympathy. While his character is saintly, it has not been perfected through struggle and conflict, but represents the triumph of asceticism which achieves its victories through the withdrawal from the world and its temptations, for the purpose of gaining its own salvation, rather than through the devoting of one's powers to the service of humanity. The weakness of the situation appears in the fact that it is the ascetic who achieves the quest and not the one who gives his life to the service of his people. Arthur never saw the Grail, though his life was so shaped as to be productive of the highest good to his people.

161. till one will crown thee king. Cf. line 482.

165. and he believed, etc. The compelling power of a pure and noble woman inspired by high devotion is irresistible.

167. a vacant chair. The Siege Perilous. Siege means a chair, and when Merlin made it he said, " There shall no man sit in it but one, and if there be any so hardy to do it, he shall be destroyed, and he that shall sit in it shall have no fellow." By one legend Merlin sat in it himself and disappeared forever. In Tennyson's Idyll, *Merlin and Vivien*, Merlin is overcome by the magic of Vivien.

213. It should be observed that the king, with those knights who were doing their appointed work, did not see the vision.

232. And four great zones, etc. The various stages through which the knights of the Round Table must pass before the quest can be achieved. Few have entered the fourth zone.

238. in the mould. In the likeness of the king.

253. Where Arthur finds, etc. Cf. *The Passing of Arthur*, lines 196–200.

254. counter. Opposite.

264. and many of those. Littledale says: "The contrast between Arthur's band of grimy warriors just back from burning the nest of robbers, and the rapt faces of the vision-struck knights, who have vowed the vow, is strikingly told. By his question, 'Art thou so bold and hast not seen the Grail?' Arthur implies that Percivale does not realize the magnitude of the task that he has taken upon himself. None of them have seen it, and he asked what they went out into the wilderness to see (*Matthew* xi. 7); in other words, did they know the meaning of what they had seen? They had all heard a voice amid the crashing thunders, but Galahad alone had 'ears to hear' it summon him to follow."

273. Darkened, because he foresaw from this the downfall of the Round Table.

300. Taliessin was one of the greatest of British bards, who flourished in the seventh century. Arthur proceeds to show by a series of metaphors that they are going on a quest beyond their powers. Galahad being pure enough for such a quest, they all deem themselves Galahads in purity; Taliessin being the greatest bard, they were all going to be Taliessins; Lancelot being first in prowess, they would all take on themselves the toils of Lancelot. They were foolish sheep who would follow the bell-wether anywhere.

In reality they were not Galahads or Percivales, great spiritual champions, but only valiant knights who had fought the heathen and not in vain. For such tasks they were fitted, but not yet for the higher quest. Still man's word was sacred, and since they had made the vow they

2 D

must go.   The pity was that while they follow the ignis
fatuus, many opportunities for doing good would arise and
be neglected, there being no knights left for such work.

350. wyvern, etc. These were heraldic devices. The
wyvern was a dragon-like creature.

358. Gate of the three Queens. Cf. *Gareth and Lynette,*
line 255.

361. And I was lifted up in heart, etc. In recounting his
adventures, Percivale speaks first of his overweening pride
in his own great deeds, then the sad conviction of his own
unworthiness for the great quest, then the allegorical tales
of temptation showing that all the things which we are
wont to hold most dear are after all but illusions. His
increasing thirst cannot be quenched by pleasures of the
senses, by love — even that highest love of man for woman
and for children, by fame and splendor, or by the highest
human pride and aspirations. All fall into dust at his
touch. It is only when he approaches the humble hermit-
monk that he finds out the secret of his failure.

449. she said. That is true humility.

462. sacring of the mass. The consecration of the bread
and wine.

466. the fiery face. "And then he took a cake of the
Sacrament, which was made in the likeness of bread; and
at the lifting up there came a figure in the likeness of a child,
and the visage was as bright and red as any fire, and smote
himself into that bread, so that they all saw that the bread
was formed of fleshy man." — Malory, XVII, xx.

478. Pagan realms. Galahad is always the ascetic, striv-
ing for his own crowning. The pagans were conquered by
the sword, not by kindness; crushed, not persuaded from

the error of their ways. There is here no social service. Arthur's aims and ideals were not those of Galahad.

489. There rose a hill. The poet may have had in mind Pisgah, the Mount of Vision, — *Deuteronomy* xxxiv. 1. The passing of Galahad is told with high poetic power and is filled with a spiritual fervor which makes it one of the most noteworthy passages in the *Idylls*. It should be compared with Addison's "*Vision of Mirza.*"

526. the spiritual city. The New Jerusalem. Cf. *Revelation* xxi. 10 fol.

545. breviary. A condensed book of prayers and services used in the Catholic Church.

547. thorpe. Little village.

558. market-cross. A cross stood in the market-place of nearly every European town in the Middle Ages.

559. small man. The poet calls attention to the homely simple utterances of the village priest as a contrast to the sweeping tide of blank verse which set forth the visions of spiritual enthusiasm and conquest.

600. the heads. The leading men.

612. when yule is cold. When Christmas is past.

633. The pelican, etc. It is an old legend that the pelican feeds its young with drops of blood from its own breast. Hence it has been regarded as symbolical of Christ shedding his blood for mankind. It was often adopted as a heraldic crest.

639. maddening what he rode. Goading his horse to a high pitch of excitement.

643. a lion in the way. His sinful love which made his quest of the Holy Grail a hopeless one.

646. his former madness. Malory tells of the madness

of Lancelot, caused by Guinevere's anger at him, when she believed him to be in love with Elaine. After two years he was healed by the Holy Grail.

661. Paynim. Littledale says: " Sir Bors meets some remnants of the old fire-worshippers, lurking in the mountain wilds amid their cromlechs (stone circles) and dolmens (stone chambers, — flat stones on pillars). Their Druid priests, wise in astrology, scoff at this quest in which Sir Bors is engaging. It is a false fire, a will-o'-the-wisp, they tell him; there is no true fire to worship save the sun."

675. hollow-ringing heavens. It was an old belief that the heavenly bodies, as they swept though the vast reaches of space, gave utterance to a majestic harmony which was called "the music of the spheres."

681. The seven clear stars. The Great Bear.

714. Heaps of ruin. Caused by the gale spoken of in line 726. This scene of destruction is symbolical of the shattering of the Round Table and prepares the way for the final scenes. **Unicorns,** a fabulous beast resembling the horse, but with a single horn projecting from the middle of the forehead. **Basilisks,** a monster of the dragon order, having but two legs, with a dragon's head at the end of the tail. **Cockatrices,** an imaginary creature, half fowl and half reptile. **Talbots,** a sort of hunting dog, with a large nose and large, round, thick ears.

737. Gawain, etc. In Malory, the account of Gawain's adventures is very different. Tennyson gives him a tale which is in keeping with the lack of earnestness and reverence with which he has endowed him.

759. like him of Cana. Cf. *John* ii. 1–10.

799. blackening, etc. Showing black against the whiteness of the surf.

810. Carbonek is mentioned several times in **Malory** and was for some time the abode of the Holy Grail.

835. crannies. Cracks.

844. All pall'd in crimson samite. Littledale says: " The Grail is clothed in white samite or a luminous cloud when Galahad sees it, but is all palled in crimson samite before the eyes of Lancelot; the sinless and sinful visions differ, but that Lancelot sees it, even shrouded in red, may be a sign that he shall die a holy man; that though his sins be as scarlet, they shall be white as snow; though they be red as crimson, they shall be as wool."

862. deafer than, etc. It seems to be a fact in natural history that albino cats are blue-eyed and deaf.

901. Not easily, etc. These noble sentiments were not in accord with the king-craft of the Middle Ages, however they may be now. Arthur's philosophy of life is embodied in this closing passage. It is clear that he does not approve of Galahad or Percivale as having reached the highest standard of manhood or usefulness.

THE LAST TOURNAMENT

This Idyll was first published in 1871. The bare outline of the story is taken from Malory. The half-humorous, half-pathetic, and wholly faithful fool, Dagonet, is Tennyson's creation.

The season of the year is the late autumn with its chill rains, its falling leaves, and its furious storms, and so the action of the play is passing on from the splendor of its high noon to the darkness and gloom of its swiftly approaching night, whose shadows have already begun to fall in the passing away of purity, honor, good faith and loyalty. In the first part, Arthur is the central figure, and here is sustained power, wonderfully graphic word-painting, and the unfathomable pathos of a noble life descending into the grave of its hopes.

6. carcanet. A circlet of gold and jewels intended to be worn in the hair.

8. Tristram is the hero of a group of romantic legends almost as extended and varied as those of Lancelot or Gawain. Littledale gives the following abstract of the Tristram story, which is necessary to a full comprehension of the Idyll.

" Tristram, having been wounded by an Irish spear, can only be healed by an Irish hand, so he goes to Ireland and is treated by Isolt, daughter of the Irish king. On his return, he gives a glowing description of her to his uncle Mark, who sends him back as his envoy to ask for her hand. On the voyage from Ireland, they innocently drink the potent philtre, and their fatal love for each other begins. Long after, when the effects of the philtre have been exhausted, Tristram is hurt by a poisoned arrow, and goes to Brittany to be cured by King Hoel's daughter, Isolt of the white hands, whom he loves and marries. Lancelot reproaches him for his inconstancy to La Beale Isoud, and the lady herself writes sadly to him. Tristram's youthful affection revives, and he resolves to go back to Cornwall to see his old love. There is a quarrel, and Tristram reproaches Isolt for her unfaithfulness to him. He goes mad and throws Dagonet into a well. After many adventures Arthur knights him, and he runs away with Isolt, but is wounded in a tournament. Mark undertakes to nurse him, which he does by putting him into a dungeon. Tristram and Isolt again escape and he goes out riding with Isolt, both of them being clad in green attire, when probably the bower mentioned by Tennyson is constructed. He fights with many knights." The similarity between this legend and that of Lancelot is noteworthy.

25. Nestling. Tennyson has apparently based this incident upon an episode in the life of Alfred told in Stanley's " Book of Birds " : —

" Alfred, king of the West Saxons, went out one day a-hunting, and passing by a certain wood heard, as he supposed, the cry of an infant from the top of a tree, and forthwith diligently inquiring of the huntsmen what that doleful sound could be, commanded one of them to climb the tree, when on the top of it was found an eagle's nest, and lo! therein, a sweet-faced infant, wrapped up in a purple mantle, and upon each arm a bracelet of gold, a clear sign that he was born of noble parents. Whereupon the king took charge of him and caused him to be baptized; and because he was found in a nest, he gave him the name of Nestingum, and, in after time, having nobly educated him, he advanced him to the dignity of an earl."

67. Pitch-blacken'd. His maimed arm had been dipped in pitch to stop its bleeding, so that he might reach the king with the defiance of the Red Knight.

90. curiously. Carefully. Arthur's high nobility is shown not only by his tender treatment of the maimed churl but also by the absence of all personal animosity against the insolent aggressor. He undertakes the expedition, not to avenge himself, but to make safe this robber-ridden country that the lives of his people might be safe.

98. head like Satan. Cf. *Paradise Lost*, V, 659. The power and prestige of the Round Table are indeed fast waning when it is possible for a rival court to be set up, not only in rebellion against the authority of the king, but to exploit those very evils which his life had been given to suppress.

114. Is it then so well? At last the king's eyes are beginning to open to the broken faith of his mightiest knight, yet he turns to him, not in anger, but in a grief so deep that it cannot be uttered. This Idyll closes with the complete disillusionment of Arthur, and the flight of Guinevere.

116. A sound, etc. Cf. *Job* xv. 21.

126. all his younger knights. Is this because he could no longer trust his older knights?

128. In her high bower the Queen, etc. Arthur goes away leaving in Lancelot a touch of remorse, and in Guinevere a feeling of vague awe and wonder. There is no tender parting, no waving of a last farewell. Careless of her husband and the issue of his desperate conflict, she stays in her high bower while he goes away, without a backward glance, firm in his purpose and the sincerity of his high resolve, but with a nameless gloom settling over his heart never again to rise.

136. The Tournament, etc. From Arthur's quest we turn aside to the doleful story of the Tournament of the Dead Innocence, rightly named, with its twofold meaning, the outer semblance of purity with the supreme mockery of it all. Contrast this tournament with the one in The Holy Grail and observe the terrible change, the shameless display, the insincerity, the listlessness of Lancelot, once the mighty champion of every joust, the soul of honor, now sitting abstractedly upon the high throne, while all the laws of chivalry and courtesy are broken and he heeds not. Modred the traitor dares to show his face. The old-time courage is gone, and when Tristram comes in his insolent boldness no one dares contest the prize with him and he wins a shameful victory.

174. A spear, a harp, a bugle. Typifying his threefold character of warrior, harper, and hunter.

177. Sir Tristram. Sir Tristram does not appear elsewhere in the *Idylls* and has no vital connection with this one, unless it is to hold up the mirror to Lancelot and show to him his own sin in its most revolting form. The story of Tristram and Isolt is a repetition of that of Lancelot and Guinevere, even to Isolt of Brittany, who is a second Elaine.

193. is red. The blood upon Tristram's hands is symbolical of the stain upon his honor, who has won the title of the Champion of Innocence. He receives the prize with gibes and flaunts his own coarse sin in the faces of the maidens in the gallery, until one murmurs

> "All courtesy is dead,
> The glory of our Round Table is no more."

206. caracole. A Spanish word meaning to prance.

213. Then fell thick rain. The melancholy gloom, the eclipse of innocence, is brought to our consciousness with wonderful vividness.

226. Variously gay. At the feast in the evening, the white of innocence was laid aside for the colors of warmth and passion, until the queen, half appalled, broke up the sports.

234. Rose-campion. A garden flower covered in the late summer with rosy-crimson blossoms. **The king-cup.** Probably the Buttercup.

240. And little Dagonet. The interview between Tristram and Dagonet places the little fool upon a higher moral eminence than that attained by any of Arthur's knights. He appears as the only one left in whom faith and loyalty to his king still abide.

258. broken music. Littledale says: "Arthur wished his knights to move to music with their order and the King, but the music has become broken music — jangled, out of tune, and harsh. Tristram has played false with his bride in Brittany, and so he has played Arthur's music falsely too. Tristram twangles his harp for Dagonet to dance, but the dwarf stands stock still. He is no jester now, but speaks some certain truths, scarce fit for Tristram to hear. Tristram and the rest have been false to Arthur, says Dagonet; they have played ducks and drakes with their holy vows; things have grown so bad that even he, the King's fool, is indignant."

291. damosels. Same as damsels. Young, unmarried women.

305. Smuttier. Smut is a fungus growth that appears on grain and destroys it.

322. Paynim harper. The reference is, of course, to Orpheus, who had the power of charming all animate and inanimate objects with his lyre. He descended, living, into Hades to bring back his wife, Eurydice.

343. The black king's highway. The king's highway is

a common phrase. The highway here referred to is "the broad way that leads to destruction."

357. burning spurge. The spurge of this variety is sometimes called milkweed. It burns with a peculiarly acrid smoke.

371. slot or fewmets. Hunting terms meaning footprint or droppings.

373. from lawn to lawn. From field to field.

392. tonguesters. Probably coined by Tennyson and used only once elsewhere, *Locksley Hall, Sixty Years After*, line 130.

419. He dreamed; but Arthur, etc. The journey of Tristram is interrupted by the tale of Arthur's expedition. This passage is Homeric and is one of the strongest in the *Idylls*. It is a Miltonic fight of the Prince of Light against the dark and deadly powers of evil. Mystic, awful, these figures move across the stage in fire and blood, and when, after the troubled night, the calm and peaceful dawn appeared, Arthur had won his last victory. Notice the high tension of the conflict, its breathless eagerness, and, finally, the peace and tranquillity of the last two lines.

421. Sallowy. Covered with willows.

423. Machicolated. Furnished with projecting galleries, with holes in the floor for pouring hot lead and other inflammables upon the heads of enemies below.

432. Field noir. In a black field.

438. That sent the face, etc. That roused to hasty flight the myriad birds who abode in the marsh.

450. scorpion-worm. There was an old legend to the intent that if the scorpion was surrounded by fire he would sting himself to death. The idea of the worm may have been taken from *Isaiah* lxvi. 24 : "For their worm shall not die, neither shall their fire be quenched."

479. Alioth and Alcor. Arabic names for two of the stars in the constellation of the Great Bear.

481. Moab saw. The reference is to *II Kings* iii. 22 : "And they rose up early in the morning, and the sun shone upon the water, and the Moabites saw the water on the other side as red as blood."

485. But in the heart of Arthur, etc. Cf. line 239.

492. one lone woman. Perhaps typical of Isolt of Brittany, whom he had deserted.

501. roky. Misty.

503. Yelp at his heart. Perhaps as foreshadowing the coming disaster, but probably they made him long to follow the chase.

509. spiring stone. The spiral stairway of stone.

549. Queen Paramount. Queen Guinevere.

555. My dole. My portion.

572. Crowned warrant. That is, the example of the queen.

594. by whom. In comparison with whom.

603. yield herself to God. Enter a convent.

611. levin-brand. Lightning.

620. leman. Sweetheart.

627. malkin. A swineherd's wench among the beech-mast, feeding swine.

668. Michael. An archangel mentioned in the Bible, who was regarded as the great leader of the angelic hosts.

692. The ptarmigan. Littledale says: "The color of this bird varies, being brownish gray in the summer and white in the winter. The changes of plumage enable it to harmonize with its surroundings at the various seasons. If the ptarmigan's feathers were to turn white before the winter's cold began, it would be seen by the eagle-owls and falcons, and would soon be killed. The metaphor is very ingenious. We are men of the earth, earthy, like the ptarmigan's summer color; if we try prematurely to become whiter than our surroundings, the rest of mankind, our ruin must follow."

695. the garnet-headed yaffingale. The green woodpecker. By tapping on the trees it exposes their hollowness.

712. Press this, etc. Stop talking.

725. Ay, ay, O, ay. Tristram's death song. The star in the sky, unattainable, is that of Arthur. His own in the mere will pass when the winds move the waters.

748. Mark's way. Cf. line 530.

749. That night. The sudden and swift Nemesis is followed by the lines in which the misery of the epic reaches its climax. No longer can the king remain ignorant of the degradation of the court. He returns in the night shadowed "in a death-dumb autumn-dripping gloom." The "Queen's bower was dark." No footstep was heard, and only "a voice sobbing" at his feet, with a message of agony too great to find utterance. The curtain falls.

GUINEVERE

This Idyll was first published in 1859. It is largely original, but is founded on this passage in Malory: "And so she went to Almesbury, and there she let make herself a nun and ware white clothes and black. And great penance she took as ever did sinful lady in this land; and never creature could make her merry, but lived in fastings, prayers, and alms-deeds that all manner of people marvelled how virtuously she was changed. Now leave we Queen Guinevere at Almesbury, that was a nun in white clothes and black; and there she was abbess and ruler, as reason would."

Guinevere may be called the Idyll of loneliness. The queen has withdrawn from the court and from all her former companionship, including Lancelot, and sought the seclusion of a convent. To her on the eve of his last battle comes Arthur, who at last knows the shameful secret of her life, and how she has brought ruin upon him and his Round Table. Yet he forgives her and passes on to his death in silent, heroic majesty. The motive of the poem from beginning to end is ethical, but it is everywhere vibrant with emotion and the despair of the queen is most powerfully worked out.

2. Almesbury, or Amesbury, is about eight miles north of Salisbury, where the old abbey church is still standing.

4. novice. A maiden who was undergoing the necessary probationary training preparatory to becoming a nun.

7. face-cloth. A linen cloth placed over the face of a dead person.

10. Sir Modred was the oldest son of King Lot, hence the nephew of Arthur. He was of a sullen and traitorous disposition, and had always plotted the overthrow of Arthur, hoping thereby to secure the throne for himself. That he was now tolerated at the court shows that the authority of the king had been seriously undermined.

15. tamper'd with, etc. Sought to secure the help of the Saxons against Arthur.

16. brood by Hengist left. The descendants of Hengist and his followers, who were reputed to have made the first organized invasion into Britain.

22. that mocked, etc. White as the hawthorn, or may-blossoms.

28. lissome Vivien. Vivien was the spirit of malicious mischief. She it was who led Merlin to his fate, as depicted in *Merlin and Vivien*. In the earlier days she would never have been permitted to come to the court. But now she not only is tolerated, but becomes one of the chosen companions of the queen. **Lissome** means lithe, active.

52. colewort. Cabbage.

56. I shudder, etc. This is an ancient superstition that is still held in some parts of the world.

64. Powers that, etc. The heavenly powers.

65. the death that, etc. That punishment which is everlasting.

73. rust of murder. Blood-stains on the wall.

75. An awful dream. Compare this dream with others in the *Idylls*.

120. sanctuary. Churches and other sacred places afforded protection from arrest or punishment for any one who had broken the law or committed a crime.

121. So Lancelot, etc. The story differs widely from the original in Malory, XX–XXI, which the student should read carefully.

147. for housel or for shrift. For the sacrament or confession.

154. Was waging war on Lancelot. Arthur supposed

that Guinevere had fled with Lancelot and had crossed
the sea to wage war on him.

166. Late, late, so late! This song is founded on the
parable of the Ten Virgins, found in *Matthew* xxv.

193. Modred had usurped the throne in Arthur's absence.

212. Will the child, etc. For the first time the queen
began to see herself as others saw her. Enveloped in
haughty pride, she had disdained the opinions of those
around, but now the artless prattle of the little maid
opened her eyes to her conduct and its results, until she
was overwhelmed with a horror of remorse which did not
yield to repentance until her interview with the king, when
at last she discovered that she loved him alone and not
another.

216. this is all woman's grief. Because the sin, like that
in Eden, came through the guilt of a woman.

243. mermaiden. From mere, a sea, and maiden. In
the belief of primitive peoples, the water was inhabited by
numerous creatures, half fish and half human. Especially
noteworthy among these were the Rhine Maidens, so
beautifully introduced in the first act of Wagner's *Rhine-
gold.*

246. little elves. Cf. *The Princess*, IV : —

> "O hark ! O hear ! how thin and clear,
>   And thinner, clearer, farther going !
> O sweet and far from cliff and scar
>   The horns of elfland faintly blowing !"

268. Before the coming, etc. Observe the fearful contrast between the joyous times of which the maiden speaks
and those which followed the coming of the queen.

283. that night the bard. Tennyson transforms into poetry the account of the coming of Arthur, which Malory gives as coming from Merlin. The simple story gains much from its poetic setting.

289. Bude and Bos. Districts in Cornwall.

294. by miracle. In Malory's account, Arthur proves his right to the throne by drawing a sword from a stone in which it had been set by magic and which no other man could move.

305. This evil work, etc. In Malory, Arthur was warned against the consequences of marrying Guinevere, yet he would not consent to give her up. In the *Idylls* there was no warning except this sudden ending of the seer's vision.

345. doom of fire. Everlasting punishment.

367. fearful. Full of fear, frightened.

370. I repent. What evidence do you find in the following lines that her repentance was not sincere at this time?

378. Cf. *Coming of Arthur*, lines 446–451.

387. over sheets of hyacinth. A similar beautiful appearance was observed by the editor on a high mountain slope near the Furka Pass, in the Bernese Alps, only the flower which colored the landscape a heavenly blue was the forget-me-not.

404. while she brooded thus. Observe how opportune and how dramatic was the entrance of the king just at this moment when her mind was swinging back from its new resolve into its accustomed channels.

420. dead before thy shame. This is the first intimation of the death of Leodogran.

421. Well is it, etc. Littledale says: " This is the one unduly hard thing that Arthur says in his otherwise just

2 E

words to her. Well it may be, now in her dishonor, that she has no children ; but how different, with sons and daughters around her, her career might have been, it is not difficult to imagine."

424. The craft of kindred refers to the treachery of Modred, for Arthur is even now on his way to battle with him and his false hordes for the kingdom.

458. knighthood-errant. Wandering knights, without organization or common purpose.

499. nor seem to glance at thee. Without seeming to cast reproach upon thee.

507. so slight elements. So fickle a nature.

509. Littledale thinks the poet should have omitted the passage, lines 509–520. " After all he has said of her sin previously, it is almost an anti-climax to divert our attention from his own particular case to the general case of the man who, either for his own or for his children's sake, lets the false wife abide within his house. He has just emphasized the fact of her being childless, and now he speaks of the general case when there are children to be considered. It may be urged that it is Arthur's nature to be didactic. This is true, but his maxims are out of place here alone with Guinevere : there is no necessity for this further justification of his course of action."

535. The doom of treason. The queen who was unfaithful to her husband was guilty of treason under the old English law.   The unfaithful wife was burned at the stake.

537. with one, etc. Meaning himself.

548. they are not mine. Cf. *Lancelot and Elaine*, line 135.

677. dole. Charity.

679. haler. Healthier, from a moral standpoint.

THE PASSING OF ARTHUR

This complete Idyll was published in 1869. One hundred and sixty-nine lines at the beginning and thirty lines at the end were added to the *Morte d'Arthur*, published in 1842. The Idyll pictures " the temporary triumph of evil, the confusion of the moral order, closing in the great battle in the West."

The Passing of Arthur covers the same ground as the twenty-first book of Malory, but in the latter work little is said about Arthur and much about Lancelot, whose later years in the monastery and death are fully described, while in Tennyson Arthur absorbs the attention from beginning to end. Nowhere do his humanity and high nobility appear in stronger relief than here, where he stands face to face with his doom, and that doom the defeat of all his plans and the overthrow of the great structure which he has spent his life in erecting. In the midst of it all, that tranquillity which is born of high courage and steadfast purpose does not desert him, and he passes on to the mysterious islands, leaving behind him the record of a noble life nobly lived.

1. Sir Bedivere. The first of all his knights to be knighted by Arthur at his crowning, and one of the three sent by Arthur to Leodogran to sue for the hand of Guinevere.

6. westward. After his departure from Almesbury, Arthur marched westward for the final conflict.

9. I found Him. Arthur is perplexed at the failure of all his plans. He has seen God undeniably in the broad heavens and the beautiful earth, but he has not found Him in the ways of men. The mystery is beyond his power to fathom, and in his despair he queries whether God has for-saken him.

25. and all my realm, etc. Cf. the passage in *The Coming of Arthur*, beginning with line 10.

78. Hath folded in, etc. The heavy gloom of mist and cloud that brooded over the world was typical of that which had enveloped his soul after his interview with Guinevere.

91. Burn'd at his lowest. That is, at the winter solstice.

117. voices of the dead. The last echoing cry of death.

160. purport. Purposes of my reign.

170. So all day long. The earlier *Morte D'Arthur* begins with this line.

180. great water. Some critic has said that Tennyson would have improved the line by substituting "lake" for "water." But the expression, as it stands, shows the fine discrimination with which Tennyson chose his words. As the weary king glanced over the scene, for the first time illuminated by the light of the moon, he was conscious of the presence of water reaching perhaps beyond his vision. He would not observe it as a clearly defined body of water.

182. unsolders all, etc. Dissolves the bonds that hold the component parts together, and they all fall apart in utter confusion.

205. fling him. Observe the personification, which shows that Arthur thought of his sword almost as a living companion.

231. water-flags. The long leaves of water plants which resemble flags as they wave in the wind.

238. washing . . . lapping. These words are said to represent exactly the different sounds made by the water rippling against a movable and an immovable barrier, respectively.

248. lief. Beloved, pleasing.

278. clouded with his own conceit. His sense of right and wrong was confused by his false conception of the value and beauty of the sword.

290. widowed. Deprived of.

293. offices of all. The duties and responsibilities of all the knights now rest upon him, their only survivor.

307. a streamer of the northern morn. The Aurora Borealis. A beautiful and impressive simile.

324. So great a miracle. So wonderful that no human hand could have wrought it.

345. nightmare. A dream in which one is oppressed with the sense of a breathless weight which cannot be thrown off.

350. Clothed with his breath. It was so cold that the moisture of his breath congealed in the air around him.

354. Dry clash'd. In this passage, Tennyson uses his vowels with remarkable effectiveness. Where the *a* dominates the line we get the sensation of hardness and clashing sounds. The dominating *o*, on the other hand, gives the impression of breadth and smoothness.

367. A cry that shiver'd, etc. The shrilling cry of disembodied spirits, rising from the face of the waters on a night when the chill and silence of winter is in the air and the moonlight floods the icy cliffs.

383. greaves and cuisses. Armor for the legs and thighs stained with drops of blood.

398. a noble chance. That is, a chance to do a noble deed of daring.

401. The holy Elders. The three magi who came from the East to greet the Christ child on the night of his birth.

403. image of the mighty world. Because here the great world struggle of the right against the wrong was carried on to the bitter end.

410. Lest one good custom, etc. Referring to the institution of Chivalry upon whose principles the Round Table was founded.

427. Avilion, or Avalon, in Celtic mythology, was the Land of the Blessed or the Isle of Souls. It was a paradise somewhere in the western seas. The only important fruit known in these northern lands seems to have been the apple, and this fruit conveyed the highest notion of enjoyment, hence Paradise was a land where there was an abundance of apples. This island is sometimes located at Glastonbury, the situation of which, on a group of hills rising out of a marsh, which even now in winter is covered with a foot or two of water, well meets the conditions. The tradition also tells that Arthur and Guinevere are both buried at Glastonbury.

435. fluting a wild carol. It is an old tradition that the swan sings her sweetest song just before her death.

443. The King is gone. Layamon, in his *Vita Merlini*, has this account of the passing of Arthur : " And I myself (Arthur) will go to Avalon, to the most beauteous of women, to the queen Argante, an elf wondrous fair : and she will heal me of my wounds, and make me quite well with a healing drink. Afterwards I will come again to my kingdom and dwell among the Britons in great bliss. While he was saying this, a little boat came, borne by the waves. There were two women therein, of marvellous beauty. They took Arthur and laid him in the boat, and sailed away. Then was fulfilled what Merlin had said of yore, that there should be mighty grief at Arthur's forth-faring. And the Britons believe yet that he is alive, and dwells in Avalon with the fairest of elves; and the Britons still look for his coming again."

INDEX TO NOTES

a beggar from the hedge, 369.

a broken egg-shell, 379.

A costrel, 371.

A cry that shiver'd, 421.

A doubtful throne, 333.

affiance, 395.

Affirming, 371.

a fuel-smothered fire, 354.

agaric, 356.

A hermit, 390.

a horror, 365.

Alas for Arthur's greatest knight, 395.

a light laugh, 358.

a lion in the way, 403.

Alioth and Alcor, 412.

All branch'd, 373.

allowed, 387.

All pall'd in crimson samite, 405.

Almesbury, 414.

altar-shrines, 337.

amazed, 327.

Among the ashes, 360.

A moral child, 387.

an, 349.

A naked babe, 350.

an ancient man, 345.

An awful dream, 415.

and all my realm, 420.

And crowned with fleshless laughter, 364.

And dreamt herself, 373.

And four great zones, 400.

and he believed, 400.

And here is truth, 346.

And I was lifted up in heart, 402.

And Leodogran awoke, 336.

And little Dagonet, 410.

and many of those, 401.

And never yet, 381.

And on the black decks, 394.

And out of bower, 347.

And there I saw, 334.

and wrote, 331.

a ninth one, 336.

a noble chance, 421.

Anton, 328.

a peacock in his pride, 359.

A prophet certain of my prophecy, 375.

a ragged robin, 373.

arms, 369.

Aromat, 398.

Arthur's Harp, 364.

Arthur's wars, 345.

Arviragus, 399.

As a wild wave, 390.

As careful robins, 379.

A sound, 408.

A spear, a harp, a bugle, 409.

As slopes, 366.

As the worm, 380.

a streamer of the northern morn, 421.

a turkis, 373.

a twelvemonth and a day, 342.

Aurelius, 325.

Aurelius Emyrs, 348.
a vacant chair, 400.
avail, 359.
Avanturine, 360.
Avilion, 422.
A voice as of the waters, 335.
Avoid, 356.
Ay, ay, O, ay, 413.

Badon hill, 389.
Bala lake, 382.
bar, 342.
battle-writhen, 392.
Before the coming, 416.
beknaved, 357.
Bellicent, 332.
bicker, 379.
blackening, 405.
blade so bright, 335.
blink the terror, 364.
Blow trumpet, 337.
bode, 390.
Book of Hours, 340.
boon, 380.
breviary, 403.
brewis, 349.
bridals, 369.
bride of Cassivelaun, 374.
bright dishonor, 332.
broach, 350.
broken music, 410.
brood by Hengist left, 415.
brother, 362.
Brought Arthur forth, 332.
Bude and Bos, 417.
buoy, 362.
Burn'd at his lowest, 420.
burning spurge, 411.
burns, 341.

burthen, 392.
But, 341.
but as the cur, 355.
But in the heart of Arthur, 412.
but Lavaine, 388.
But one was counter, 354.
But when he spake, 333.
by miracle, 417.
By overthrowing, 381.
by two yards, 351.
by whom, 412.

Caer-Eryri, 350.
Caerleon upon Usk, 367.
Caerlyle, 386.
caitiff, 358.
Cameliard, 325.
Came lights and lights, 364.
Camelot, 343, 386.
caracole, 409.
Carbonek, 405.
carcanet, 406.
carrion, 356.
Castle Perilous, 353.
cate, 359.
Cavall, 368.
cave, 363.
cedarn, 367.
censer, 345.
central bridge, 361.
Chair of Idris, 372.
charlock, 348.
clomb, 341.
Clothed with his breath, 421.
clouded with his own conceit, 421.
colewort, 415.
comb, 363.
comfortable, 341.

common sewer of all his realm, 365.

coppice, 370.

corselet, 377.

counter, 401.

cousin, 348.

cowl, 397.

crannies, 405.

craven, 349.

Crazed, 356.

crescent, 390.

cressy islets, 379.

Crowned warrant, 412.

crystal dykes, 379.

cubit, 376.

curiously, 407.

damosels, 410.

Darkened, 401.

dead before thy shame, 417.

deafer than, 405.

delegated hands, 381.

Delivering, 348.

Did I wish, 376.

did their days in stone, 347.

dim brocade, 370.

dis-caged, 340.

distant walls, 372.

Divinely, 386.

dole, 418.

donned, 355.

doom, 347.

doom of fire, 417.

dragon-boughts, 345.

drave the heathen, 328.

dreaming, 368.

drops of water, 345.

Dry clashed, 421.

dry shriek, 379.

Dubric, 337.

Dull-coated things, 355.

each by either, 366.

eagle-owl, 357.

Edyrn, son of Nudd, 372.

Effeminate, 376.

Elaine, 388.

Elaine the fair, 385.

elfin Urim, 335.

errant, 378.

errant knights, 372.

erred, 377.

error, 363.

ever highering, 340.

evermore, 349.

Excalibur, 335.

Except the lady he loves best, 372.

face-cloth, 414.

fair permission, 365.

Fairy changeling, 335.

false doom, 378.

fantasy, 354.

Far off, 344.

faultless, 387.

fearful, 417.

Field noir, 411.

fighting for the blameless king, 382.

fineness, 364.

fling him, 420.

Flow'd in, 372.

flower, 362.

fluent, 350.

fluting a wild carol, 422.

for, 352.

For all my pains, 367.

For an your fire, 356.
For Arthur, 367.
forester of Dean, 367.
forge, 376.
Forgetful, 366.
For her, 394.
for housel or for shrift, 415.
for pledge, 369.
For who loves me, 387.
foughten field, 330.
four rivers, 381.
frequent, 341.
from lawn to lawn, 411.
from my hold on these, 363.
From the great deep to the great deep he goes, 336.
from the moment, 354.
frontless, 359.

Galahad, 399.
gap-mouthed, 351.
Gareth, 340.
Gareth and Lynette, 338.
Gate of the three Queens, 402.
gaudy-day, 375.
gave upon a range, 354.
Gawain, 391, 404.
Geraint and Enid, 375.
ghostly man, 394.
glanced at Guinevere, 389.
Glanced first, 386.
Glastonbury, 399.
God's rood, 371.
God wot, 349.
good lack, 341.
Good now, 358.
Gorloïs, 328.
gracious, 381.
Great lords from Rome, 337.

great plover, 376.
greaves and cuisses, 421.
grimly, 358.
Groan'd for the Roman legions, 327.
guerdon, 378.
Guinevere, 413.
gyve and gag, 348.

Had marred his face, 388.
haler, 418.
half my realm beyond the seas, 393.
haling, 358.
happy mist, 381.
harden'd skins, 362.
Hast mazed my wit, 362.
Hath folded in, 420.
haunting, 340.
Have I not earned, 352.
head like Satan, 408.
heathen host, 325.
He dreamed; but Arthur, 411.
held the lists, 390.
Here, by God's grace, 370.
her pearls, 394.
he speaks, 328.
he that told the tale, 364.
highest-crested, 354.
his former madness, 403.
His honor rooted in dishonor, 392.
his younger knights, 408.
Ho, 329.
hollow land, 381.
hollow-ringing heavens, 404.
holt, 356.
holy life, 353.
hostel, 369.

Ho ! they yield, 329.
huge, cross-hilted sword, 334.
humorous ruth, 378.
hurled, 367.

idiot tears, 380.
I found him, 419.
If there be such in me, 376.
I know thee for my king, 330.
image of the mighty world, 422.
in-crescent and de-crescent, 351.
In her high bower the Queen, 408.
instinctive, 368.
in the mould, 400.
inveterately, 345.
I repent, 417.
I shudder, 415.
Is it then so well, 408.
Isle Avilion, 350.
is red, 409.
I trust thee to the death, 330.

jousts, 341, 372.

King, 346.
kings, 329.
kitchen-knaves, 342.
knighthood errant, 418.

Lady of the Lake, 334.
Lancelot, 349.
Lancelot and Elaine, 383.
Lancelot of the Lake, 394.
lanes of shouting, 355.
Leodogran, 325, 331.
lap him in cloth of lead, 349.
Late, late, so late, 416.
lander, 370.
laughed upon his warrior, 330.

Lay a great water, 420.
Lay like a rainbow, 390.
leash, 340.
leman, 412.
Lent-lily, 360.
Lest one good custom, 422.
Let love be blamed, 347.
lets, 386.
Lets down his other leg, 363.
levin brand, 412.
lief, 421.
liege, 330.
lightly, 361.
like a sudden wind, 351.
Like flaws, 375.
like him of Cana, 404.
like the cross, 345.
Limours, 371, 378.
Lion and stoat, 359.
liquid note beloved of men, 370.
lissome Vivien, 415.
Listless annulet, 378.
litter-bier, 380.
little elves, 416.
lived in fantasy, 386.
Livest between the lips, 388.
long-lanced battle, 329.
loon, 357.
Lost footing, 340.
Lot, 341.
lovers' quarrels, 378.
loves you no more, 379.
low splendor, 373.
Lo ye now, 349.
lusty, 352.
Lynette, 353.
Lyonesse, 386.
Lyonors, 353.

Machicolated, 411.
maddening what he rode, 403.
malkin, 412.
manchet bread, 371.
Man's word is God in man, 330.
marches, 376.
Mark, 348.
market-cross, 403.
Mark's way, 413.
Marred her friends' aim, 392.
mavis, 362.
May-blossom, 352.
meadow gemlike, 377.
merle, 362.
Merlin, 331.
Merlin's hand, 347.
mermaiden, 416.
Michael, 412.
mixen, 373.
Moab saw, 412.
Modred, 416.
molten, 366.
monstrous ivy stems, 369.
Morning Star, 354.
Most noble lord, 395.
muse, 394.
My dole, 412.
My free leave, 378.
myriad cricket, 387.

nameless king, 390.
Nay, said the knight, 398.
Nestling, 407.
never built at all, 346.
Never man rejoiced, 375.
news, 351.
New things and old, 345.
nightmare, 421.
noble, 353.

noble maintenance, 373.
noise of falling showers, 390.
Noonday Sun, 362.
nor seem to glance at thee, 418.
novice, 414.
Not a hoof left, 380.
Not an hour, 341.
Not easily, 405.
Not knowing that he should die
    a holy man, 395.
not obey, 377.
Not proven, 342.

offices of all, 421.
O friend, 331.
often, 341.
oilily bubbled, 358.
old knight-errantry, 353.
one, 342.
one lone woman, 412.
On heaps of ruin, 404.
O purblind, 376.
oriel, 394.
Orkney, 333.
our courtesy, 392.
Our true Arthur, 392.
over sheets of hyacinth, 417.

Pagan realms, 402.
painted battle, 330.
palfrey, 367.
passion, 369.
Paynim, 404.
Paynim harper, 410.
peacocked, 356.
Pendragon, 328, 390.
perilous, 380.
Peter's knee, 351.
Phosphorus, 363.

pilot star, 378.
Pips, 369.
Pitch-blacken'd, 407.
place of tombs, 420.
playing on him, 346.
Powers that, 415.
Press this, 413.
prodigious, 351.
prove her heart, 372.
puissance, 326.
purport, 353, 420.

Queen Paramount, 412.
quest, 352.
quick, 342.
quit, 393.

ragged oval, 351.
Ramp, 363.
rapt, 389, 390.
rathe, 390.
reave, 349.
red berries charm the bird, 341.
refectory, 398.
restless heart, 391.
reverence thine own beard, 347.
riddling triplets, 336.
roky, 412.
Roman wall, 338.
Rose-campion, 410.
rosemaries and bay, 362.
Rose-red, 399.
rough humor, 348.
roundelay, 350.
rout, 359.
rout of random followers, 379.
rustic cackle, 369.
rust of murder, 415.
ruth, 360.

sacred mountain cleft, 346.
sacring of the mass, 402.
Sallowy, 411.
sanctuary, 415.
scape, 354.
scorpion-worm, 411.
Sea was her wrath, 395.
seen the good ship, 346.
Seer, 345.
Serve, 342.
Serving man, 357.
set on, 377.
settle, 380.
shall we fast or dine, 380.
Shame, 341.
She answered, 342.
she made a little song, 393.
she said, 402.
she sang, 361.
shingly scaur, 386.
shallow shade, 377.
shoaling sea, 381.
shook her pulses, 377.
shore, 381.
Short fits, 377.
showerful, 340.
shrilling, 356.
shrive me clean, 394.
sickens nigh to death, 380.
silent life of prayer, 397.
Sir Bedivere, 419.
Sir Fair-hands, 350.
Sir Galahad, 394.
Sir Kay, 348.
Sir Lancelot, 337.
Sir Modred, 391, 414.
Sir Morning Star, 360.
Sir Percivale, 394, 397.
Sir Tristram, 409.

sleuth-hound, 350.
slew the may-white, 354.
slot or fewmets, 411.
slowly past the barge, 394.
small man, 403.
smoke, 380, 398.
Smuttier, 410.
so, 356.
So all day long, 420.
sod and shingle, 357.
So fine a fear, 392.
So great a miracle, 421.
soilure, 385.
sold and sold, 373.
So Lancelot, 415.
so slight elements, 418.
Southwesterns, 362.
spate, 340.
spears, 380.
spiring stone, 412.
spire to heaven, 347.
Spit, 357.
Spleen, 369.
sprigs of summer, 367.
spurs are yet to win, 367.
staggered, 351.
standeth seized, 348.
still, 386.
storm-strengthened, 355.
stubborn-shafted, 377.
Suddenly honest, 379.
supporters of a shield, 378.
swallows, 335.
Sweet brother, 399.
sword, 345.

Table Round, 326.
tact, 393.
Taliessin, 401.

tamper'd with, 415.
tarriance, 391.
tarn, 386.
tarns, 350.
tawnier, 394.
Than sister, 399.
that best blood, 353.
that ever answered Heaven, 381.
that I live to hear is yours, 392.
That listens, 377.
that mock'd, 415.
That night, 413.
that night the bard, 417.
That sent the face, 411.
That she ride with me in her faded silk, 374.
that shrine, 395.
That were against me, 393.
The black king's highway, 410.
The craft of kindred, 418.
the cuckoo, 332.
the day of darkness, 399.
the death that, 415.
The doom of treason, 418.
the dusty sloping beam, 369.
the face, 394.
The fair beginners, 337.
the fiery face, 402.
The fire of God, 389.
the garnet-headed yaffingale, 413.
The Golden Symbol, 328.
the goose and the golden eggs, 340.
The green light, 390.
the heads, 403.
The holy Elders, 422.
The Holy Grail, 396.
the Holy Grail, 398.

the King hath passed his time, 356.

The King is gone, 422.

the King's calm eye, 352.

The Lady of the Lake, 344.

The Last Tournament, 405.

the lily maid of Astolat, 385.

the lions on thy shield, 352.

The lord of half a league, 353.

The Marriage of Geraint, 365.

the morning star, 328.

the old serpent, 380.

the pale, 398.

The Passing of Arthur, 419.

The pelican, 403.

the Phantom of the house, 393.

The ptarmigan, 412.

The sacred fish, 345.

the sacred shield of Lancelot, 385.

The seven clear stars, 404.

the song, 370.

The sparrow-hawk, 369.

the spiritual city, 403.

the spiteful whisper, 382.

The Tournament, 408.

the White Horse, 382.

the wolf would steal, 326.

the violent Glem, 389.

Then fell thick rain, 409.

Then suddenly, 392.

there is the keep, 379.

There rose a hill, 403.

they are not mine, 418.

They prove to him his work, 388.

thine, 349.

Thine enemy, 348.

This evil work, 417.

this is all woman's grief, 416.

this king is fair, 335.

this Order, 353.

this vermin to their earths, 368.

this world's hugest, 386.

thorpe, 403.

those of old, 374.

three dead wolves, 377.

three queens, 345.

Thus — and not else, 364.

till one crown thee king, 400.

tinct, 386.

Tintagil castle, 332.

Tip-tilted, 352.

To blame, 387.

to make him cheer, 389.

tonguesters, 411.

Took at a leap, 360.

took the word, 378.

To plunge old Merlin, 344.

topple, 354.

To quicken to the sun, 372.

to stick swine, 359.

to that stream, 394.

to thy worship, 395.

Traitor, 392.

Travail, 328.

trefoil, 362.

trenchant, 355.

Tristram, 406.

twain, 372.

twelve great battles, 338.

two brothers, 386.

Unbound as yet, 395.

under-shapen, 371.

ungentle, 357.

unsolders all, 420.

urged all the devisings, 364.

2 F

Urien, 327.
Uxoriousness, 366.

Variously gay, 409.
vermeil-white, 370.
vermin voices, 387.
vexillary, 363.
vext at having lied in vain, 387.
vicious quitch, 381.
victim's flowers, 392.
victual, 378.
vile, 369.
villain kitchen-vassalage, 342.
voices of the dead, 420.
vows impossible, 387.

wan 358.
Wan=sallow, 349.
washing . . . lapping, 420.
Was waging war on Lancelot, 415.
water-flags, 420.
Wattles, 399.
We are green, 398.
Weed, 381.
Well done, 362.
Well is it, 417.
westward, 419.
What the rough sickness meant, 392.
when yule is cold, 403.
where we see, 376.

Where Arthur finds, 400.
Whether would ye, 348.
while she brooded thus, 417.
white sails flying on the yellow sea, 375.
white samite, 334.
Whitsuntide, 367.
Whom Gwydion, 374.
widowed, 421.
wilding, 369.
wild land, 371.
will poison, 350.
windy walls, 377.
with all ease, 390.
with one, 418.
With one main purpose, 381.
Will the child, 416.
With white breast-bone, 364.
world-old yew tree, 397.
Worn with wind and storm, 345.
worship, 366.
worthy to be a knight, 354.
wrack, 332.
wreaked themselves, 358.
Wroth to be wroth, 368.
wyvern, 402.

ye are overfine, 356.
Yelp at his heart, 412.
Ygerne, 332.
yield, 340.
yield herself to God, 412.

Printed in the United States of America.

English Poetry

Its Principles and Progress, with Representative Masterpieces and Notes. By CHARLES MILLS GAYLEY, Litt.D., LL.D., Professor of the English Language and Literature in the University of California, and CLEMENT C. YOUNG, of the Lowell High School, San Francisco, California. *Cloth, 12mo, $1.50*

A manual for the general reader who takes an interest in the materials and history of the higher English poetry, and seeks a simple statement of its principles in relation to life, conduct, and art. The introduction on "The Principles of Poetry" aims to answer the questions that inevitably arise when poetry is the subject of discussion, and to give the questioner a grasp upon the essentials necessary to appreciation and to the formation of an independent judgment.

"The Introduction on 'The Principles of Poetry' should be an inspiration to both teacher and pupil, and a very definite help in appreciation and study, especially in the portion that deals with the 'Rhythm of Verse.' The remarks on the different centuries, in their literary significance and development, are helpful, and the notes to each poem, lucid and sufficient." — HARRY S. ROSS, Worcester Academy, Worcester, Mass.

For More Advanced Students

A History of English Prosody

From the Twelfth Century to the Present Day. In three volumes. By GEORGE SAINTSBURY, M.A. (Oxon.), Hon. LL.D. (Aberdeen), Professor of Rhetoric and English Literature in the University of Edinburgh. Volume I — From the Origins to Spenser.

Cloth, 8vo, xvii + 428 pages, $1.50

"What strikes one is the sensibleness of the book as a whole. Not merely for enthusiasts on metrics, but for students of literature in general, it is a good augury toward the probable clearing up of this entire blurred and cloudy subject to find Omond's mild fairness and Thomson's telling simplicity followed so soon by this all-pervading common sense. . . . The most extraordinary thing about this volume is that, unintentionally as it would appear, the author has produced the one English book now existing which is likely to be of real use to those who wish to perfect themselves in the formal side of verse composition." — *The Evening Post*, New York.

THE MACMILLAN COMPANY

Publishers   **64-66 Fifth Avenue**   **New York**

He begins in the mid[dle]
of the action of the Slo[?]
and then goes back to
[w]hat precedes. (L + Cla[?]
Indirect method.

(1809 - 1892) Tennyson
Queen Victorian Age